Todd's L

The early years of a "not very tall boy" growing up with good friends & a slight disability in the "Perfick" Countryside of South-East Kent during the 60s &70s

Kevin Pilcher Aged 6

Dedicated to the memory of Alf Coombes (my grandad)

The names in this book were changed to protect the innocent, but then I thought…

"Blow it, we're all guilty of being who we were"

So, I changed them all back again to their true identities!

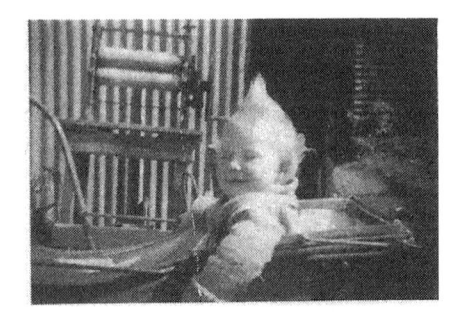

The Author, aged under 18 months. Please note the mangle, this was used by mum to get that "sticky up" pointy bit in my hair. I would be held, horizontally, so that my hair could be trapped between the rollers. This was long before "Childline" came into our lives!

Chapters;

Chapter One – And it came to pass...

Chapter Two – Life on the farm

Chapter Three – It's a what...?

Chapter Four – A little bit of snow

Chapter Five – Do you find the defendant guilty of G.B.H.?

Chapter Six - A Demolition job!

Chapter Seven – The times, they are a changin'

Chapter Eight – A Brave New World

Chapter Nine – Growing Pains

Chapter Ten - Diagnosis "Hippy shoes"

Chapter Eleven – A sentence, a stadium and a slipper!

Chapter Twelve – Testing my luck, same again

Chapter Thirteen – Caribbean Angels

Chapter Fourteen – Clomp, Kick, Snap!

Chapter Fifteen – Big Boys, Bad Words

Chapter Sixteen - Who's dishing up my dinner? You must be joshing!

Chapter Seventeen – Standing on my own Two feet

Chapter Eighteen - Small Gains and a Big Loss!

Chapter Nineteen- Who's nicked our Meadow?

Chapter Twenty - It's all Greek to me!

Chapter one – And it came to pass...

It was a cold, Wet and windy night in the small hamlet of Court at Street, overlooking the dark and windswept Romney Marsh on the South Kent coast.
The date was 17th January 1958, and I was about to make my entrance into the World.
There was no guiding star to be seen over the tied farm cottage to show the way to any trio of Kings from Leyton Orient, nor were there any wise men or monkeys present to witness my birth. So, there were no little pressies then, and I'm rather partial to a bit of Myrrh. Just my mum (obviously), my nan who lived next door, and the midwife were in attendance, although a pride of sheep could possibly be heard bleating in a nearby field, or so I'm told.
As the chimes of the clock struck approximately twenty-three minutes past eleven that evening my first plaintive cry could be heard echoing from the front bedroom of the, now cooling house.
An owl may have hooted from the barren branches of a tree outside, or it may not have given a hoot, I don't know. I was too young to know what an owl was at that age.
So, into the World I came. Not with any thunder and lightning, nor with a magical firework display, but with a larger than average nose that would possibly lead to a life of ridicule and name calling for the next sixty plus years.
I think that the midwife may have slapped my mum instead of me, for producing such a scrawny little specimen, that was when she'd finally stopped laughing!
When all of the messy bits (including me) had been cleaned up, my

dad was allowed to enter the room. The first thing that he could see was the look of unbridled love on my nan's face (this would stay with her for me, for all her life), then he looked at my mum with the red welt on her cheek where the midwife may or may not have struck her.

"There, Dave" she said, for t'was his name.

"It's a boy....... I think".

The midwife removed her slapping glove and nodded.

"Yes, it's a boy" she grunted

"Look, he's got a willy, only smaller!"

They must have known that I'd grow up trying to make folk laugh because as the midwife presented me, he looked at my mum in dismay and said...

"Is this a joke?"

Once convinced that it wasn't, he took me into his grubby farm labourer's arms and held me up to the rain lashed window.

"Behold" He may or may not have said. Remember I'm only guessing as I was too young to know or understand Kentish Yokel.

"You will grow up on this land and it will seep into your bones and very soul, and the love for this place will never leave you" He may have said, but if he didn't, he should have done because it came to be.

"You will play in these fields and you will be known as 'The King of the Sheep Turds'" I definitely invented that bit!

The midwife, keen to be on her pushbike and back along to Aldington, grabbed my dad's arm causing him to juggle with me and she looked at me as if I was the runt of the litter without there actually being a litter, and grunted...

"And what shall you call your undersized (apart from the nose) son?"

My dad peered down at my little shrivelled being, choked back a tear of possible disappointment, although I like to think, pride. He held me aloft, and matter of fact stated...

"We will call him KEVIN!"
So there you have it. I wasn't born under any wandering star, more like a leaky roof.

*

We lived in one of a pair of farm cottages. The adjoining one was my nan and grandad's, who was the farm foreman prior to his retirement. I have pictures of me with my grandad, my dad's dad, but not any actual memories as he passed away when I was only a toddler. Apparently he thought the world of me (who wouldn't?) and I have a treasured photograph of me on his knee, sitting on our old well outside the two cottages. I believe that the well could have been our only source of water at that time.

We also had a single toilet for the cottages down at the bottom of the back garden that had to be emptied by granddad each day. It was said that where he tipped the bucket in the orchard, the best apples grew. I don't know if that was true but I wouldn't have been eager to sample them. Obviously, in later years I would have been happy to take one to school for the teacher.

Like many farm or country family's, we had dogs and cats and we also kept chickens and rabbits, though not as pets. As a kid growing up I wasn't aware of the real reason for quite a while, but I did often wonder where my favourite rabbits had gone. It seemed that lots "escaped" according to my dad.

Mum and dad got a little kitten, bought especially for me. It went by the name of "Peter". I can't explain why, neither can mum or dad, but it was called "Peter".

Personally, I can't believe that anybody can actually recall incidents that happened when they were a mere baby. All of the things that I mention from my earlier days have either been related to me by relatives or I have gained the information from old grainy black and white photographs.

My family have pictures of me in my pram as a baby in which I appear to be dressed up as a girl!

That may help to explain my desire for long hair from my early teens onwards to today.

I have no explanation for my love of pretty dresses though!

Only joshing..... I've sold them all now, anyway.

*

As I progressed from babyhood into a fully-grown toddler, I was given the run of the large plot and farmyard. I didn't have to venture too far as there were plenty of things to play with, and on, and plenty to eat on the vegetable patch and in the small orchard out the back.

I'm told that I would chase after the chickens, clucking and squarking. I don't know what noise they made though!

They always managed to escape from me because their legs weren't quite as spindly as mine were.

The very same spindly legs that would power me on my bike across and around this vast land in many years to come, but for now, with only a year or so under my nappy, I would be happy to motor around the garden (like a teddy bear, one step, two steps and a tickly under there!) in my "Baby walker contraption". Yes, they were around in the late fifties, just bigger, heavier and much more cumbersome.

It was such a great time to grow up in (although I've been told I'm still trying to grow up now).

That's not the case though, as I'm not really trying!

My dad was a fully paid up "Brylcreem Boy" with a large motorbike for transport. It was a Triumph Vincent or a BSA Norton, I think. He would soon have transport more suited for a family when he obtained a sidecar!

Mum would be seen in the billowing dresses that were the fashion of the time when they ventured out, either to the pictures at the "Ritz" cinema in nearby Hythe or up the road to the "Welcome Stranger" public house.

You have to remember that televisions were only just appearing in some houses and they were mainly rented black and white sets with a very limited choice of programmes. The popular alternative was the radio or wireless, which is what I recall more.

It was a time when music was starting to change the World, even in a rustic backwater such as Court at Street, and music would mean a lot to me as I grew up in the 60s and 70s. It may have been a slower, turnip crunching way of life in the country, but we still heard all the same music as those in the towns and cities.

It was around about this time when I had just started to notice things that my grandad Pilcher passed away and my dad left his job as a farmhand to become a milkman.

*

All this turmoil meant leaving the cottage of my birth. My nan moved to East Langdon, near Dover to live with her sister, my old Aunt Kate, in a large detached house with its own large gardens and orchard, whilst my dad loaded up a tractor and trailer to move us the colossal distance of approximately four hundred yards along the road, nearer to the Welcome Stranger pub, opposite Manor farm. We could have all been humming "Travelling light" by Cliff Richard & the Shadows which had been at the top of the charts a couple of months previous. We had gone from a tied farm cottage to a council house that was

much more modern than what mum and dad were used to.
It even had an indoor loo!
Holy smoking Cortina's!

There was also a bathroom instead of using the old tin bath that we had to before.
This was more luxury than a snotty large nosed toddler could cope with.
There were still the rats, mice and other creatures associated with the countryside to contend with, but this was certainly a large step up for my parents.
Blimey, we even had water from a tap instead of the well.
Luxury indeed! Well it was 1960.

*

It was around this time that my dad decided that a short break to see his Aunt Jess would be in order. The only problem was that she lived in Stafford and he only had a motorbike and (now) sidecar.
No problemo! (apparently).
Mum could ride pillion and the little spindly legged kid with the big nose could be secured in the sidecar along with the luggage.
Hey Ho!
It must have taken a couple of months to travel the two hundred miles or so to Stafford, or at least it would have felt like that, cooped up and wedged in like the fifty first sardine in a tin made for fifty.
We would stop at Greasy spoon transport cafes along the way so that we could all thaw out for a while. Mum and dad would indulge in a hot cup of tea each, so strong and sweet that you could stand the spoon up in whilst I was left to suck on an old Rusk soaked in milk, and then it would be time for a nappy change, then off again.
The nappy change was for me, in case you're wondering.

Just a thought, but Politicians and nappies have one thing in common. They should both be changed regularly, and for the same reason!

We would finally arrive at Aunt Jess's house and my dad would disappear with the menfolk to the local pub whilst mum and Aunt Jess would chase me around the lounge (she was very posh), trying to stop me from grabbing and throwing all of her fine porcelain ornaments about to see if they bounced. I don't believe that any did! I would then be cordoned off in a safe area of the room, out of reach of anything worth grabbing, and I would be given some old dolls and teddies to play with. They would then try to amuse me by play dressing the dollies. Were they attempting to turn me into a little girl?
Or worse still, an early version of Danny La Rue?
I just wanted to throw things, well, that was after I'd discovered that I couldn't eat them.
For the few days we were there, I was trapped in my "padded cell area" within the prison of Aunt Jess's posh abode with just the occasional toddle outside for my exercise. This was only carried out under supervision of two heavily armed guards whilst cuffed and on a restraining lead!
There wasn't any pushchair or pram available for me there, so I was "Convict Kevin" of Stafford.
It was while we were there, I'm told, that my family nick-name that would follow me throughout my younger years came about....
I was called "TODD".
That was because, allegedly, I was a "Sod".
Can you believe that?
Well wipe my socks in a bowl full of porridge!
I'd been accused, charged, found guilty and condemned of what

most, if not all children from about eighteen months onwards would do, get into little bits of mischief or bother.

I was, in my mind, blamed for every little mishap, accident or whatever that would or could occur within our household.
Even if I was responsible for most, I was barely two, for Farley's sake! That was the sort of thing that could mentally scar a young whipper snapper for life. If I wasn't careful, this cruel nick-name could stay with me until it was replaced by an even crueller one by wicked bigger boys in my later years.
If I didn't nip this accident prone, mischievous little "Todd" in the bud, it could eventually grow into a "Jonah Lucky" creature of blame and ridicule as I progressed unsteadily along life's path.
If I thought that being blamed for a few china breakages and stuff in Stafford was bad, I'd have a lot more issues to deal with in the next few years.

*

Me and grandad Pilcher sitting on the well (he's the one with the cap)

Chapter Two – Life on the farm

Back at Court at Street in our new home, life felt pretty good. My nan would come to visit us for some weekends, and she would look after me while mum and dad popped to the Welcome Stranger with most of the other local folk.

Our little hamlet consisted of two farms, five council houses, two corrugated tin houses and about four or five bigger private ones... oh, and the pub. There would be a grocers van that would come round once a week from Sellinge stores, about four miles to the North. There was a post office, shop and school in Lympne, a larger village two miles to the East, and the same a couple of miles West in the village of Aldington.

There was a bus that would pass through between Hythe and Ashford every few hours or so. I can remember that it was the No. 111.

Mum would sometimes get the bus down to Hythe to do some shopping or she would walk with me, sometimes being carried, sometimes walking, running, stumbling and falling over, down to her own mum and dad's house at St. Georges Place at the western edge of Hythe.

It was a good three to four miles, all downhill off the top of the Roughs (the edge of the North Downs) onto the edge of the Romney Marsh. We would reach the Royal Military canal at the bottom of the Roughs, near the old Roman ruins of Portus Lemanis situated below Lympne castle, and we would follow it to their house.

The only problem was that it was all uphill from the canal, across the fields going back home but that never really seemed to matter.

Just to be out with mum in the fields or along the canal with the animals and birds was great, playing and running amongst the cows and sheep and sometimes even managing to avoid what had fallen out of their bottoms.

Sometimes even mum managed it too!

I had another nan and grandad to dote over me and I even had some aunties and uncles and cousins in Hythe. My mum, unlike dad, came from a big local family.

As I would grow older, my grandad, Alf Coombes would become a big influence over me, and he would also be my confidante and greatest friend. But that was for the future.

For now, I had several new Worlds to explore and find out all about.

*

The year of 1961, my third year, was a traumatic time for dad and also quite a bit for mum as well.

On the morning of 13th May of that year, my dad, in his capacity as a Milkman discovered the murdered body of Alice Buxton, lying in the porch area of her home "The Pantiles" in Frith Road, Aldington.

As fast as his milk float would carry him, he drove to the house of the local Police Constable who, upon being told in a rather high pitched voice what had occurred (I'm guessing at that bit), followed dad back to the scene on his sturdy black Police push bike (And no, he wasn't shouting "NEE NA, NEE NA, NEE NA).

This was serious!

Following their rapid return at 5mph to the house, they parked their respective vehicles, dad's Slomans Dairy milk float and P.C. Dixon's (that wasn't his name) pushbike and entered the building.

There, they discovered Alice's husband, Hubert.

Both had been shot and battered to death.

Eventually, in July of that year, Polish/ Ukrainian refugee Hendryk Neimasz was on trial at Lewes Assizes. He was convicted and would be the last murderer to be hung on Wandsworth Gallows on 8th September 1961.

My dad had to attend Lewes Assizes as a witness to the crime and so, obviously, my mum and I went along to support him.

Unfortunately, the judge, Mr Justice Somebody or Other, asked for me to be removed from the court as I was (allegedly) being disruptive, loud and unruly. I think that I cried a lot as well. Well, it's not the place for a three year old, is it?

There is a book (or perhaps several) with this murder in it and also a picture of my dad, the Milkman. He looks like a young Des O'Connor!

*

This was also my last year of comparative freedom as school was looming over the horizon.

I was only three and a half and it wasn't fair.

Also, mum was apparently putting on a bit of weight, although I hadn't really noticed. I had more important things to worry about.

I expect she had eaten too many chips!

I wasn't the only kid on the block, so to speak, in Court at Street. There was my best friend Robert Harden who lived two doors away in Manor Farm cottages, and the Banyard clan. Although I only really knew Robert, the eldest of us all, Johanna, in the middle and Sally Anne, who we all knew as either "Winky" or "Boo Boo".

Don't ask me why we all called her by those names, none of us know. We never once called her by her actual name to my recollection.

In fact, I still call her Winky or Boo Boo when I see her now!

We would have been the "Famous Five" if we were famous, and if one of us was a dog called "Timmy", but we weren't.

Our little gang would all play in the surrounding fields and woods and also in the farmyard across the road.

The local farmer, Mr. Duthoit, never minded us roaming around the farm, and as we got older, we would "muck in" and help with various jobs around the farm. In fact, the two Roberts, being three years older were already helping with things.

As kids, in the summer after the baling of the straw was completed at the back of our houses, we would make castles or forts and play on the bales and haystacks, chasing the rats and mice away as we did.

There was also our favourite field called "Five Acres" that nearly always had the sheep or cows in it. With the sheep there was a ram who we called "Larry". We didn't have a great imagination at that age for names.

The thing about Larry though, was that he'd let us ride on his back. Only us, mind. If anyone else went even within a sniff of a gnat's crotchet near him he would butt them.

No if's or butts, he would butt them good and proper. He would chase them back across Five Acres field and it was a jolly good laugh to see them try to scramble over the five-bar gate with Larry's horns close behind!

Oh, how we all loved that ram.

Playing in amongst the sheep pooh and the cow pats never bothered us in the slightest. In fact, if you kicked the cow pats and the Sun had dried them sufficiently you could fling them like a Frisbee at each other.

On the other hand, many a time you would kick one and your little red plastic sandal would disappear right up to your white(ish) ankle sock and everyone would laugh. It happened to all of us, all of the time, and it was an occupational hazard playing in the country.

The sheep turds (when hardened) became great missiles and grenades as well.

I can't actually recall any of us eating any but if anyone did, it would have been Boo Boo!

As sure as a vicar poo's in the woods.... well he would if a bear was chasing him!

Just over the bank, with a panoramic view out over Romney Marsh and the canal, stretching out to sea, with a sighting of France on a clear day, there was, and still is, the remains of a chapel.

"Bellirica chapel" is its official title apparently.

The chapel is associated with Elizabeth Barton, the Holy Maid of Kent, built sometime between the 12th and 17th century. To us little Herberts though, it was just "the old chapel", a great place to play. Right beside it, just on the lower wall, was and is an old second World war pillbox with a vast field of fire over the marsh to machine gun invading Nazi hordes or to sheep pooh Joanna and Boo Boo as they sneaked up on our camp.

To us young 'uns caked in cow pooh, these two buildings, almost joined together but from ages far apart, built for totally different purposes and reasons, were just our own personal playground.

We would grab elderberry branches and other bits of bush and scrub to make camps and forts and we would even sometimes take sandwiches and water or juice from home to have picnics there. It was to either have a pleasant picnic or to dig in for a long siege, the two variants would almost certainly always overlap. We would even share our food with the animals, if they asked us nicely.

Many a jam sandwich has been consumed by a flock of cows!

There were the woods and small copses to play in as well, in fact, most daylight hours were spent out on the farm and surrounding area.

*

In a way it was just as well for me to be out because I was always getting in the way if I were indoors, especially as the year went on and mum seemed to be getting even fatter than before!
Was she a secret pie eater who only gorged themselves when I was out?
I liked pies, and if that was right, then it wasn't fair.
"Oh no!"
"What if it was chocolate?"
"Please don't let it be chocolate!"
As the wintery colder months came, I found that I couldn't get out as much to play so mum pestered dad to take me with him on his round for Sloman's Dairy.
Well, at least on his round to collect empties and collect the money. I wasn't getting up in the middle of the night to deliver milk while folk were still asleep, snuggled up in their warm beds.
"No way, Pedro!"
We were still living in a time, in the country, where milk churns were put out and collected in a big lorry from the farms.
In fact Robert Harden's mum, Mrs. Harden (I never knew her as anything else) was the milkmaid, cow herder for Manor farm, and as we got older we would help her bring the cows in twice a day for milking.
She even taught us how to do that as well!
What a well-rounded little Todd I was becoming.
At least by being out on the farm I wasn't causing any grief or getting into any bother.
Yeah, right.
So, out I went with dad in his float. It was a good few years before Benny Hill's "Ernie, the fastest milkman in the West" came along. It

was fun being out with my dad, helping to collect the money (I thought) and to meet some of his customers. Some even gave me some sweets or some pennies. Lovely folk.
After much pleading, dad allowed me to collect some of the bottles for him while he dealt with the money.
This went well.... until I dropped and smashed a couple and badly gashed my hand.
There was blood everywhere, I was crying, not because I was a girly baby or owt. No, I was crying because it hurt, and there was blood. Lots of it.
A lady wrapped my hand in a towel and told dad to drive me up to Doctor Fitzgerald's house and surgery.
I cried some more.
After a rapid dash to the surgery at 5mph with dad a swearing and a cussing and me a bawling we jumped the queue of a couple of wobbly old ladies chatting in the waiting room (or large porch).
Doctor Fitzgerald cleaned it up (I think, I wasn't looking) and put some gunky stuff on that stung, I cried again!
When we got home, mum took one look at my three and seven-eighth year old hand and started lecturing dad quite loudly (she may have been shouting) about "Knowing what he's like, for Christ's sake!", She wasn't very happy and completely forgot to comfort me in my time of patheticness (I know, I know, I've just made that word up, but I'm allowed to, my hand was hurting).
She then shouted at dad to "Put the cat out!"
I didn't even know it was on fire!
Dad thought it best not to mention the kind old lady's towel that would need cleaning. I don't know why she was so grumpy at us.
Perhaps we'd interrupted a secret chocolate eating session.
I couldn't see any wrappers though.

*

Christmas was soon upon us. Not just us, everybody.
We were all in it together.
I was excited, but I didn't really know why. It was the same for most kids, I suppose. There wasn't a lot of spare money about at the time, well, at any time really, especially for extremely poor families in the countryside, who had to ask the church mouse for a hand out.
That Christmas eve I pulled the blankets up until just my nose was peering ever so slightly over the top.
I strained my ears in the silence, listening out for sleigh bells or Reindeer panting or some fat old man wheezing as he tried to squeeze down the chimney without burning his bum on the burning embers in the grate.
All I could hear was a sheep fart out in the back field.
Apart from that, I could detect beggar all.
So, I cast my agile mind to the thought...
"Does Satan get a lot of letters from dyslexic kids at Christmas?"
Not really, I wasn't even four yet.
Christmas day dawned at Hammel cottages and, to be honest, everywhere else as well.
It wasn't a lot different from other cold wet days. The one big difference was that dad didn't have to deliver milk. Instead he enjoyed a big fried breakfast, chopped some wood, fed the fire and then paced about until "The Welcome" opened its doors for the thirsty local folk.
Mum sang tunelessly along to the wireless as she got the Christmas dinner prepared and I played with my new Games compendium and teddy. I was saving my dandy annual until later in the day as I didn't want to peak too soon.

When I say I played with my new Games compendium, I mean that I flicked tiddlywinks all over the carpet, seeing how many I could get to land in the fire. Well, I was until mum clouted me around the ear and told me to stop tiddling!
I could just about understand snakes and ladders, but I thought it was easier to go up the snakes as well as the ladders.
It wasn't so much fun playing games on my own, but mum and dad had other things to do. It was at times like these that I wished that I had someone to play with, but I had to make do and use my imagination and play with myself!
No, stop it, you know what I mean.

*

Chapter Three – It's a what...?

As times moved on, our Christmas's would change but that was all to come. For now, it was a Yuletide spent in virtual solitude until the Welcome Stranger opened its door.
This was a lunch time for the elders to dress in their Sunday finery whilst us young 'uns would all be adorned in our new Christmas jumpers, shirts and dresses (That's just the girls for the last one). We were then turfed upstairs into the front room over the bar (there was only the one bar).
The highlight would then be a tray brought up to us by Claire, the landlady, with a bottle of Vimto each with a straw and a packet of Smith's Salt and Shake crisps. They even had a little cupboard with comics and annuals to read and a few toys to play with.
It was also a great opportunity to be with the other kids, especially for me, although it was a shame that Robert Harden wasn't there. His mum and granddad didn't go to the pub or drink at all as far as I know so he missed out on this rare treat.
All the Banyard clan were there though so we spent a happy time trying to blow bubbles with the straws, well most of us did, all that Boo Boo managed was to get Vimto up her nose!
After our hour of festering frolics, it was back home to see how black the chicken had gone in the oven, and just how many spuds were still edible.
This ritual happened in a lot of houses because gas ovens were still a thing of wonder to many a housewife, especially in rural areas where gas was supplied. It wasn't always totally reliable. That's what mum

said anyway (although I expect a few Babychams didn't help).
In a couple of days "Moon River" by Danny Williams would replace Frankie Vaughan's "Tower of Strength" at number one in the charts. Notice that it was Danny Williams and not Andy Williams, it was the same song though and I still love it today.
The Christmas and New Year period would soon pass for us kids in the country, the same as the Townies I suppose, except that we had the Aldington Hunt to look forward to. I don't really know what the town kids had as I wasn't there.
I'm not sure what made it such a special event in the country, possibly the sights and sounds of all of the hounds and horses running over the fields and hedges and through the gates as they chased after some fox that was almost always too fast and cunning to be caught by them.
Also, there was the daft spectacle of the "Toffs", all dressed up in their poncey red coats and other "Huntsman finery", with rosy red cheeks, flushed by them being completely out of condition, in some cases, and the biting wind that flew up from the marsh.
Sometimes one would fall off their horse, much to the merriment of the land workers accompanying them. They daren't get caught laughing though. It was more than their jobs were worth.
It was still a time of tugging forelocks and "Yes Sir", "No Sir", "Three bags full Sir", to the landed Gentry and their ilk.
To be honest, as a country boy now, I can definitely say that these Hunts hardly ever caught the cuddly little foxy, but I have seen firsthand what damage to livestock the little blighter can do and how it can destroy so much.
A lot of Townies don't actually have a Scooby Doo about things in the country and that's understandable.
Why should they?
I don't understand or know a pigeon's fart about life in a large town

or city (and I don't need to, it's none of my business).
Anyway, that's one modern day rant out of the way. Let's get back to the start of 1962.

*

It was a cold start to the year although, at the time, nobody could envisage twelve months on!
I was really starting to take things in and notice stuff. For a start, I was aware that I was going to be four in a couple of days, and I was sure that nowt was going to spoil or upset my special day.
Yeah, right!
Mum weren't doing a lot indoors and seemed to be tired or snappy a bit more of late. I was being shipped off to my Aunty Dot and Uncle Jim quite a lot. They weren't my real Aunty and Uncle, they were next door neighbours, but everyone was an Aunty or an Uncle in those days.
I liked going next door because Aunty Dot was always baking cakes and me being allowed to lick the bowl was always something to look forward to.
The cakes weren't bad either.
The excitement of reaching a new number was really mounting for me on the day before my big day, but instead of being at home in front of the fire playing with my few old toys, I was shepherded once more around to Aunty Dot, who pampered me as usual.
There seemed to be activity going on in my house but I wasn't involved. Perhaps they were getting a big party ready for me!
Every time I asked Aunty Dot where mum was, she said I would see her later and she would have a special present for me.
I wanted a new bike!
As Cliff Richard and The Shadows sang the new number one hit "The Young Ones" on the wireless at Aunty Dot's, I was finally taken back

home to see mum.

But where was she?

I was summoned upstairs with dad to be confronted by the sight of mum sitting up in bed.

But it was daytime!

Was she ill?

In her arms was a large bundle. As I was led nearer, I could hear noises, like a cross between a contented baby gurgle and a dog licking its bum.

Then I could see it.

"IT'S A BABY" I shouted. Only to be told off for making it jump.

"It's your new baby brother" said mum, smiling.

"I wanted a bike!"

"You've got a brother, now be quiet so you don't frighten him" said my dad, a little disgruntled at my confusion.

"Why's he all red and wrinkled?"

"He's just come out of mummy's tummy" said Aunty Dot, who had just sneaked in.

"Is that why mum was so fat?" I asked, still confused.

"That's right" she replied, grinning at my innocence.

So, mum hadn't been stuffing herself with pies and chocolate behind my back. I hadn't missed out.

"He's ugly" I boldly stated.

"He's not, don't be naughty" said dad, giving me a little clip around the lug hole.

"But he's got a face like a monkey's bum, dad" I robustly replied, only slightly smarting from his clip.

"He's called 'BARRY'", stated mum, trying to end this particular conversation.

Well you could have blown me down with an Angel's fart!

"He looks more like Barney Rubble" say's I, attempting to get the last word (The Flinstone's comic cartoon had come out in 1960 and I'd seen it on the Banyard family's black and white television that they'd just got).
"Do I still get my birthday tomorrow?" I said, starting to get a tad worried.
"Yes, but you'll have a little brother to share it with now".
"I don't want to share it!" I stubbornly stated, whilst shuffling my feet around and dipping my chin down onto my chest in a perfect sulky stance.
It was a very deflated (almost) Four-year old that was ushered out of the bedroom and back downstairs.
The slightly haunting lilt of Acker Bilk's clarinet playing "Stranger on the shore" could be heard coming from the wireless and it kind of matched my melancholy mood.
I'd get over it.
Yes, I was happy that I had a little brother to play with and annoy (I think), but my birthday had been scuppered and ruined now forever as, every time I had one, it would be the day after his! Whatsisname!
Mine would now always be "After the Lord Mayor's show", if we had a Lord Mayor living with us.... er... and if he then gave a special show on "Thingy's" birthday.
My World had changed forever.
I had been pushed further down the food chain. My position in the pecking order in this household appeared to be moving "backerds".
As I reached the kitchen it occurred to me that I should do what I'd seen my mum do in the past when she yearned for a change of fortune, so I threw some salt over my left shoulder as mum had told me that it brings good luck......
Unfortunately, I chucked it too hard and broke the kitchen mirror

with the thick glass salt cellar!
Hey Ho!

The next seven years could be interesting. Obviously, I didn't think that at the time as I wasn't old enough to know these things and I was crying with a sore bum after getting smacked for throwing and breaking things.

*

As it turned out over the next umpteen years, little Barry would gain the family nick name of "Charlie Choops" for his little chubby cuteness, whereas I would always be known simply as "Todd".
I did develop my own names for my brother as we grew up....
Barney, Big Ear, Rodders, Lurch. I certainly wasn't going to call him "Charlie blinking Choops". Not on your Nelly!
Still "Every picture .... er... has a silver lining" as the saying goes.
The big day arrived, and I became Four. Soon I would be a big boy as school would beckon.
Yep, ahead lay eleven years of purgatory, apart from P.E. and games, that is.
My birthday passed by pretty much in a blur. A sort of non- event due to the fact that mum had a chubby little package of sick and pooh to occupy her time. Dad was at work so I was just left again to play with myself.... You know what I mean.
Smutty minds are lonely minds.
I was FOUR! For the love of Hedgehog's!
The day passed with a little birthday tea (it was just a normal tea with "Happy Birthday" sung to me, out of tune, by mum).
AND I DIDN'T GET A BIKE!
A few weeks later it was time to enter a more grown up world.
School held very little fear for me as all, bar Boo Boo, were already

there and she would be starting very soon as well, so it would be "The Court at Street kids on tour" to Aldington, a massive two miles or so distance along the road.

When I say that school held no fear, it didn't. East Kent buses, on the other hand may have done as, to start with, as mum was fully engaged in feeding the rapidly fattening blob of a baby brother, I was placed on the No. 111 single deck country bus to Ashford each morn, opposite the Welcome Stranger, whereupon mum would return home, a few yards away to have a cuppa with Aunty Peggy, Boo Boo, Johanna and Robert's mum. In fact, she would mostly just watch me walk from the gate to the bus stop with the others, and then go back indoors. It was a different age then.

So, as they were sitting in the front room slurping their tea and watching out as the bus drove away towards Aldington, Aunty Peggy would turn to mum and say ...

"I'm sure that I just saw a little blond head walk past the front hedge, Marge".

Give it a few more seconds then the back door would open and in I'd walk.

"I don't wanna go on the bus" I would sob.

Mum would then smack me around the legs, shouting...

"I'll give you something to cry about in a minute!"

She did.

And I did.

This little event would occur on most days, to the merriment of the two Roberts and Johanna.

They were even told to make sure I stayed on the bus, but it was too much fun to watch me out of the back window as I walked home.

I don't know why I did it then and, to this day, I still don't know.

I'm guessing that it was because all of the other kids on the bus found it funny, I was making them laugh. Even at that early age I loved to make folk laugh.

But it was a routine that soon ended. My little routine was.... to walk up to the bus stop.... watch the bus pull away.... walk back home.... get shouted at by mum.... cry.... get smacked by mum....cry some more.... get sent to bed till dad got home for his dinner....get shouted at by dad.... cry.... get smacked even harder by dad.... cry even more.
Boy oh boy, was I a glutton for punishment?
Eventually mum asked the bus driver to keep me on the bus and to actually, physically escort me into the school building as it was quite feasible that I would scurry back home from there, given half a chance!
Sometimes, especially during the colder winter months, the bus wouldn't run on the country routes as there were lots of narrow, winding hilly little lanes and we very rarely, If ever, saw any gritting lorry's up there, so we would all pile into a private taxi driven by Mrs. Duell, who's family ran a garage, and still do, down at Bonnington, just below Aldington. The car in question was an old 1950s Triumph Mayflower, and although it isn't, by today's standards, a large vehicle, it seemed absolutely massive to us kids.
Mrs Duell was such a lovely lady, and I believe that she's still alive today in Bonnington, although I may be wrong. I hope not.

*

My first and only teacher that I can recall at Aldington school was Miss Stanley. I have a vision of her today with her hair tied up tight in a bun, wearing a bottle green or grey cardigan with a buttoned up to the neck blouse, a long skirt and woollen tights. A very staid and prim lady, but I have only good memories of my time there, so she must

have been a very good and nice teacher.
Oh, and when I say that her hair was "in a bun", I don't mean a sticky or currant bun, but a hair style. Just thought I'd mention it.

We would have our lunch, or dinner as it was called, at our desks as it was pretty much then, a one or two classroom school with a small kitchen at the side.
We would pull our plastic tablecloths out of our desks which would also contain our cutlery, along with our books.
I can recall the smell from the school kitchen even now, in fact, in my capacity as a school governor and P.T.A. chairman at my daughter's school many years later, I still encountered the same smell emanating from the kitchen and it never failed to bring back my own childhood memories.
I really did enjoy Aldington Primary school, and I started my sporting, mainly football at the time, interests there.
I became the school goalie!
What a lofty position to hold.
Well it would have been lofty, but I was only knee high to a Billy goat.
I had a hand knitted roll neck dark green jumper, full of holes that was slightly too big for me. In fact, I had to roll the neck over twice otherwise I couldn't see.
Mum said that I would grow into it.
Yeah, when I was about 27!
It has to be said now that mum wasn't an expert at knitting or sewing.
I actually preferred to have holes in my clothes because mum's way of mending the holes was to just gather all of the edges of the hole together and roughly (and I mean roughly) darn it, making blister like stars in the shape of a cat's bottom all over the place!
Sewing up the holes in trousers around the knees weren't ideal

either because if it wasn't a cat's bum, it would look like a toothless granny smiling!
TURN UPS? TURN UPS?
Don't get me started!

When any trousers had to be turned up, my friends in later school years would all have little neat hems, mainly machine or invisibly stitched around the base, all of this, lovingly done and ideal for young lads reaching an age when perhaps, impressing girls is starting to be a part of the growing up ritual.
MINE?
I would have a Three to Four Inch fold under turn up, that looked like it had been harpooned by a One-armed drunkard, using an extra-large needle and string!
One other little pointer on my mum's prowess in the needlework department........
It didn't have to be the same coloured cotton!
Not even similar!
Any old cotton would do.
You wanna try being at big school wearing black trousers with four-inch turn ups, sewn in blue or grey with a cat's bum shape on the knee, and not get a complex!

*

Anyway... life continued at school during the week and playing around the farm and in the fields and woods the rest of the time. It was all about making our own fun in our own little world.
The only time that we would be indoors in the daytime was when it was really bad weather, and during the summer months there didn't seem to be much of that.
A special highlight in the summer would be a walk to Lympne, about

two miles to the East, to the summer fete. We would all set off, mums and us kids, along the road all eager with excitement to see what may be on offer to us. It was usually some ice cream, candy floss and a drink of pop whilst there was always a chance to win something on the many stalls.

For me, as I recall, the main highlight of the walk there would be passing Lympne Airfield, where the old DC3 Dakota's, and then the Avro 748 Turboprop Airliners took off and landed on a grass runway. Yep, grass!

They did put a concrete one in place after an Avro landed and turned upside down after digging into the soft ground one evening in the summer of 1965.

The planes would fly between Lympne and Le Touquet in France, and I think they may have also flown to Paris.

The big deal, especially for us kiddies, was that, if you timed it right, you could be walking along the road by the Airfield fence when a plane was either, coming in to land or taking off.

As they came in to land they would only be a few feet over your head, just missing "The County Members" public house, and any traffic on the road. It was a good job that no double decker buses went that way as the planes would have picked up anybody on the upper deck.

They were, honestly, that low.

I jest you not.

It was a great sight for a young boy or girl.

"Mind yer heads". Coming in to land at Lympne Airport. The County Members Public House is the white building in the background.

At four years old, a round trip of about four miles was nowt. We all just did it, playing on the way. There was no hurry in those days to get anywhere and we would almost always stop at various places on the way to pick blackberries or whatever.

There were all sorts of wild berries and stuff that our mums had us picking. There were even wild gooseberries, or "goosegogs" as we all called them.

It's strange, but as I've got older, I can't stand the things. I possibly indulged in too many as a kid.

There were also summer fetes at Aldington, on the village green, and to the north, a couple of miles across the fields or down Harringe Lane, at Sellinge. It didn't take a lot to please us simple country folk.

It was also around this time that dad changed his job again. He became a lorry driver for Hythe Town Council (or Corporation), working on the roads. Apart from a short "blip" he would remain with the Council, in its many guises until he retired as a Highways Supervisor many years later. I would follow a very similar course myself as I grew up, and my dad was actually my foreman during my early twenties.

*

Chapter Four – A little bit of snow

The summer would end, autumn would pass, and the trees would look naked after shedding their once green foliage.

As the weather got colder, we would still play out around the farm and fields, only now we would all be adorned with big thick coats and woolly jumpers and horrible, sweaty, smelly, rubbery wellington boots.

And most of them leaked, leaving us with wet socks and squelchy toes that would become ingrained with dirt that was carried through the boots, then socks, and then onto our cold, wet and shrivelled feet.

Most times it wasn't just mud either as we careered around the cow shed, playing chase or Cowboys and Indians.

The cows, at the time tucking into their luncheon, were totally oblivious to the sight of five young dung covered halfwits running through their front parlour shouting...."Wa Wa Wa Wa" whilst pretending to be Apaches, firing twigs from an elderberry bow and baling twine, whilst covered in their "leftovers".

Playing this game in the summer, I would tie some baling twine around my head and stick feathers in from the many lying around in the fields. This became much more difficult and less realistic in the colder months as our mums would insist that we wear balaclavas. But these wouldn't be any expensive shop bought woollen items, Oh no, they would be home made hand knitted balaclavas that, in my mum's case, would be based on her vision of a deep sea diver's

helmet!
This would cause the problem of not quite being an exact fit.
It would sometimes turn or spin around so that I could only see out of one eye, or it would slide down so that I would have to look out of my mouth.

This oversized, misshapen balaclava also had the benefit of being able to wipe my snotty nose without having to delve into my coat pocket for my hankie. The only drawback was that it would then smear the aforesaid mentioned snot all around my face.
I do hope that you're not eating whilst reading this bit!
Oh, and mittens.
Yep, mittens!
Apparently, these were easier for mum to knit than gloves as mum couldn't "do fingers".
Again, in my case they were the size of a small carrier bag with a little knobbly bit on the side for my thumb.
Well, one was.
The other one was based roughly (and, again I mean 'roughly') on an oven glove with only just enough of a knobbly bit for a partially dismembered thumb.
It didn't really make no never mind, as these large water gatherers would become so wet and heavy that I would have to hang them over a five-bar gate to drain (about a six week process).
The balaclava and mittens never matched either, as they were knitted from wool left over from my hand knitted jumpers (that never fitted), and there was never enough wool to make both items the same colour.
They were always grey or dark green though!

*

So, then came our first Christmas as a family of four.
Mum went out and collected a fattened turkey (or pigeon) whilst I stayed home with Aunty Dot and played with a fattened little brother. At the rate he was growing, I'd be wearing his "hand me downs" soon.

Christmas day was as any other Christmas day in the country, the same build up and kiddie excitement, the same presents and the same anti-climax!
"Was that it?"
Only this year, that wasn't it.
Oh no, Fernando!
It was much colder than normal, and dad had gone down to Hythe to put the gritter and snow plough on his lorry as it had been snowing a bit for a few days.
Well, that was the last that we saw of dad for a couple of weeks or so because on Boxing Day it snowed...and snowed...and snowed...and snowed (are you getting the picture yet?).
In fact, it just kept on snowing. At first, on Boxing Day, we thought it was great despite the Hunt having to be cancelled for obvious reasons (The cunning little foxy woxy had got a white coat for Christmas and they couldn't find him!).
We could get out into our gardens to make a snowman.
After a short time, it was hard to pick out the snowman from the snow falling and my mittens had become so heavy that it was difficult to lift my arms. My balaclava had done a ninety-degree swivel causing a complete "Greenout" on my snot covered face.
As I couldn't lift my soggy, snow laden mittens to my head, I had to scream to Robert, who had joined me in the garden, to turn my balaclava round so I could see. His balaclava was fairly dry as he had the hood of his duffel coat up.

Cunning lad, eh?
It was easy for him to adjust my headgear as the snot acted as a lubricant!
As my mittens dropped to the ground from my white, shaking, withered little hands I could wipe my, now Bluey coloured nose, with my anorak sleeve (You can't buy class).

Eventually Robert's mum called him in as she had to get the cows in early because of the worsening weather. She wouldn't let us go with her, down over the bank, this time as she didn't need to worry about us as well as getting the flock of cows in.
She went out in a Black coat, boots and a headscarf, and she came back completely White!
Inclement weather wouldn't stop a proper country lady like Robert's mum from getting on with things. Animals still had to be fed, milked, cleaned out and bedded down, no matter what the conditions were like.
We realized that we couldn't play out the following day as we couldn't get out of the door. The snow was halfway up it and it was still snowing. We were lucky that we had some coal in and wood for the fire. Dad had made sure that he had chopped a load for us.
But we were stuck!
Outside, the road had at least three feet of snow on it. Dad was stuck down the hill in Hythe. At least he would get a lot of overtime using his snowplough and he could stay with nan and grandad.
How do Jamaican snowplough driver's fiddle their overtime?
Anyway, that meant that I was the eldest male left there.
I was now, for a while, the man of the house.
I cried because I couldn't go out to play!
The White out continued with large snowdrifts of several feet. Our world in Court at Street was restricted between the few houses and

the pub, as we, like many other hamlets and villages, were completely cut off. This silent White world lasted for many weeks. Some of the braver souls managed to gain access across the fields on an old tractor to Sellinge, to replenish supplies while they still had them.

Supplies certainly needed replenishing in our house as my little apprentice "Sumo Wrestler" brother seemed to be devouring more than his fair share. There weren't the ingredients in the house to bake a birthday cake, not even a joint one. Although it's doubtful that there would be any left over for my birthday, even if there was. So, my fifth birthday passed with just the wireless for entertainment, until the batteries ran out!

Mr. Cliff Richard seemed to be making a habit of having hits around my birthday time as he was at number one (again) with a double A side, "The next time" and "Bachelor Boy".

I didn't know it at the time but, musically, for this little five-yearold, along with many, many other young kids, life would be changed and so magically enhanced by a new four-piece pop group.

The Beatles came along, and alongside them there were so many other new pop groups appearing like Gerry and the Pacemakers, Freddie and the Dreamers, The Hollies, Bee Gees etc. Also, at this time, a new phenomenal sound called "Merseybeat" hit our lug holes.

It's strange how today, we can still remember the words of the chart hits up to sixty years ago, but we would struggle to remember owt about this modern stuff. It's all base, bongo, talking fast noise with no guitar playing or melody at all.

Oh no!

I'm turning into my dad!

"You call that music?"

"That's not music, that's just bloody noise, that is!"
There you go.
So, back to me being a fully grown up Five years old.
The thaw finally reached us in the back of beyond in early March, but here's a strange thing, once the roads were passable, despite them having up to four feet high side walls of snow in some places, we all went to school!
Yep, incredible as it may seem today, us Court at Street kids either got our taxi, thanks to Mrs. Duell, or we walked and slithered all the way to Aldington and back.
There was none of this Health and Safety malarkey. Oh no, heavily weighed down with wet sliding, snotty balaclavas and sopping wet gloves and mittens, we all donned our duffel coats, anoraks or macs, and with icy water sloshing around in our leaky wellies we made our way eagerly through the White, silent world (well, silent apart from our shouting, laughing and playing) to the comparative warmth of the school.
I say comparative warmth because you would only benefit from it if you were seated near to one of the few radiators, and that privilege was usually reserved for the very little ones (some of them who were actually younger, but bigger than me) and the girls.
If only I'd kept some of those outfits that I was forced to wear as an infant (Hindsight is a great thing to have).
I can remember sitting with the ends of my fingers and toes really hurting so you would have to keep stomping your feet (in wet socks) and rub your hands together.
As your digits warmed up, then came the itchy very uncomfortable bit till it all gradually got back to relative normality.
Still, what's a bit of frostbite to a young whipper snapper?
Come playtime, we would all be pleading to be let out to play in the snow again and to make slides across the playground. There was

nobody to stop our fun by putting salt down on our slides, in fact many grown ups would have a go themselves when they could. We wouldn't worry about falling and banging our heads or owt. We had thick woolly balaclavas on as protection, and anyway if we did bang our bonces and see a few stars we would be told that it may have knocked some sense into us.

It was our own fault!

There would be many incidents of other kids sliding into you or pushing or tripping you into the snow. There was no crying to the teacher or anything. Sometimes you would be "accidently" shoved, head first, into a deep drift. There was no "Where there's blame" culture.

Oh, bless my giddy Aunt, no!

We all just got on with having fun. Cuts, grazes, bumps and bruises were par for the course in those days and I think that we were better for it.

For the walk back home after school, we would grab our, now dripping and slightly steaming, togs and off we would toddle. The five of us together now, up past the old Rectory, on to the top of Knoll hill and from there we could just about see the smoke coming from the chimneys, over the tree tops and hedgerows in the distance. We would still lark around on the way as there were very few cars about, even when the weather was better, and none of us were in a hurry to get indoors and be given chores to do. We were our own bosses when we were out.

*

Spring, and then summer came around and I was given an old bike by my grandad Coombes. He had got hold of it for me and had fixed it up as a surprise for me when I walked down there with mum and that "little fella" chappie in the pushchair.

He didn't do a lot of walking yet, preferring to be pushed or carried around. Well, he was only eighteen months old!
Blimey, I'm sure that I had started shooting Apache Indians and building dens at that age!
Well, in my mind I had, even if he was nearly as big as me already. I reckon I must have been left out in the rain too much and I'd shrunk. When grandad took me out to his shed and presented me with my first bike, I do believe that he was as happy and excited about it as I was myself. I'm sure, looking back, that there was a great deal of pride and pleasure in him as he sized me up on it and lowered the saddle accordingly (quite a bit, actually).

It was bright blue with a white saddle and handlebar grips and it had white tyres.
It was my first bike!
And grandad had sorted it for me. It was better than any new bike. It was to me, anyway.
I knew that, as grandad said, it was "A good 'un", it couldn't have been anything else. As I wheeled it around his back garden, I couldn't then imagine, even in my sixties, how much fun I would have on a bike. That was in years to come though. First, I had to learn to ride the damn thing!
I insisted on pushing it myself, all the way home along the canal and up the roughs, through Aldergate. Not once would I allow mum to put in on the pushchair and I wouldn't let her persuade me to let dad take it home in the old Austin A35 van he'd just bought. Not while I could propel it myself.
Mind you, the pedals kept hitting me on the shin and the upwards slog took about three weeks (or so it felt).
Barry already had a little metal tricycle that he sat on and got someone to push him around the garden on, or he would push

himself with his little chubby feet on the ground. He didn't know what the pedals were for and I wasn't telling him.
I wanted to learn to ride mine first, so it was across the road to Mr. Duthoit's Manor farm I went.
I pedalled and fell off round and round the farmyard for ages until I could pedal without falling off so much.
I had taught myself to ride a bike!
I was as chuffed as a fly on a cowpat.
My little brother could only sit on his old trike and stare out through the slats in our old front gate as I zoomed around the farm. I could even pedal on the road without fear of any fast traffic hammering past. The only traffic that we had was the occasional tractor, farm lorry or car. The Ashford bus would pootle along every hour or so, but that was it.
I'm almost convinced that Pop Larkin would frequently trundle by in his old lorry but, obviously I know that he couldn't have done because he was a fictional character like Dixon of Dock Green, Sarah Brown's little toy "Hoppity" and Bobby Charlton.
There were several "Pop Larkin" type characters around at the time though and it was definitely "Darling Buds of May" country.
In fact, it was mainly filmed around the area.
It was "Perfick".
H.E. Bates could have been writing about any one of us growing up here. Obviously, he only wrote about the good bits though.

*

All five of us had bikes of one sort or another, either too big or too small or in Boo Boo's case, a Three Wheeled tricycle with a basket behind the saddle. But none of them were new, we would bound along the farm tracks, keeping either in the left or right tyre track, depending which one had the smoothest course.

Through the ruts and puddles and bouncing over the protruding rocks we'd go, swerving to avoid the worst of the dips and bumps. It was harder for Boo Boo on her old red tricycle with largish wheels and a flapping front mudguard. She'd hit virtually every obstacle going as she'd just plough through them.

The bikes went up in size with Boo Boo's three-wheeler, then my white tyre bike, Johanna had a bit bigger girl's bike and the two Roberts had even bigger ones. Robert Banyard had an old racer whereas Robert Harden had a very old adult's black bike with metal brake rods. It was a big old heavy thing which he would eventually get replaced by a smaller bike, more suited to his stature in the group, because riding the old bike, he couldn't sit on the saddle and reach the pedals. He had to stand on the pedals or sit rather gingerly on the crossbar. Yes, he did have one or two, shall we say, "testicular moments?" Still, it made the rest of us laugh when he was doubled up on the ground using words certainly unbecoming of a 1960s young schoolboy.

*

It was around this time that I got invited to a birthday party at The Old Rectory, on the Aldington road. It was a girl at school's party and she had invited all her friends, all girls, and me. Dad had taken me there in the family vehicle. He was just going to drop me off and pick me up at a given time later, but as the Rector (the girl's dad) came to the door surrounded by about half a dozen excitable five year old girlies, I just started crying and refused to go in, no matter how much dad and the Curate tried to push me in or persuade me. In the end I was just given a few sweeties and a piece of cake to take home, loaded back in the van, still sobbing, and driven back home. Mum wasn't too impressed, nor was dad as he said that I made him look stupid.

I think that it was that I didn't want to make too many of the girls jealous if I ignored them in preference for the birthday girl, also all the boys that weren't invited might have taken my invite as an excuse to hit me!

Oh, and I was pooping myself as the only boy there!

*

The summer days seemed endless. "Perfick" sunny days with only the very occasional white fluffy cloud in a clear bright blue sky. The smell of the harvest as the combine harvester did its work, followed later by the baler, making straw bricks that we would play on, turning them into camps and forts in the large field behind our houses.

By golly, did that straw hurt if the end caught you on the leg which, of course it did all the time. We'd all be covered in scratches, cuts and abrasions as we would dive into the bales trying to avoid those pesky injuns or Germans, depending upon who we were fighting at the time.

When the bales were stacked in the farmyard to form what we all knew as a Haystack, we would climb all over it and fire down on those Apaches from a much greater height (obviously sometimes we were the Apaches, then we could shoot our homemade arrows on those nasty cowboys!).

None of us ever fell off or had any fear of falling off the haystack to the ground. We did sometimes either fall or dive down onto the bales, which was great fun for a Five years old adult!

If my memory serves me right, the only mishap that occurred in the haystack was when Johanna once dropped a needle, and we never did find it!

Summer would end, and the nights would close in with darkness descending earlier, sending us indoors to play alone. I can't recall ever spending any time in each other's houses. The Banyard clan all had each other, plus younger siblings as well, I had my big little chubby brother to play with, but poor old Robert Harden had only his mum and grandad in his house.

*

I was ever so slightly concerned about our rabbits. Soon after I had named any, they seemed to "escape". At the time I couldn't fathom out how they had got out of the hutch or where they had gone to. They were all well looked after and fed well. It was very confusing and a tad upsetting. Still, mum would always console me saying…

"Never mind Todd, stop crying and come in and have some stew, that'll cheer you up".
And you know what?
It always did. It was very tasty!

It was during October that Gerry and The Pacemakers had their hit "You'll never walk alone" at number one. By 'eck, that song would reverberate with me on the many occasions in the future when I would bellow it out with Twenty-Seven Thousand other souls on The Kop at Anfield during my teens, but that's to come in the distant future.

As the year came to an end, the Christmas decorations had been up and had been taken down as the big day both came and went. I could play with my new games compendium (again) and read my Dandy and Beano annuals. I also had some Airfix soldiers to play with. Brilliant! They were placed in strategic positions behind table legs and along the edge of the rug in front of the fire. I'd spend hours indulging in war games, making all the relevant machine gun noises…
"De Gu De Gu De Gu De Gu De Gu De Gu De Gu"
"Dum Dum Dum Dum Dum Dum Dum Dum" and…

"KABOOM" as machine gun nests would be blown up. (Get the picture?).

It was hard work doing all the voices as well as the (brilliant) sound effects, but as a kid with an imagination that only a kid can have, I managed.

Between stuffing his face with Jelly Tots and Smarties, my little bloated brother would attempt to join in and annoy me until I pushed him away and shouted at him. This would almost always cause him to cry or "grizzle" as we called it.

Then mum would come bounding into the room, shout, give me a slap for upsetting her little "Charlie Choops", pick him up and carry him into the kitchen to lick the oven or whatever it was that shut him up. I would be left again, sobbing with a red mark on my leg, but left alone to continue my game of soldiers. If I was lucky, I'd get a Caramac or a Crunchie from my selection box. If I was very lucky, I'd get a Bar Six or a bag of Maltesers. If I wasn't at all lucky, mum would keep them out of my short reach on a cupboard shelf in the kitchen. They may have been out of my reach but not out of Barry's reach when he was in mum's arms. He only had to whine and point to the sweets and, just to keep him quiet, I'd usually see him chomping on a Kit Kat or something. Usually MY Kit Kat or something.

Hey Ho!   *

Chapter Five – Do you find the defendant guilty of G.B.H.?

At least there was some great music to raise your spirits around that period.
"I want to hold your hand" & "She loves you" by the Fab Four. There was Freddie and the Dreamers, Dusty Springfield and The Dave Clark Five, who were number one on my sixth birthday.
I certainly was "Glad all over".
What a great, incredible time to be growing up!
Also, on the first of January 1964, a new pop programme would start on the BBC.
"Top of the pops" was born, and it would run for just over Forty-Two years. It had presenters such as David Jacobs, Pete Murray, Alan Freeman and Jimmy Savile, who was the longest serving DJ on the show, presenting the first one and finally finishing in1984.
Yes, we all know now what a monster he was, but back then everybody just thought him very strange and eccentric. To be honest, I'm sure that a lot of folk thought he was very creepy at the time and during the ensuing years, but as I've said before, hindsight is a great gift.
It would be nice to know that he's rotting in Hell though!
Okay, let's lighten up again.

*

Of course, being six years old at school did come with responsibility. I was made a "Milk Monitor".

This meant that, along with another boy or girl (duel responsibility), I had to get the crate of milk from the main door front step. It was a third of a pint for all children at morning playtime. If it was sub zero degrees outside the milk would obviously freeze and so it would have to brought in early to defrost before the allotted slurping time. In the summer it would be the opposite as little Blue Tits and Robins would be the worst culprits for pecking open the tops to get the cream before we'd got the bottles inside.

To be honest, after my track record with milk bottles as a young 'un, I was surprised to be given the responsibility but also, in a pathetic kind of way, I was very proud.

I was even given a "Milk Monitor" badge.

I lost it!

There was another event that had entered my world, and that was Sunday school. It was held in a hall that still stands today down Forge Hill in Aldington. It was always held on a Sunday, strangely enough, and it was where you would learn all about Religion, whether you wanted to or not.

I can't say that I didn't believe in Religious stuff at such a young age. I think that at six or so years old, you would believe most of the things that you were taught. I suppose it's called "Learning". You might start to question some things as you got older, but most things, especially Religion, you would take as Gospel!

Har De Har! That tickled me.

I Suppose you should believe, as they reckon Reincarnation is making a comeback!

Oh Yes! Boom Boom!

During bad weather we would get a ride to Aldington but otherwise we would walk there with specific instructions to walk straight home after, with no playing or detours as we all had our "Sunday Best" clothing on. We could lark about in the sheep and cow pooh laden fields once we had changed and had dinner, which was always a midday meal.

Well, ours was. Dad's would be shrivelled up in the oven whilst he was supping brown ale or whatever with landlords Albert and Claire at the welcome Stranger.

That was the way it was, and our family was no different to any other. The women cooked the Sunday roast whilst the menfolk went to the pub, came home, had dinner then a kip for a couple of hours. As kids, you knew not to make a noise around the house during that time or some beer stinking ogre would come hurtling down the stairs, shouting and arms flailing at whatever as they had been woken from their drunken Sunday afternoon slumber.

I'm not saying that every house was like that though, no, only the certain ones that I knew of!

Oh yes, there were a couple of other things regarding Sunday school that I can remember.

Once, the Sunday school teacher made me stand on one leg all morning until I thought...

"I'm not having this anymore"

And I put my foot down!

Only joshing.

No, one thing that did happen was that we were all presented with our own little Blue bible with our name inside.

I lost mine.

As I've said before, I'm not a religious person but I do wish that I still had that little book, if only to remind me of that happy time. A shame really but ne'ermind.

*

As a child of the time, Easter was always a big occasion. And yes, I'm talking Easter eggs here. There was no hunting of eggs in my house. Oh no, the Idea was to grab mine and get them out of the way before little "Gutsy Malone" could get his chubby little mitts on them.
Chocolate button ones or Smartie ones were the norm. Rarely you might get a Cadbury's Milk Tray one or a Terry's All Gold (Yuk) or even a Weekend box of chocolates and jellies (Yum), but it was, for us poorish yokels, pretty much the standard fare. Mind you, the eggs were bigger, thicker and tastier then and you weren't just paying for the box.
There weren't any posh ones for us kids like Ferrari Rochetoe's or Thornton's chocolate. If we were lucky, we might get a Mars Bar egg with two Mars Bars inside. I'm talking about proper Mars Bars now. Big chunky things with thick toffee, nougatty stuff and thick chocolate. Not the poor imitations that they churn out today. They're shameful. Mr. Mars Bar would be turning in his grave. They're not fit to wipe the bum of the proper good, old style Mars Bar!
There, another worthwhile rant over.

*

It was around this time that my little brother Barry decided to get me into even more strife than usual by having an accident.
He had the audacity to BREAK HIS NECK!
Well, as Jethro would say...
"What 'appened was"...
We were just playing in the front room with a balloon, as you do, knocking about to each other, you know the sort of thing. Well, he was getting excited as he hit it up into the air, so I just belted it back past him as he retreated towards the fireplace.
As he toppled back'erds, his partially full nappy prevented any major

impact on his ample, yet gooey, bottom in the grate, but as he fell, he just missed landing where a blazing fire would usually be, instead he hit the fire surround reasonably hard with his bonce and fell a bit awkwardly.

As per usual the grizzle started, like one of those old wind up Air Raid Sirens, building up to a high pitched crescendo.

He may have even squirted some matter out of the side of his nappy and down his leg as his red-faced scream led me to believe that he may be in a bit of pain.

"Mum" I shouted

"Barry's hurt his head"

In she came, like a whirling dervish with a fitted turbo.

How she managed to swoop, pick him up and smack me at the same time, I don't know, but she always seemed to be able to, and to chant at the same time between smacks…

"I…told… you… to…watch…him…,I…knew…you'd…make…him…cry…"

"It weren't my fault mum, he fell over" I cried

"Little…Sod…wait…till…dad…gets…home…"

"There, there, Choopsy, don't cry, he's nasty to you" she said as she cuddled him and patted him on the back.

He cried even more when she did that, so she took him off into the kitchen, leaving me to rub my legs again and wipe my eyes.

It was always my fault.

The upshot of all this grizzling palaver was that the following day, after a night's sleep interrupted by much wailing over the marsh, mum took my little red-faced blubber box to see Doctor Fitzgerald at his Aldington house/Surgery.

His examination led to dad driving them to Ashford hospital in the A35 van. I was left with Aunty Dot next door.

After x-rays, it was discovered that he had broken bits of his neck, this meant that he was kept in for a bit whilst they fitted him up in a plaster cast space suit that only left a facial opening and went all the way down to his chubby waist. The thing about this plaster cast outfit was that when they did it, they unfortunately bent one ear forward.

From recalling the cast, I'm now sure that they based the children's programme "The Teletubbies" on his look at the time (One of the hospital staff must have taken and kept a photograph), although I'm not sure that either Tinky Winky, La La, Dipsy or Po had a "sticky out" ear as they grew up!
Barry did!
So, the poor old sausage had to wear the plaster cast for weeks, while the story abounded around the family and neighbours that Todd broke his little brother's neck whilst playing too roughly with a balloon.
I was only six!
A violent child beater!
Can you be charged with such a crime at that age?
Was I responsible for my little brother's horrific injury?
Would I carry the burden and scar of that accusation for years to come?
Would he have a "sticky out ear" all his life?
The answer to the first two questions is... No.
The answer to the second two questions is... Yes
A definite YES!
I was made to stay indoors for a while to watch over the poor little mite whilst mum carried out her housework and a little cleaning job that she had, along at Aldergate, for a posh family with a big house (I just hope that they didn't ask her to do any needlework!).
In this day and age, it could be said that I was "grounded", but there was no such saying then, so I was just "kept in" or "not allowed out".

It's said that "Plenty of being Mollycoddled and lots of sweeties is a healer" or something like that. Anyway, that's what he got. Eventually the spaceman suit was prised from his, now overweight, wibbly wobbly body and he was back to his usual grizzling self, apart from the sticky out ear.

*

I was let off the leash once more, back into the fields and woods around us. I'd missed being outdoors.
Sometimes we would go all the way down, past the old chapel, to the Royal Military canal, which, at that section was called "Ashford Water", although it was still the Royal Military canal, which ran all the way down to near Rye at the South Western end. At West Hythe, below Lympne, a dam had been built, splitting it into two.
We had a rope swing out over the canal even though not one of us could swim. I think that may only have been three or four feet deep, but we were only three or four feet tall, if that, in mine and Boo Boo's case.
Luckily, we never did fall in, but after a good few hours swinging, it was a long, steep climb back up the hill for tea. There was a wood above Honeypot cottage down by the canal called "Bluebell Wood" for obvious reasons. We would all grab as many as we could to take home when they came out. The same happened with Primroses, though we lost most, or they died before they made it home to the jam jars. Lots of our time would be spent gathering these flowers and various berries. Obviously, as I've said before, blackberries were a favourite to take home to our mums as they were plentiful.

*

Collecting grass and dandelions to feed the (disappearing) rabbits was another little pastime.

One day I was told to clean the rabbits out with Barry.
It was only when mum came out and saw my little brother covered in dirty wet rancid straw and rabbit pooh that she screamed at me that she meant that I should use the dust pan and brush and not his sticky out ear and hair to do the job. Why didn't she say that before?

By the time that she had cleaned him up, changed him and given him a choccy biscuit, I had stopped crying and the bright red mark on my cheek had ceased stinging, so she told me to go out with Robert and collect some wood because I couldn't be trusted to look after my brother.
He just stood there, biscuit in his paw ready to direct it back to his cake hole where it would first mix with the snot that was creating its own path from his nose to his top lip. Urrggh!
Robert and I would scurry off to the little wooded area just below the ridge where we would collect as many dead branches as we could carry back to our little cart that we left in the farmyard by the pig pen. He could see my reddened cheek clearly but didn't comment. We were all used to seeing these things on each other from time to time, so no words were needed. We all understood though.
We would spend ages on this chore because firstly, it was a job that we both loved and secondly, it kept us out of the house and sometimes earned us praise when we carted a full load home (That's three things). We all had our stockpiles at the rear of the houses, ready to be used in the cold winter months.

*

On one of our excursions out, this time checking through the trees and bushes over the edge of Five Acres, Robert decided that he urgently needed a disposal of…, and there's no easy way to put this, pooh!

He was only about three hundred yards from his house containing a perfectly serviceable lavatory plus several rolls (well, two at least) of toilet paper, but he insisted that he needed to go, there and then. His bomb doors were ready to open. Squatting himself down in a gulley, hopefully out of sight of any peeping sheep, he instructed me to find him some paper, pronto.

"What for?" says I, a little perplexed.
"To wipe my bum with, what do you think it's for?"
"Where can I get paper from, we're in a field?"
He replied, rather desperately now with a whimpering voice, bordering on slight panic
"Please, just find some. Anything, but hurry!"
Well, I did my best for him and I frantically ran back to his gully, steam now starting to rise, with my find.
On reaching him, I came to an abrupt stop….
"Cor blimey Rob!"
I mumbled with my face, and especially my nose, buried under the collar of my oversized jumper….
"Cor, it stinks!"
"It's because you've got a big nose" A tad hurt, I fear.
"You've got a bigger nose than me" I stung back.
"Haven't!"
"And where's my paper?"
I handed him, with my head turned away, the only thing that I could find.
A dark Blue Golden Wonder crisp packet!
"Is that it?"
He questioned with a bewildered stare at the crinkly gift offered up.
"It's a 'Ready Salted' one!"
I said, pointing to the packet and stating the obvious.

"I can't use that!"
"There's nowt else here, only grass or stinging nettles. It's all I could find", I pleaded in self-defence.
"I did my best!"
"I wanna wipe my bum, not scratch it!"
"I did my best!"
"You could've run back to my house and got me some loo roll"

He wasn't a happy bunny!
"You could've run back there yourself and used the bog!"
I shouted, still with my face buried deep in my woollen wear.
"It's a bloody crisp packet" He sighed.
That was a big swearword for a Ten-year old like Robert.
"I couldn't run home, it was nearly hanging out!"
He said, giving far too much information, whilst attempting to clean himself with one of Golden Wonder's finest.
"At least it's not Cheese and Onion, so it won't smell!"
I said before realizing what I'd said.
"Well thanks anyway".
There was a smile starting to crease his face.
"Don't worry Rob, we won't tell your mum or anyone".
"No", he pleaded.
Don't say owt to anyone, I nearly poohed myself!"
"Don't panic", I reassured him
"I won't let on to anyone, ever"
"You're my best mate, it's our secret"
"You promise?"
"Yes!"
"You promise me you'll never mention it".
"I promise, I'll never mention it"
"Ever!"

And I've kept that promise to this day!
That's what mates are for.

*

The walks and jolly capers that the five of us got up to all over the land around our little hamlet had us out all day, every day while the daylight permitted.

After teatime we would help Mrs. Harden get the cows in for evening milking until our mums called us in.
Every so many weeks, dad would pick his mum (my nan) up from the Red Lion Square in Hythe after work. She would get the bus down from Dover to visit us for a long weekend. I absolutely loved these visits as I had such a special relationship with her. It would be an opportunity for mum to accompany dad to the Welcome Stranger for a night out with nan Pilcher babysitting.
With nan, we would watch the local regional daily news programme "Day by Day" on Southern Television, followed by The Weather with Trevor Baker, and then a special treat. We could watch "Batman". This was all on the new Black and White T.V. that dad had got from Southern Rentals. It had a fourteen Inch screen and was set in a large wooden box like case. The thing about renting a television (which nearly everybody did) was that, when it broke down, which they did frequently, the van would come around to collect it for repairs and they would leave you a replacement. That was a very good thing in years to come as, sometimes they would take your old Black and White set away and leave you with a colour one. Brilliant!
I'm sure now that they did that to get you to want a coloured set, well it certainly worked on me.
I can remember on the opening credits for "Day by Day", there would be a close-up film of seagulls flying over the White cliffs of

Dover. I can also remember it being presented by Barry Westwood and Fred Dineage (Blimey, he's still presenting the up to date version "Meridian Tonight" as I write, some fifty odd years later, now that is an achievement!).

After the early evening's televisual entertainment, I had to go "up the wooden hill" to bed with little Charlie Choops, as He would always whine or grizzle if I was permitted to stay up later. I was four years (minus one day) older than him, for Griffin's sake!

But no, the little "Curly Wurly Gulper" was given in to every single night, so I had to climb the flaming wooden hill at the same time as him so that he would go to sleep (that's what I was told, anyway). He did like his curly Wurly's though!

If mum or dad remembered, I was sometimes allowed back downstairs if, and when he finally went into a "fully stuffed" slumber.

They rarely remembered.

It was different with nan Pilcher in charge. She liked nothing more than sitting quietly with me either next to her or on her lap, so up I would toddle with the little tubby toddler, with a crafty wink from nan. She would settle "us" down in our large double bed that we shared in the big back bedroom. Nan had the box room when she stayed.

On this bed we had cold cotton sheets, about Forty-three thick blankets and a top duvet. Well that's what it felt like when they were on top of you. It was hard to move, never mind turn over. I would lay there, very slowly forcing my way out from under the containing blankets so that I was half in and half out of bed, and then I'd pretend to be asleep, all the time with one eye half open, watching. Both ears fully tuned, listening.

Waiting until the time I would assume that he was nodding, gently dreaming of "Milky Way's", the sweet you can eat during your sleep and not spoil your appetite.

When I finally judged that the time was right, I would sidle out onto the cold floor and sneakily tip toe around the bed in my socks (always with my big toes gawping out), we had no slippers in our house.

The amount of times I reached the stairs, creeping down until a creaking step gave me away…

"WAAAAAHHH!"
"NAAAAAN"
"WAAAAAHHH"

Back I would trudge, back to bed until I had to go through the entire process again.

Sometimes it would happen three or four times, then it was obvious that the little git wouldn't go to sleep so I had to stay there. In the end though, after a while, nan realized how unfair this all was on me and she came up with an ingenious, though looking back, slightly cruel cure.

If I had made it downstairs, or even halfway before the little walking Sumo wrestler stirred and came hurtling down the stairs after me, nan would simply just take her teeth out and chase him back up again, clicking them together and threatening to bite him with them! Har De Har!

The poor little food bubble must have had nightmares. He always ran back up to bed screaming, then grizzling, but then he would be quiet for the rest of the night.

Laying there in utter terror, possibly!

Oh, but it did make nan and me chuckle though. She was very aware who was spoilt and who always got the bum deal.

It was always nice to spend the evening alongside my nan, with Peter the cat purring away on her lap.

Barry always tried to blub to mum that nan Pilcher took her teeth out and chased him. We both just said that they fell out as she told him off for being naughty and not going to bed.

*

When nan wasn't down at our house we would often, on a Sunday afternoon, load up in the A35 van and drive to East Langdon village where she lived with Aunt Kate, her lovely sister.

They lived, with a soppy old dog, in a large rambling detached house surrounded by lawns edged by flowering borders and an apple orchard at the rear.

To play around the garden and orchard in the summertime was sheer joy for us

Aunt Kate would often have deck chairs and a table out on the lawn and there would be sandwiches and homemade cakes with real tea in a large china teapot for the adults and homemade lemonade for us two whippersnappers. There would even be jelly and ice cream and Aunt Kate would always let us get out the old comic annuals that she kept there for us. Rupert Bear, Beezer, Topper, Beano, Dandy and other ones like the Victor and Hotspur.

As we got older, we were sometimes allowed to take a friend with us as well.

There was a massive big black old Aga type cooker and Aunt Kate and nan baked many a tasty thing in it.

It was a proper big farmhouse kitchen with a large table and chairs in the middle. Many a happy Sunday was spent at the "Four Winds" in East Langdon.

*

Chapter Six – A Demolition job!

Very soon, Christmas was once again upon us. At school we had our little Pantomime productions, but they were just for us kids as far as I can recall, and they were performed during the school day.
There was no "coming back to school" for an evening show for the parents. The children's houses were scattered far and wide from the village of Aldington, various small hamlets or individual cottages or houses from Court at Street in the East to almost as far as Mersham in the West and Sellinge in the North to Bonnington and Bilsington to the South.
We would occasionally play football against Lympne school or Sellinge or Brabourne school and also, I believe against Mersham school.
I can't remember any of the results from then but, with me between the sticks for Aldington, I would imagine that we won most games, with hardly any goals conceded and several heroic Penalty saves by yours truly!
In my mind that's what happened anyway, and it's my story so, as the Fonz would say…
"Sit on it!"

*

There was a place at Court at Street that I haven't mentioned yet, and that was a tin corrugated cottage, in fact there were two of them, just above Upper Park farm cottages, where my story started, and a couple of hundred yards or so from Manor farm, opposite to where we now lived.

I can remember a little old lady who was friendly with nan Pilcher who lived in one of the little tin houses. I would frequently take supplies such as milk, sugar, vegetables, cakes and pastries down to her from mum, and I would often tarry a while for a chat or to hear a fascinating story about her life from long ago.

The inside of the building was lined with tongue and grooved timber, all painted a faded shade of white or cream, and her table and sideboard was covered with finely embroidered cotton and lace cloth with separate matching doilies.

An old wireless, made from wood and beautifully shaped would stand on the side and a couple of old, small comfy armchairs, one a rocker, would be strategically placed around the room.

There was an old wood burning stove for cooking on, and for heating, and that was it. An outside toilet and a well for water, was all that was required by this lovely old lady from a bygone age.

Oh, how I wish that I could remember her name, but my memories of that distant time have sometimes dimmed like the faded fingerprints on an abandoned handrail (Thanks for that one, Bob). I do believe that she was possibly a spinster of the Parish. I don't have any recall of the person or people that dwelt in the other cottage. I only know that it was lived in.

There's no trace of the corrugated cottages today, they are both now long gone, and the land has returned to farming. The well still exists though. It was shown to me a few years ago under some old wooden boards. Mr. Duthoit, the Manor farm owner once told me that they were erected to house folk involved locally in the War effort around 1940.

There were other buildings on his farm that were used for storing supplies and equipment as well.

The usual fare abounded at Christmas, the excitement for us young 'uns was still as intense but after the initial high at the crack of dawn, with the tearing open of the paper to release your presents, a more usual run of the mill boredom would descend as it was always a day that we were made to stay in with the family and not go out into the fields.

So, it was a time of reading the Christmas Beano and Dandy annuals to update on the antics of Dennis the menace, Rodger the dodger, Billy Whizz, Minnie the Minx, The Bash Street kids, Desperate Dan, Korky the cat, Biffo the bear, Lord Snooty, Little Plum, Corporal Clott and Brassneck (Remember him?).

After the initial ripping open of the Games compendium, it was left where it was until there was nowt else to play with, then out it would come. The usual Snakes and Ladders, Ludo, Draughts etc. would all make an appearance at some stage.

It's funny but it was usually the Draughts that went walkabout first. Perhaps that was because they would also be used as soldiers and football players.

Now, to be added to our toy collection was a box of Beta Bilda bricks. We did, over time gather a large plastic box of this and we would spend hours making houses, forts, castles or whatever we could, fighting over various pieces such as doors and windows. There were green tiles for making roofs and I made many buildings for my little Airfix soldiers to fight in.

This was the one thing that we could both play with together without too much hassle, that was until the little chubby one's snot would run down off the edge of his top lip onto the bricks that he liked to put up to his mouth (when chocolate wasn't available).

It wasn't only the roofing tiles that ended up green thanks to the little snot machine!

We did have some Lego as well but Beta Bilda was our preferred building material of choice.

Around this time, I was also starting to gain an assortment of Dinky toy cars and lorry's, and some larger Corgi cars as well. The big treat would be if you were given a sort of cardboard mat with a road marked out on it, especially if it came with a garage. As luck would have it, this Christmas that's exactly what I got.

It had a little plastic garage with a ramp up to a car park on the roof. Brilliant!

Out came all my assortment of miniature traffic and I was given permission to play with it on the front room floor. At least, pressie wise, things were starting to look up.

"Wait till I tell the others" I said to no one in particular.

To my limited knowledge, nobody else would have a road system and a garage.

I felt like the cat that had got all the cream, then found a tasty fish hiding behind the bowl!

Over the Festering period we played together quite well with hardly any arguments and very few Beta Bilda bricks pushed up the podgy urchin's nose.

*

We all got into the little Austin van and headed down to Hythe for a Boxing day afternoon and evening get together with the rest of mum's family at Aunt Daisy and Uncle Bill's house in Palmarsh. Aunt Daisy was my mum's older sister. She also had two brothers, John and Ron, and a younger sister, my Aunty Bett, who I don't ever recall calling "Aunty" as she was only eleven years older than me. I always had a special relationship with Bett who, as I grew older, would become a great friend and advisor and, also a shoulder to cry on, many times in the future.

At Aunt Daisy's house, my nan and grandad Coombes would also be

there, and the grown ups would all sit and reminisce over old times with light hearted arguments and gales of laughter. They would also play cards and bingo (compulsory), and drink Uncle Bill's home brew.Well, most of the men would. The womenfolk would drink Cinzano, Martini, Sherry and Wine or Advocaat. Obviously not all together, well, perhaps one Aunty would!
I would see my cousins there, John, Paul, Gary and Stephen. I think there may have been a cousin Lynn, Gary's younger sister, I do know that, sadly, she died at a young age so I'm not too sure.
Also, I had Aunt Daisy's daughters there, Theresa, Maureen, Kathy and Patsy (hang on, they were cousins too).
My little favourite cousin Karen, Bett's future daughter hadn't shown her face yet.
So, there were a lot of the Coombes clan present with my grandad Coombes at the head with my nan alongside.
Nan would always have a cigarette hanging out of her mouth and we'd all wait for the long length of ash to fall off onto her pinafore and into her lap. It would always amaze us how long it would hang there whilst she was talking. The ciggie seemed to be stuck to her bottom lip all the time. Grandad, on the other hand, would smoke his pipe. He would sit in the corner, watching proceedings through a cloud of baccy smoke. I was certainly drawn to him from a very early age and I would remain close to him until he finally passed away, just nine months short of his century.
I couldn't have had a better friend or mentor.
The women all loved their bingo, as you will find out as my story progresses. Personally, I would rather staple my private parts to a stable door. Luckily, in this life, we're not all the same!
These, now annual Boxing day get togethers at Palmarsh would carry on throughout my childhood and partly beyond.
After dad had consumed only several pints of quite potent home

brew, we would all pile back into the van and pin ball our way back home via West Hythe and Lympne hill.
It was certainly so different in the World back then.

*

The day after Boxing day would start, for us kids, with bags and shovels as we'd trail the hunt's route, picking up whatever had descended from a horse's bottom. This was good fertilizer for our dad's vegetable gardens, and it got us out again in the fields.
The only problem was the cold, and cold meant balaclavas and mittens, not to mention the old wellies.
I said not to mention them!
If it was just a cold, crisp clear sunny frosty day, your breath would hit the inside of your woollen facial prison and sometimes freeze. If it didn't freeze, it would just remain wet and cold and feel totally unpleasant, especially if your balaclava had a mind of its own, like mine did.
I'd be running around with the others, with a wet freezing face, wet numb fingers and toes and a bright red and painful end of my slightly large nose, whilst carrying a bag laden with smouldering horse's doo dah, and I, like the others, would be enjoying every sodden minute of it.
Well, I was until we all stopped running about and then the reality would set in and your blazing fire at home might beckon a tad quicker.
Once I was back indoors, I had to get mum to take my mittens and wellies off as my hands were too cold to hold anything. As each wellie was pulled off, you would look down to see at least half of your sock, soaking wet and dangling from the end of your foot, with the darned big toe dripping water onto the floor.
My wet woolly gear would be hung on the fire guard to steam and

dry, snotty balaclava as well, and then I could resume my indoor games. While I had been out collecting big brown smelly lumps for dad, sleeping Bunty had been having his "after feeding time" nap and he had just woken up in a grumpy, grizzly mood (no change there then).

I was just settled down, not too near the fire, as I was instructed not to be, just driving my little Dinky delivery lorry around the road system when Grizzly features, half asleep, staggered in.
He stepped straight onto a Beta Bilda building brick and fell back screaming, and his big fat bulbous arse landed directly on my plastic garage, flattening it quicker that the Luftwaffe would have done twenty years earlier!
My mouth sprang open, but words wouldn't come out.
"M…..nnggg"
Then off he went….
"WAAAH" WAAAH" WAAAH"
Mum came running in and, seeing him sitting there with the garage flag just visible between his chubby legs, picked him up.
"WAAAH" "WAAAH"
"Mum, he's just bro….."
Whack!
"Why did you leave that there for him to fall over?"
Whack!
"Mum, he's just broke my garage!"
Smack!
"Ow!"
"Mum, it's not my fau…"
Smack!
"Tidy this up now!"
"It wasn't me" I cried.

Smack!
"Tidy it up, you shouldn't have had it there, now put it away!"
"My garage is smashed up" I cried again.
"He doesn't know"
Mum yelled at me and carried the little fat blitzkrieg into the kitchen.

Between sobs I loaded all my Dinky toys into the box along with the road mat. Hopefully dad would be able to fix my garage later.
I wouldn't hold my breath though.
Life moved on and The Beatles topped the charts with "I feel fine". My garage didn't feel fine though and nor did the backs of my legs where they'd been clouted.
Oh well.

*

The snow came and went but it was nowt on a couple of years back. We would venture over the fields at the back, towards Birch Rough woods and Sellinge. Just before reaching Sellinge we'd cross the Southern British Railways line from Dover and beyond, and up to London. That would be a different World up there. We rarely walked to Sellinge though, only going there if one of our mum's wanted something urgently from Sellinge Stores, and that was rarer than a pig with three eyes!
Do you know what you call a pig with three eyes?
A piiig! Okay, sorry about that one.
Sometimes whilst around Birch Rough or near the Otterpool Manor estate to the North West, we would see, or most certainly hear the farmers, or possibly, poachers, out shooting pheasants, rabbits, honey badgers and the like.
The noise from their shotguns would reverberate across the land and it would penetrate though ones very being. We tried to be as far

away from those folk armed with big guns, as we could. Our guns were only plastic or sticks, these could do some serious damage. As kids around the farm, we had all seen these large shotguns up close as we had been shown them by Mr. Duthoit and his sons, but only to warn us never to touch them or go too near them. To this day, I've heeded that advice. I've never felt any yearning to either touch or go near them.
Just a thought here….
I wonder if Gun manuals have a "Troubleshooting" section in them!

*

There was one incident just after my seventh birthday (and Charlie Choop's third).
We were astounded one morning to see Court at Street overrun with officers from the Kent Constabulary.
There were Police cars everywhere, and a Police van and some Policemen on motorbikes.
The Police cars weren't these revved up, turbo charged super-duper fast beasts of today's Force. Oh no, these were little Morris Minor's and Mini's, with a large Austin Cambridge as well, and they all had a dollop of a spinning flashing light on the roof. I think that the driver had to lean out of the window, shouting…
"Nee Na, Nee Na, Nee Na, Nee Na".
Maybe not!
Anyway, the whole point of their presence in our little quiet hamlet wasn't owt to do with poaching or any minor traffic infringement such as driving a tractor or lorry after consuming several pints of local ale, no indeedy.
This posse of Police was because there had been an escape of two prisoners from the local HMP Aldington, which was about a mile down the hill from our school near Bonnington, where Mrs. Duell's

family garage was (and still is).

We all stood there open mouthed as we watched a couple of motorbikes bounce across the field in front of us. It was like an early version of motor cross, except the riders were Police Constables and didn't have numbers on their backs. Their white helmets bobbed up and down as they attempted to stay in one furrow on the muddy ground.

I couldn't work out why they were in the field at all and not on the road, then I heard our local bobby on a bike say that there were Police in the wooded area under the hill trying to flush the fugitives out if they were in there.

Exciting or what?

He then asked mum if she could go with them to unlock the big house at the far end of Aldergate where she cleaned as the owners were away.

She could only do it by loading a Curly Wurly chewing, garage busting yobbo into the kiddie seat behind her saddle and cycle there.

Obviously, he didn't sit there with his mouth open very long before a long stick of chocolate covered toffee was wedged in.

Despite her saying that I couldn't go, I decided that I would also cycle there with her on my trusty little Blue bike as I might have been of assistance in arresting the two hardened criminals.

Well, in my mind I may have been, but to be honest I just wanted to see all that was going on as things like this were as rare as a nun's fart in sleepy Court at Street.

As it turned out, I had to stay at the top of the steps to the house with Munchy, the chocolate boy, while the Policemen went down with mum to unlock and have a good old sniff around. I kept myself busy by scanning the trees to see if the convicts were perched up in the branches but alas, I could only spot a squirrel that was possibly munching crisps. Ah Ha! That may explain how I found that empty

packet for Robert's plop plops that time (this looked like a ready salted packet too!).
Or did I just imagine that bit?
Perhaps time has once again puffed the smoke of age across the windmills of my mind. Hang on, I'm getting into a song there.

The drama (the one about the escapees, not the crisp eating squirrel) ended when some other Police Officers, possibly "The Sweeny", apprehended them along by the canal near West Hythe.
They'd travelled approximately three and a half miles as the Cormorant flies (Yes, we do get the occasional one or two here).
Aldington Prison went from a closed prison, when I was a lad, to an open prison, then to a Detention Centre for young offenders, before finally closing in the mid / late 1990s.
I did eventually make it inside when it was a Detention Centre, but only as a visiting footballer when we played against them in a local match. I was playing for "The Prince of Wales" pub team and I can say that it was terrifying just driving in through the gates, and as fellow human beings we all felt very sorry for the poor lads in there. I know that quite a few possibly deserved to be there but the regime seemed very harsh and totally frightening. Perhaps that was the point. I don't know. I do know that we all tried to slip the lads a few ciggies, and that I was glad and grateful to be able to drive out again after the game.

*

Anyway, back at least twenty years, possibly more.
On 30th January 1965, the country bade farewell to possibly our greatest ever Prime Minister, as the whole land bowed their heads in grief, respect and thanks to Winston Churchill, who's State Funeral was sombrely televised. I can still recall the sight of his coffin being

transported down the River Thames on a cold bleak day. The Black and White footage added to the sadness of the occasion.
The passing of a truly great man. I just thought that I'd add that as I felt it was important.

*

Looking out over the marsh from Five Acres, we couldn't help but notice a massive construction taking place out at Dungeness Point, some ten miles in the distance, on the coast.
This was the commencement of the building of Dungeness Power Station. It was an enormous blot on an otherwise unspoilt landscape. A desolate, but none the less, beautiful location.
As time would go on, we could watch the site becoming bigger and, obviously more permanent.
Our view from the Downs was dramatically changed forever, and now it is just part of the scenery and it's hard to recall a time when it wasn't

*

Chapter Seven – The times they are a changin'

There was another change for our little gang of five after the long summer holidays. It was a time when we could really relate to The Hollies "I'm Alive" at number one in the charts.
The Power Station would be the first of our irreversible changes.
The two Roberts would be going to Secondary school in Ashford. Johanna would also be going next year.
As we marched off to school in the September sunshine of 1965, we were waved to by two very nervous looking faces from the early bus, on their way to Ashford North Secondary school. We would really miss them, as I'm sure that they would miss us (at first, anyway).
It suddenly occurred to me half way into the walk to school, just as we crossed the top of Knoll hill, that I was the eldest man in the group, in fact I was the only man in the trio.
We became men at an early age in the country. I was a very mature seven and a half and it was my job to look after Winky and Jo Jo (Boo Boo and Johanna to non- gang members).
I still held the responsible position of Milk Monitor, although I wasn't given a replacement badge. We all had our school photo's taken in the playing field a week after our return to school. We had to tell our parents that this was about to happen, so they could dress us in our best school clothes to make sure that we were half presentable for the occasion.

*

After school the two Roberts came home, full of themselves, and loaded with stories of the "Big school". They were both quite big strong lads, as most were that were bred in the countryside. I must have been the runt of the litter as far as Court at Street kids went. It was still my one footballing ambition to be able to touch the crossbar when playing in goal. Luckily there weren't many boys at school that could really kick the ball too high to worry me.

Football, and sport in general really was starting to become a big interest for me. I would refine my main tastes down to football, rugby, cricket, tennis and cycling as I grew, and I would have a few tales to tell as time went by (mainly on the football pitch).

As the two Roberts started to play different sports at school, they tried to introduce the rest of us to some of them. I was an easy convert, but the girls took some convincing.

We would mainly play cricket and football in Five Acres. We had an old cricket bat and made stumps from old bits of chestnut fencing. Any ball would do to play with, although it did get harder to hold the ball, the more it got stuck in any brown gooey stuff that the cows or sheep had left behind.

It could be great fun bowling a pooh coated tennis ball at an unaware batsman and to then fall about laughing as they splatted it with their bat and got a face full of the brown stuff. It would always end up with the bowling offender being chased around the field whilst lumps of Sheep's pooh went whistling past their ears.

While all of this was going on of course, somebody else would be reloading the ball, keeping it poohy side down so that the already brown splattered batsman wasn't aware!

I bet that Townies didn't play games like that.

A lack of livestock fodder, I suppose.

We had to make up our own puerile fun, and I must confess, it was a lot of fun.

Unless you were the batsman!

*

Our bike rides would extend to Lympne, where we would spend a lot of time standing by the fence of the Airfield and wait for a plane to land or take off for France. There would always be small aircraft flying about as there was a flying club based there, but it was best watching a Dakota DC3 leave the one and only terminal, then taxi out onto the runway, and with both propellers going like the clappers it would charge towards the fence and adjacent road, only just rising at the last minute and missing it and any traffic on the road at the time.

Oh, and the noise!

It was quite a posh little Airport at the time. There was another one down at Lydd on the Romney Marsh that also flew planes to areas of Northern France and possibly, Southern Cyprus (I might have made the last bit up!).

Lympne was one of the main fighter Airfield's during the Second World War, with both, Hurricanes and Spitfires based there.

An Avro 748 trying to take the lid off an unsuspecting Ford Cortina as it comes in to land.

There's a lot of history around Lympne, with the Roman ruins of "Portus Lemanis" on the slope of the Roughs, just below Lympne castle and St. Stephens church.

We could do a circuit on our old bikes from Lympne, down to the old Royal Oak Motel at Newingreen and along to Sellinge, then past the race course at Westenhanger. From there we could either pedal back up Harringe Lane to home or carry on to the Aldington turning and cycle home that way. There were many detours and variants from this as well as we had a lot of time to use up.

It was at the weekends that we had our main times together, what with the two Roberts being away at Ashford school during the week. One Week day during a school holiday the two girls had gone with their mum to Hythe to do some shopping, so it was Just us three boys left to fill our time.

We were mooching around the farmyard when I got hold of a piece of old fencing wire that was laying on the ground. With this bent and twisted around a few times I managed to fashion (in my mind) a rather passable boomerang. The only problem was that when I threw it, it never came back!

So, I had to fetch it.

It didn't make no never mind, we all made them and started aiming at targets around the yard, this was quite good fun for a Seven and Three- quarter year old with his two older mates.

It was decided that we'd drained every last drop of enjoyment out of the game so we all agreed to have a walk to Knoll Hill woods, so as my little snotty nosed sibling stared at us from his tricycle through the front gate slats, we made our merry way, only for me to realize that I was still holding onto my rather good, but cumbersome boomerang. The other two had tossed theirs away (they didn't come back either).

On seeing mum come out of the front door, I shouted to her that we were going off...

"Mum, we're going down to the woods" I shouted.

"Don't be late back for your tea!"

How we knew what the time was, I don't know as none of us had a watch. I think that it was just instinct that told us.

"Mum, look after my boomerang!"

I yelled out as I flung it high over the baby baboon's head. I watched it, along with the two Roberts, as it unerringly made its way directly through our large front porch window!

CRAAAASSSHHH !

The sound of the window pane shattering and falling back into the porch (along with the offending boomerang) could be heard right up the road to the Welcome Stranger.

The next thing that I knew was that I was grabbed by my ear (not a sticky out one.... Yet!) and dragged up the garden path, with my feet only just contacting with the ground every fourth step, to the accompaniment of mum shouting and screaming at me at the top of her voice. I caught some of the words, none of them too complimentary though, and some were bad words that I'd not heard from mum before.

I think that she was upset about something!

I was traipsed over the broken glass with it crunching under mum's feet (I think I flew over that bit, aided by an ear lift).

Once inside the house I was flung down on the stairs and told to get to bed till dad got home. I was sobbing that I was sorry but that didn't do owt other than incur the usual smacks on any part of me within reach, so I scrambled upstairs to my room and cowered on the bed. Mum appeared so angry with me that she had stopped shouting and screaming and just left me to stew. I knew when dad got home, I wasn't going to get any good news so... "Hey Ho"

"There be it" as my grandad would say.
As this entire debacle happened, the two Roberts amazingly ran off, lest they get involved in the punishment dished out, and my little turd shaped younger brother just stared over the handlebars of his bike, with possibly just the slightest smirk, as he knew what was coming my way. For what seemed like ages I lay there, sobbing into the pillow as I listened to the sound of the broken glass being swept up, interspersed with further information screamed up to me, telling me what sort of person I was, how good and helpful around the house I was (alright, not that bit), and just exactly what dad would say and do when he got home.
I was ahead of her on that bit.
I knew what was coming my way and it wasn't a packet of Spangles or a repaired garage!
I was right.
That little indiscretion only kept me indoors for a day because, apparently, I was getting under mum's feet, so I was free to roam with my cowardly chums once again.
I never saw my boomerang anymore though.

*

The year moved on and Christmas passed by once more. "Day tripper" and "We can work it out" by The Beatles topped the Christmas charts and they were still there for my Eighth birthday in January.
The only memorable present for Christmas was, for some unfathomable reason, a teddy that I received. It was obviously just the Ideal gift for a young macho short-arsed, big nosed lad with a penchant for getting into mischief. The odd thing about this teddy though was that it's golden hair, or fur, was brushed upwards, so he was completely different and at odds with any other teddy. The

possible runt off the production line.
I called him "Michael!"
Nope, I've no Idea why.
There were, I thought at the time, two impending events this year, 1966.
The first was that the school would have to construct a "Grizzle corner", because the baby hippo that was my little brother was about to be foisted upon the Education system. By making it past his fourth birthday without exploding from chocolate and biscuit overload, his reward was to be entry to Aldington school as an Infant. I thought that it could be okay to have my little sibling at school as I would grow as an older brother, with all the experience and responsibility that it would entail in looking after him during his early days at school.
Oh dear, if only I knew then what would happen, I'd have got myself expelled before he'd got there!
Secondly, in July this year, the World cup was to be held in England (although no matches were scheduled for the Romney Marsh area). As my interest in football had now become full on, I couldn't wait. Some games were even going to be shown live on T.V. albeit in Black and White in our case along with most other folk. I hadn't properly picked a team to support yet, although I did have a liking for Liverpool (This would grow), and I had cheered them to victory against Leeds United in last year's F.A. cup final. I'd also watched them on Match of the day on BBC2 when it started in 1964.
You try watching a grainy screen in Black and White featuring two teams that look like their both playing in the same strip as they all looked the same. Liverpool vs Chelsea or Manchester United vs Everton was virtually impossible to follow, or once when Leeds United, in all White, played Tottenham Hotspur, in their away kit of all Yellow, the commentator said…

"For those of you watching in Black and White, Spurs are in the Yellow socks!"
I'm sure that it wasn't the King of the commentators, Kenneth Wolstenholme.
It was hard work following sport on the television in those days. My grandad, in the subsequent years, used to watch Pot Black snooker in Black and White, and how he managed to follow it, I just don't know. There was one event that I wasn't prepared for though, and although my recall isn't great about this occasion, I was to be Christened along with Barry at St. Stephens church, Lympne.
Now, I was Eight years old and it had never ever been mentioned before.
Why had mum and dad waited to get me Christened with my brother?
Was I not good enough to merit my own Christening when I was younger?
Was I just added on to my baby brother's Christening as an afterthought?
Was it "Dip one, Dip one free"?
Anyway, that was the situation. A done deal.
Prior to Barry starting school, we had a joint Christening.
I expect that the vicar used his sticky out ear as a paddle in the Font. I have since been told that I just had to stand and tip my head back to the water for mine and I just shrugged it all off really. Little Charlie Choops, on the other hand, apparently whined all the way through the service.
No change there then.
Oh, how I wished that the vicar had Christened him "Charlie Sticky Out Ear Choops" instead of Barry. There was another family name for him that was being used more and more now, especially by mum, and that was...

"Baa".
Yep, she would call to him by shouting out…
"Baa", "Baa".
"Are you upstairs Baa?"
Mum was turning into a sheep impersonator!
Why did he get lots of family nick-names, yet I only got the one?
Okay, I know, some of the names for the Sticky out eared, Curly Wurly, chocolate munching little fat blob were only used by me, but that's not the point.
I was sometimes called by other names than Todd, but they were only abusive swear words and they don't count.

*

Easter came and went, and after consuming 50% of East Kent's chocolate egg supply, the little chuckle brother joined Boo Boo, Jo and me in Mrs. Duell's taxi.
As the old Triumph Mayflower laboured up the gentle rises in the road, carrying much more weight now than the car was used to or built for, the girls regaled Barry (I wouldn't do any sheep impression for him) with tales of how good school was and how much fun he'd have , to keep his little mind occupied and to stop him grizzling again.
On reaching school, he was taken off my hands by his infant teacher. I don't mean that she was an Infant, he was the Infant and she was the teacher. The Infant teacher.
I think that I've explained that fully now.
So, off he went, and I could get on with my own class and forget about him for the day.
Wrong!
Just after I'd helped to bring the milk in for the morning playtime slurping session, I was called to the secretary's office. Oh no!

What had I done wrong now?
No, I'd done nowt wrong, perhaps they had my replacement Milk Monitor's badge, or even some new goalie's gloves so that I don't have to use dad's old driving gloves anymore.
Nope.
Before I'd even knocked and opened the office door, I could hear the familiar sound of a Sticky out eared grizzle!
And there he was, in all his glory standing in front of me.
But something was different....
"They're not his shorts!"
I pointed out to the kindly old school secretary.
"I'm sorry Kevin, but Barry's had a little accident".
I was handed a newspaper wrapped package. The smelly wetness from his pants and shorts was starting to seep through.
"Mrs. Duell is on her way, you'll have to take him home, I'm afraid, Kevin".
"But Miss, it's games later!"
"Sorry Kevin, but he can't go on his own, there's a good lad".
We stood, the two of us, in the main porch waiting for Mrs. Duell to arrive.
When she did, she gave me a sympathetic smile and put newspaper down where the little pee and pooh fountain was going to sit, and off we went back home.
Luckily Mrs. Duell said that she'd wait while I ran indoors to tell mum what had happened, although a blind man looking the other way with no sense of smell would have been hard pushed to not notice. At least this time she couldn't blame me. I handed over the sopping wet parcel and in went the little squelch monkey.
Before you could nail a jelly to a tree I was out of that door and back in the car, screaming..."Go, Go, Go!"

Thanks to Mrs. Duell, I wouldn't miss games after all.
Unfortunately, I didn't know it at the time, but this was to be a regular occurrence and not a "one-off".
I was to spend many days, standing in the front porch of the school, clasping a newspaper bound package, sometimes containing more than just widdle, with a pong that could knock the starlings out of the sky, whilst all the snot covered little sewerage producer could do was to stand there and grizzle.
There were times when the school's supply of replacement togs for such an event got so low that even the skirts became a viable option. I think that they may have been used once or twice as well!
I can't recall when the situation ceased, but it went on for a good few weeks until he'd learned to become a proper human and used the toilet.
I can't cycle or drive past the old school today without looking at the old main door and remembering those times.
Oh, happy days!
Not!

*

During the early summer, the cottage that separated us from Manor Farm cottages was being restored after being bought by a man called "Robert". Another one, although this older, nice chap lived alone. He may have been Gay, which was not a thing talked about nor recognised back then, especially in the outback where we roamed. He was certainly very polite and always impeccably dressed. Whatever his leaning, it didn't make no never mind to us which side of the toast he buttered. He seemed a class or three above us peasant folk in his manners and appearance, but he would never flaunt it. As I say, a very nice chap.

The thing was, that when his cottage was being renovated prior to him moving in, I was given permission to help the builders. They let me believe that I was really assisting them, I would carry bricks, wood, anything they asked me to, and I would sweep and tidy up for them. When they had their tea breaks or dinner, I would sit with them, eating my sandwiches and Kit Kat and swigging out of my bottle of orange squash. They had a thing called a Transistor Radio blasting out tunes of the day, such as "Sunny Afternoon" by the Kinks, "Bus Stop" by the Hollies or the Beatles "Paperback Writer". We would all be singing along whilst laying bricks, or in my case, passing them up.

For years and years, I had it in my mind that we were constructing or building the cottage until, in recent years, a local told me that it was possibly built in the 17th century or sometime around then. So now I know that we were renovating it. I still say "we" as I feel that I contributed a lot to the job, although now, thinking about it logically, I may have been a hindrance or at worse, used as a glorified "Gofor", a skivvy, unpaid of course.

*

Never mind, the World Cup was upon us and everyone was displaying their Willies!

Yep, "World Cup Willie" was everywhere. He was the symbol of our World Cup. You could get him in all sorts of various guises from shops, petrol stations and the like.

There were "Willie" stickers everywhere!

It was an incredibly exciting time to be a fan, as everybody was during the tournament, especially watching on the T.V. as England, in either all White or in White shirts and almost Black shorts played Uruguay, who were in light Grey shirts and Black shorts, Mexico, who played in dark Grey shirts and White shorts, and then France, who wore a slightly darker Grey, almost Black shirts and White shorts, winning two and drawing the other to top the group (it was quite a boring group).

The team that everyone wanted to see was Brazil in their almost Cream coloured shirts and darkish Grey shorts, with the great Pele playing in their side. Unfortunately, his opponents appeared to mistake him for the ball as they tried to kick him out of Everton's ground, so that was that for both him and Brazil. At least, hopefully he got to appreciate how good our Elastoplast plasters and our bruise creams and liniments were!

We then got to play some nice chappies from Argentina who played in Grey and White striped shirts (different) and Black shorts whilst we wore a natty all White outfit which I think they got a bit humpy about, and their captain kept shouting at the referee about how our brilliant White shirts were too bright and were dazzling their goalie. While the goalie was hunting in his bag for some sun glasses, Geoff Hurst headed a goal for us.

That really put the goat among the pig pens, I can tell you, the little Argentinian captain started arguing again with the referee and poked and prodded him. Anyone watching this display of petulance would have thought that the referee had just broken into his house on Christmas day and widdled all over his children's presents!

(I have tried to Google this, but I can't confirm if the referee did do this or not, nor does it state whether the Argentine captain has children. I do like to be factually accurate where possible).

I'm not entirely sure what else the captain may have said to the referee, but whatever it was, the referee took umbrage and he sent him to the dressing room to put the kettle on (I think). The programme notes did say that the referee liked a very strong cup of tea, so that would have been a sensible move on his part. After that, and much kicking, pinching, punching, spitting and shoving, we won.

Referee's really shouldn't behave like that, they should set an example!
And don't forget, I was relatively new to the game so some of the rules, maybe I didn't understand fully.
Next, we played Portugal in the semi-final. They played in quite dark Grey shirts and White shorts and we stuck with those lucky brilliant White shirts, but we toned it down with darkish, almost Black shorts again. There'd be no dazzling this goalie as it was played at night under floodlights.
By now, even the mums were getting into it. Many a mum dashed into town, trying to grab a "Willie" to wave around their head.

World Cup Willie

Everywhere, folk were singing…
"Red, White and Blue!"
"World Cup Willie"
I can't remember the rest.
As if you didn't know, we beat Portugal to play our old foe West Germany in the final.
In houses all over the Country, families gathered around the television set to watch the game together…except in ours, we didn't. Dad had found out that one of mum's brothers had a colour set so, ignoring my pleading face, he buggered off down there to watch it, while we stayed at home to see England, this time, in natty Grey shirts and White shorts, beat West Germany, who were actually in White shirts and Black shorts, by 3.5 – 2.

Well, come on, we all know that it wasn't really over the line, don't we?... Don't we?

Still got the blinkers on, have we? It doesn't matter now.

When that Swiss Referee, who didn't speak any Russian, asked that Russian Linesman, who didn't speak any Swiss, if it was a goal or not, the Russian Linesman, apparently got confused, thinking that the Swiss Referee was asking for directions to the nearest bakery, pointed with his flag to a baker's shop in the general direction of the centre circle. The non-Russian speaking Swiss Referee then thanked the non-Swiss speaking Russian Linesman, and excitedly pointed, and ran off towards the bakery, being chased by several non-Swiss or Russian speaking German footballers, trying to shout their orders for Chelsea buns and chocolate fingers, in German to the non-German speaking Referee and Linesman.

If only they'd all spoken in English, they could have asked Alan Ball, who was nearest to the situation, and he could have told them, in his very high, pitched voice, that the aforesaid mentioned bakery was closed as the baker was at home watching the game.

There, problem solved!

It's worth pointing out, at this juncture, that none of the England players requested any cakes or pastries at that time as they were concentrating on the game, although Sir Alf Ramsey was photographed secretly nibbling on a Macaroon!

It must also be pointed out that the Russian non-Swiss speaking Linesman came from Azerbaijan!

Obviously, it was easier to say that he came from Russia in those days of the Soviet Union.

I got all these facts from Winklepedia, so they must be true!

As Mr. Kenneth Wolstenholme said at the time, as Bobby Moore wiped his grubby mitt before shaking the Queen's gloved hand...

"It's only twelve inches high, made of Gold, and it means that England are World Champions!"
He wasn't talking about "World Cup Willie".
I remember that everyone was in the Welcome Stranger that night. Us kids were upstairs with plenty of Vimto, Coke, crisps and choccy to keep us going (if we could keep Barry's nose out of the trough for long enough). We could hear singing, laughing and cheering down in the bar, and that infectious good spirit reached all of us.
It was a time when all the Country came together as one to celebrate, whether football was your thing or not, it mattered not a jot.
It was a time when we all knew that England would rule the football World for many, many years to come, with frequent World cups and celebrations such as this one.
Our little World Cup Willie's would grow and grow!
Ah well.

*

Life in our little Dingly Dell would return to its normal meandering course.
The two Roberts had started to make some new friends at the big school, so they didn't always spend their time with us so much with us now. It was a new World for them, away from their childhood haunts. A time to spread their wings a bit and to see new things. Well, it would have been, until they realized that they didn't have any wings, so they had to catch a bus instead.
Johanna was also off to school in Ashford now, so that only left Boo Boo, me and the mini cesspool tanker.
Sometimes mum would take him to school on the bus, and she would carry on to Ashford to do some shopping. At least that meant that Boo Boo and me could walk. It wasn't as much fun, just the two

of us though. With five, there was always someone messing about, we would play chase or run across the fields pretending to be all sorts of characters. With just the two of us, we'd generally chat about the charts, singing different songs, invariably unintentionally using different words and laughing.

Sunday school was becoming less frequent as well, as sometimes it would only be one person wanting to go. We'd had enough schooling through the week, and as we all got bigger and older, there were more important things to do at home, and more places to explore, either on foot or on our bikes.

Some of the bikes were now being outgrown, so saddle posts had to be hoiked up in some instances, like the two Roberts. Mind you, they were very low down to start with. Johanna got a newer, bigger bike so Boo Boo could have hers, but she couldn't reach the pedals.

As luck would have it, grandad made any adjustments that I needed. I suppose it was obvious to anyone with eyes that both, Boo Boo and myself tended to be the Dwarf element of our group. We never seemed to grow much at all. In fact, we're still both quite short now. I'm only about Five feet seven, and Boo Boo is around Two feet shorter.

Only joshing.

She's about One foot six shorter!

By now, I reckon that most of our bike's tyres had more patches than actual tyre, as punctures were a common hazard with plenty of Hawthorn, Gorse and other prickly, thorny bushes lining the lanes and tracks around the area.

Stinging nettles were heavily involved as a source of injury, especially if you were the unfortunate one to be pushed into them. We'd hide in amongst them as well when we were playing war games, or our favourite Cowboys and Indians. You'd always give yourself away though as you got stung and yelped out in pain.

We would also cut them off at the stems and hold a bunch with some sacking or our sleeves, and use them as a weapon of attack, thrashing out at each other whilst shying away from the lunge of your opponent's nettles. (I'm sure that's what the Apache would have done if they'd have had stinging nettles there).

What with these weapons of pain and torture, and the many meadow cakes and sheep grenades at our disposal, I suppose that you could say that we all led a safe, sheltered upbringing at Court at Street.

We'd also have a different way of using our sheep grenades. We would get a nice springy Willow or Elderberry branch, Willow was best, and attach the grenade to it by just prodding it onto the end of the branch, and then flinging it off the end, like a catapult or grenade launcher. An expert launcher could get brilliant results, hitting the recipient with a splat, to the ribald laughter of the others. The two Roberts were our experts.

They could have flung sheep pooh for Britain!

I suppose we gave another meaning to the words "Pooh sticks".

We never raced them under any bridges though.

*

As 1966 headed towards Christmas and 1967, we seemed to be spending a lot more time in Hythe, at nan and grandads house. There were a few boys around my age, and I was told that I could go out and play football with them in the Square.

It was never explained to me why it was called "The Square" as it was a circle in shape.

It was just down on the elbow bit of a dead end, leading to some garages, off the main Dymchurch Road, and, really, I think that it was mainly a turning area for cars, but there were hardly any about, so it became a football pitch. I think that the residents knew not to park in

the Square as they might get some dents from the football.
The boys, who I'll introduce later, took me straight into the group. Their parents were all tenants at St. Georges Place. Nan and grandad lived on the main road bit, facing Hythe Ranges and the sea.
Whilst passing through nan's front room one day, to go and see grandad in his shed, I overheard mum saying that the family in the house next door were wanting to move to Folkestone, the next town along the coast, and that their house would then be up for rent.
Although I didn't know it at the time, mum wanted to get a transfer down to Hythe to be nearer to nan and grandad, as she was feeling cut off up at Court at Street.
Now, I've heard of people moving to be nearer their kinfolk, but this was the house next door.
Although I liked coming to Hythe, I lived in Court at Street.
It was what I knew. It was all I knew!
I was happy there, although times were changing, and as kids, we were growing older, I didn't want to move.
I wasn't going to be given a say or have any choice in the matter though. I wasn't quite Nine yet.
It was discussed a lot by mum and dad over a very subdued Christmas. Nan Pilcher was consulted as well when she came down to visit (teeth and all!).
Any arguments that I tried to put up were answered with…
"You'll do as you're told!"
So, that was my contribution ended.
Alarm bells should have been deafening me by now…
Then it happened.
The family from number 5 St. Georges Place had got their Council transfer and they'd invited mum and dad round to see the house layout. It was identical to nan and grandad's next door, just the other way around.

Mum explained to me that I'd have lots of new friends to play football with, and that I'd still see my old friends (I don't know how), and she said that I'd also have my own bedroom, and that I would...
"Do as you're bloody well told!"
So, that was it then. A done deal.
It was made clear to me that it would be better all round for us to move from one number Five to another number Five, on the Western edge of the town of Hythe, on the Eastern edge of the Romney Marsh.
Mum was as chuffed as a squirrel who'd got all the nuts as the transfer was confirmed. My Ninth birthday passed in a blur. We would be leaving, what I would describe in later years as "God's own Country", and we would be getting ever so slightly closer to civilization.
I would still be a country boy, although not so rural!

*

One other tiny incident occurred in Hythe, around this time. Mum had decided that one of her young Pilcher offspring required a haircut so, along with my lovely Aunt Nell (Nan's sister, who I'll mention more of later) she took the young, stroppy lad to the barber's shop in Chapel Street, whereupon the, obviously upset boy decided to drop a couple of "Richard the Third's" out of his trouser leg, onto the floor of the shop. Mum immediately left the premises, totally embarrassed (I don't blame her), leaving Aunt Nell to confirm, when the barber noticed the steaming pile, that she was the naughty child's mother. She had to clear up his mess, before leaving with hIm in shame.
Another little moment of my chubby little brother's bottom fall-outs?

Nope, on this occasion, I must confess that it was me!
Obviously, a dodgy turnip or something.
After that unfortunate event, mum vowed never to take me to the barber again (she bottled it and ran away, anyway. Poor old Aunt Nell).
From that day on, we had to sit on a board across grandad's Carver chair while he attacked our heads with scissors, clippers and shears!
I've still got his hair cutting kit in my collection of his old stuff, today.

Chapter Eight – A Brave New World

The move down the hill to Hythe was gradually carried out by dad and a couple of his workmates from the Council. I believe they may have used his Ford Council lorry as well.

All that I had to do was to pack my few toys, books and comics into a couple of boxes, and that was that. In our old chest of drawers in the back bedroom, one drawer was half full of prehistoric old seventy-eight records, which we proceeded to smash in the back garden and dump in the dustbin. There could have been some priceless classics in amongst them but, hey ho! We didn't know, nor did we care.

With all my sad, stifled goodbyes said to the others, Boo Boo, Johanna and the two Roberts, I left the part of my life where I lived in Court at Street behind. I would still go there frequently in the subsequent years, as that's the place I loved and where I was born and bred.

The place that shaped me.

Even today, my heart and soul are still there, in fact, I have made a clause in my Will about having my ashes scattered in Five Acres field, overlooking the Romney Marsh and the sea. Obviously, I don't envisage that event occurring for many, many years, hopefully near to my one hundred and fifteenth birthday or beyond, depending on my unbelievable good looks, fitness and my continued ability to fool myself that I'm still a child at heart.

It was a bit ironic that, just prior to moving, on my Ninth birthday, Tom Jones was manning the number one spot with "The Green, Green Grass of Home".

Still, ne'er mind, eh! These things happen in life.

*

"Onwards and upwards" as the saying goes…Or in my case, it was downwards to sea level and our new abode, next door to nan and grandad.

It was a busy period with very little time for brooding, as me and the Curly Wurly kid had to both start and settle into our new schools. I was bound for St. Leonards Primary school in Hythe, and Mr. Nibble was in the Infants school, just across the Green. This was certainly a new World for us, as there was no Mrs. Duell and her taxi now. We had to get on the number 105 double decker bus through to Hythe Red Lion Square on most days, and then cut up over the canal to the schools. There was a whole new motley array of children to get used to as well. The bus journey was only two miles, and of course, all the kids headed straight upstairs to the top deck.

I would be in the Second year of Four classes for a bit. I made some good new friends straight away at St. Georges Place, or "Nanny goat Square" as some folk referred to it as. That was because a field next to the houses, on Bluewater farm contained goats in earlier years, and they used to stray through the fence, into the small estate. Now, Bluewater farm had changed to a caravan site with a shop selling sweeties, so that would do very nicely. The shop was only two hundred yards from my front door.

This was a complete contrast with our old house in Court at Street, where the sweetie shop was miles away!

A further couple of hundred yards along the main road to Hythe stood the Prince of Wales pub, then it was on past Pennypot estate, which was also once a farm. After Pennypot, would be Princess Terrace Council houses on the main road, then the large building that was the Kengate Laundry. This establishment took all the laundry from the various hotels and businesses in the Hythe and Folkestone area. Further onwards, towards Hythe, was "The Gem" Newsagents shop, opposite on the seaward side of the road was Reachfields, a small group of Army corrugated tin houses, surrounded by some rough, scrubby ground and backing onto a football pitch.

Three hundred yards further Eastwards was the Light Railway station, or to use its correct title, Hythe station of the Romney, Hythe & Dymchurch Railway. It's the smallest running public railway in the World, and it runs from Hythe to Dungeness.

It chugs along behind our houses, and the sight of these trains, and the smell of the steam from the engines are two of the senses that I've grown up with and never stop loving. I could look down on these trains from Five Acres at Court at Street. They were very small caterpillars, snaking their way across the marsh with the steam puffing out. You could hear their whistle in the distance, given a fair wind, and now I've got them as a permanent fixture, running alongside us.

What a beautiful background sight and sound to grow up with.

On the other hand, on the opposite side of the road from us, all the way from Hythe fishing boats to the Redoubt to the West of us, was the Hythe Ranges. It was only about a four hundred yards stretch from our house, across the Ranges to the sea shore.

After a short while, the noise from the guns firing when the Army were in residence on the Ranges, never bothered us. We sort of became immune to it and never even noticed.

Believe it or not (and you should believe it, because it's true!), those sounds and smells from the trains and the guns firing are still with me as I now, fifty years on, live back in Palmarsh!

*

Anyway, back to 1967, and settling into my new house and school. The one concession that I was given as the eldest son, was the choice of bedroom. Would I like the large back bedroom with lots of room to play with my soldiers and cars on the floor on the warmer

Western side of the house, or would I prefer the much smaller box bedroom with barely room to swing Peter the cat, on the much colder Eastern side of the house with the wind whistling up the alley next to the bedroom wall?

I'm not accepting bets, but have a guess which one I opted for?

So, it didn't take long to move my stuff into my cupboard... er... I mean, bedroom. Yes, I know that it was about a third of the size of Lardy Bum's room and I couldn't even fit Peter the cat into it, never mind try to swing him, but I could see it's potential. Well, I thought that I could. As it was so small, it could only fit a single bed in it, which meant that I would get a new bed (sort of), and he would keep our big double bed (he would grow into it), also, the window would be near my head in the middle of the room so I could sit on the bed and look straight out, over the back gardens, railway, caravan and camping site, over towards the canal and right up the Roughs to the large Radar mirror from the Second World War. Us kids would have many a jaunt up there over the next few years. The one bonus, although I didn't know at the time, was that directly below my window was our flat back porch roof. I would climb out of the window and sit on the roof in future summers, listening to the record player that I hadn't yet got.

There would be a major move for me in the future, but that's to come!

The thing was, mum, dad and Barney Rubble all thought that he'd got the best deal. Who was right?

*

Two of the boys that I knew, Steve Miller and Mick O'Brien, called for me as soon as we got into the house and I was allowed out, to get me out of the way, to go and play football in the Square.

These two would be very good mates over the coming years as our mutual love of football grew. Mick had a younger brother called Carl, and there was Kim Maycock (who would later be known as "Cecil", I don't know why) and Robert Hyson (yet another Robert), and sometimes Brian and Lynton Warne would all join us, with others to play football and, I suppose, generally annoy all of the residents around the Square. Some other boys would join us as the years moved on as well. It was a fair old tribe!

At the end of St. Georges Place, by the garages that backed onto the railway tracks, was an area called "The meadow".

Now, this can conjure up images of grass billowing in a warm summer breeze, festooned with wildlife, buttercups and daisies. A truly beautiful vision, is it not?

But, oh no, our meadow was not as this.

No, our meadow consisted of shingle and Gorse bushes, plenty of them, with some nettles and various pieces of broken glass and china from very old bottles, cups and plates. Some, or most of the glass was dark Green or Blue in colour. Sometimes we would come across an almost complete old bottle from times gone by.

There were dirt (or mud, depending on the time of year) paths snaking through the Gorse, mainly leading across the meadow to the Dairy, Mr. and Mrs. Nicholson's VG store and Palmarsh hall.

The meadow area was approximately four hundred yards by two hundred yards of what I've described. In the middle of it was a small clear area where we created some sort of football pitch on the uneven, shingle, gorse and glass ridden ground.

On this little God forsaken patch, with the trains puffing and tooting alongside, we had some of the happiest times of our young footballing lives.If it was too wet or muddy, we'd play in the Square, if it wasn't too bad, we'd be on the meadow. Don't forget that this shingly, beachy area was all ground that was reclaimed from the sea many, many moons ago. It was on the Eastern edge of the Romney Marsh, so the drainage was quite good, we had, in effect, the largest "Soakaway" in Kent.

Of course, playing sports such as football, rugby and indulging in war games of all types on such ground, surrounded by gorse, would have a detrimental impact on our clothing, especially the knees of our trousers. This was where mum's needlework skills and prowess came to the fore yet again, giving me so many "cats bums" and "toothless granny smiles" sewn up areas that I looked like a misshapen clown. Unbelievably, at one time, when she was in a hurry to sew up my knee with a toothless granny smile, she sewed (and I kid ye not!) the front and back of the trousers together, so I couldn't get my foot down past the sewn area...

"Mum, you've sewn my trousers up"

"I know I have Todd, you idiot, now don't go ripping the arse out of the knees again"

"But mum, I can't get my leg in"

She looked, agog, at me trying to force my leg down the dead end of my trouser leg, half way down.

"What have you done now, you sod, you know I'm in a rush!"

"Mum, you've sew..."

"Give them here!"

She shouted as she yanked them off me, causing me to topple back'erds into the chair.

"Oh, for Christ's sake, look what you've made me do! I've got to go, I'll miss the bus" Screeched my intrepid seamstress as she vigorously snipped and pulled at the thread with her blunt scissors.

"There, now go! I need to get the bus!"

I could just about squeeze my foot past the "repair". I stood there with a trouser leg that looked like it had sucked its cheeks in as well. So, I had a large toothless granny smile with a deflated face around

the knee region!
She was then, further annoyed when I refused to go back out looking like that.
I got a smack for my troubles.
And I'm not making this up!
There were a couple of other mums who weren't quite sure which end of the needle to thread, but they were second division compared to my own championship contender.

*

Fortunately, this was at a time when a big event in the calendar was the "Jumble Sale".
This major social event happened frequently at Palmarsh hall, with my nan seeming to organise most of them, to raise money for various local things, especially our new to be football team that was being planned by some of the dads.
This meant that, with mum and Aunt Daisy also heavily involved, I could get into the hall on the Saturday morning and, on the pretence of helping to sort the jumble, I would gain a few of the best toys, cars, soldiers and annuals before the doors opened to the queue of folk outside (and there was always a big queue).
Getting in early to pick out the best toys was offset by the crappy clothes that mum was able to pick out for us, and she truly excelled at this rummaging pastime.
My wardrobe consisted entirely from cast off clothing from better off families, as did most of us around St. Georges Place at the time. If any kid was wearing a new outfit, it would automatically be assumed that their dad had had a "touch" on the horses, or a little "tickle" on Vernons, or the more upmarket, Littlewoods pools. The totally embarrassing bit would be if you were out, wearing something and another boy said…

"Hey, that used to be mine, but my mum chucked it in the jumble!". Nowt made you run home and change quicker than that, I can tell you.
To be perfectly honest, I am telling you.
As you're reading this!
But, all in all, jumble sales were a very good way for us young 'uns to get some new togs and toys, but even more so, there was no greater pleasure than getting hold of someone's old football or Christmas annual to read. It made all the handling of some old lady's undergarments seem almost worthwhile, not quite though, especially if you were rummaging through a large bag, pulling out old clothes, hoping to find some goodies or hidden gems, when you happened to grab an old pair of bloomers with unexplained stains on them, which had got too near to your face before you had time to chuck them! Uurrgghh!!!! (And I had a big nose, remember!).
With our ill-gotten gains secreted away in a back room with mum's "perks of the job" bits (all the mum's were at it), us kids would then disappear around the back of the hall, or over to the meadow for a game of football, whilst the general "Hoi polloi" were let in to pick over what was left. There was always a strong musty smell at these events. I wonder why that could be?
After it was all finished and tidied up, we would walk the hundred or so yards back home with our "swag bag", and then we would empty our goodies out onto the front room floor. Any toy cars would join the others in the box, the books sorted into order for reading and the toy soldiers of all shapes, sizes and descriptions went into their own bag. I'd got plans for them.
Luckily my smaller, but larger, little brother didn't interfere too much with my stuff now as he had his own preferences. I could tell a lie now and say that he liked dolly's, but no, that's not my way. He had discovered a love of marbles, and he'd now got quite a collection,

mainly in a large sweet jar. He'd also gained quite a few ball bearings as well. He would play for hours with his new friend, David Warren, from the other side of the alley at number 4, next door. His big brother, Adrian, was more into gardening and growing stuff.

Lynton and Brett Wilson from over the back would play marbles with him as well. They all went to school together. By this time (he was five now) he was allowed out to play, just locally, near the house (his restraining chain wasn't too long!), and he still didn't have a bike though.

In fact, I don't think that he ever had one.

He would have had the balance of a warthog on a roller skate, so perhaps it was for the best.

*

Me and "Charlie Choops" in our new back garden (I'm the handsome one on the right).

Chapter Nine – Growing Pains

It was around this time that I started to feel a lot of continuous pain, all the way down my right leg from my hip. I had, in fact, had these pains for quite a while, gradually building up over the past year or so, but I had "just got on with it", putting it down to the fact that I was always climbing trees or running up and down the uneven fields and hills around my Court at Street home, and we all had some form of ache, cut or pain so I thought it was no different from the others, although sometimes, the pains would make me cry when I was on my own in the bedroom. I didn't want to make an issue of it because I thought that mum and dad might make me stay in, and I didn't want that.

But now it was different. I could be out all day, playing all sorts of stuff, mainly football though, and at the end of the day I would come in and the pains were so bad, like a shooting sharp stabbing right down the leg, and a constant aching sensation around the hip joint, that I'd be crying, and as you know, I'm no big girl's blouse (I'd fought Red Indians whilst covered in cows muck!), so the pain must have been bad.

At first, for a long time, mum and dad, understandably, put it down to "Growing pains". It was nan Coombes, I think, who said…

"There's summat wrong with that boy, that's not normal, he's in pain, look! Get him to the doctor!"

So, mum took me into Hythe to see my new doctor, Doctor Barham. He gave me a thorough examination. Mum said…

"Is it just growing pains, Doctor?"

"Well he is growing, Mrs Pilcher".

He looked again, down at my gentleman's vegetable region…

"Well, parts of him are, anyway!"

Hmmm!

"But he does seem to be in a lot of pain around his hip, I'm not entirely happy about this".

"Aren't you", said mum, looking a tad concerned now.

No, I'm going to refer him to see a specialist at Ashford Hospital"

"Oh, okay Doctor", said mum, thinking it was a fair old way on the bus.

"There may be quite a wait though, so you'll have to manage it till then".

In other words, "Get on with it".

So, I did.

*

I was straight back out with Steve and Mick, playing football, we'd even arranged a bike ride up to Court at Street. I had managed, through a complicated phone procedure, to contact Robert Harden to arrange to meet up.

I would go to the telephone box at the top of Palmbeach Avenue, just past the VG store, and telephone the telephone box that was outside Robert's house in Court at Street. Somebody, usually his mum, would then hear it ring and answer it. On being told who you wanted, they would go and get them. I would then telephone the telephone box again from the telephone box that I was in, about five minutes on (if nobody else was waiting to use my telephone box), and if he could have been located, he would answer. The job's a good 'un!

You see kids, that's how we lived without mobile phones back then, and when we were out walking along the road, we could look all around us at what was going on because we weren't just stomping along, eyes down, staring at a little thin boxy, type thing in our hands all the time. We had lives that we controlled then…and…and…

It's okay, I'm feeling better now for getting that off my chest.

I know that we didn't have instant contact, interweb and stuff like that but, boy oh boy! Wasn't life simpler?
And there speaketh a child of the times!
A man from a bygone age!

*

So, Robert cycled down to us for the day, he would have dinner at my house and meet the others, then we'd all go off on our bikes. At the end of the day we would all ride with Robert, either all the way to his house, or we would all push our bikes to the top of Lympne hill and he would carry on home from there and we would then freewheel back down the hill to home.
We did this frequently for a few months, but then it just gradually tailed off. Robert now had new friends from his school in Ashford and I had my new friends, now in Palmarsh. It was such a shame to lose touch with him.
I last heard, some years back, that he'd moved to some village or town in West Kent, after being in London for a while. Blimey.
I still think about him and our childhood days together and I so wish that we were still in touch but, hey, ho! Such is life, I suppose.

*

At my new school I had settled in quite well, making some friends there as well. Andrew Maytum and Geoff Underwood, being two of my best chums there, along with others.
Although I still, so very badly, missed my old life and friends at Court at Street, I was starting to adapt quite well to my new life and friends down at sea level in Hythe.
My Uncle Dick (he was actually my dad's friend from the Council) and my Uncle Stebby (dad's driver's mate from the Council) came around to our house a lot and I thought a great deal of them both. Uncle

Dick would travel up to London a fair bit, he did something in the Labour party, I think, I'm not sure what though, all I do know was that he was a staunch Labour supporter, as my mum and dad were. I don't do politics or religion. It's easier that way.

Anyway, that Autumn he had bought me, from one of his many trips to London, my first Subbuteo football set. The F.A. cup final that year was between Tottenham Hotspur and Chelsea, and those were the two teams in the set, not the usual No.1 and No.2 teams, Manchester United and Everton.

This simple, but brilliant thought and gift from my Uncle Dick would, although I didn't know it at the time, start a love for this game that would last through to adulthood.

I was allowed to set it up on the table, behind the sofa as soon as Sunday dinner was done and dusted, and so commenced hours and hours of sheer joy. I was suddenly transported into another World, a World of miniature football figures. The annual games compendium would remain unopened from now as I had something worthwhile to seriously open my imagination (on all things football, that is!).

My World appeared to be overrun with little midget footballers because, as well as the new Subbuteo teams, I had turned some of my soldiers into mini football stars. My own "Star team", which I had imaginatively called "Soldiers United" would, over the next few years, gain total World dominance in the mind of this young boy.

To show how cosmopolitan and ethnically aware I was, even way back in the good old sixties, my goalie was a rather bulky Gorilla, whom I called "Peter Bonetti", I had a big centre half captain called "Bobby Moore", obviously, he was a large Arab in full Bedouin regalia. There was a Red Indian chief, made from lead. That was very clearly "Dennis Law". My two main forwards were "Jimmy Greaves", one of the greatest ever goal scorers, who was a Cowboy in a surrendering pose, with both hands held up. He had an absolute "rocket" shot on him, and his chief scoring partner was "Mike O'Grady" who, to keep the cosmopolitan theme of this great team, was a Spaceman in an astronaut's suit, that had his base removed so he couldn't stand, but boy, could he score goals! There were others that made it a complete team but again, time has blown the cobwebs to a forbidden track, barely travelled.

Soldiers United had very serious contenders (in my mind) in Milda United. There was also a Milda City, Enderton, Beldom City, Petamy Athletic, Tordery Albion and Daggington Hotspur, to name just a few of the teams that played in the simple mind of this young, football mad child.

In the times to come for me indoors, along with Subbuteo, these games of soldiers would whisk me away to my own little World, whilst I played on the floor behind the sofa for hours, making silly high-pitched noises as I gave a running commentary on these games. Ooh, I've just remembered, "Rose" and "Brown" were the main forwards for Milda United, and they were both... Knights in armour! A young child's brain has many facets, and absolutely no boundaries. To help me with the set up for my Soldiers United games, grandad let me loose in his shed so that I could make a proper goal out of his bits of kindling wood. I'd build the goalposts and crossbar by the simple task of hammering nails into the bits of wood to join them. As my Uncle Pete would say...

"It's not rocket salad!".

Then I would shape a bit of wirey metal to form the stanchions behind the goal. These would then be wedged in between the post and crossbar, and for the net, well, grandad let me use some old cast-off bits from an old shrimping net of his. I would secure the net to the carpet by sliding some tin tacks in. Brilliant!

I know that I've spent a lot of time describing all of this with the soldiers, and I'm sorry but I make no apology...

Hang on, I've just inadvertently made one!
What I'm trying to say is that it became such a massive part of my young, schoolboy life, especially when times for me, got rather grim, as you'll see further on.
So, I'm sorry for apologizing for saying sorry, as I'm not sorry really! Does that make any sense to you?
I'm blowed if it does for me.

*

The Subbuteo really got going as well. Steve Miller had also got a set, so we would play it together when we were permitted to in the evenings. I started to get other teams to join the two that I already had. To be truthfully honest (can you be both, together?), mum went to town and bought them for me. She was a good old stick, really. Very soon, I had a league up and running, using my Subbuteo log book to keep a record of the results, and this sort of thing went on in many households throughout the Country. We had never heard of the word "computer". Every child would find things to occupy their time when they couldn't get outside, even Barry had his marbles.
I must have lost mine!

*

It was a very different Christmas for us this year. For a start, I had two houses to use so I could, sometimes, get out from under mum's feet so I wouldn't get blamed for everything. I loved spending time with grandad in his shed (he seemed to be keeping out of the way as well). I would sit, just watching him sharpen his scythes, bill hooks and bagging hooks, or I'd sometimes help him to clean and try to fix his mowers or our bikes. At the time that we moved down, grandad had a big old black bike with a box on it. He used to do some gardening for folk as well as chopping wood and, best of all, he would take me shrimping.

In nan and grandad's front room, you could hear the cacophony of several different clocks ticking, mostly old wooden framed timepieces. They did have quite a few and they all told the same time. It was quite a racket when they all chimed together. That was another hobby of grandads, fixing clocks and watches, and he was very good at it. He'd sit there at the table with a clock in pieces, but he still knew how it all went back together again. I was amazed how his big old gnarly fingers managed to perform with those intricate parts of machinery. He gave me one of his pocket watches. I've still got it today but, alas, it doesn't work now. I wish I still had grandad here to fix it for me.

Grandad had two sheds, one was for storing things, and an old greenhouse, constructed on the side of an old Anderson shelter that they had in the garden. There was a mangle by the kitchen window in the garden (still in use), and mint would always grow around the dustbin area, where sometimes the ashes would spill. It wasn't a large garden, by any means, but it had more in it than we had. We did have a big old rotten shed at the bottom when we moved in, but that was soon knocked down and onto the fire, so all that was left was a grassy bit with a narrow border. We could at least play out the back and up the alley. We would have many games of football up the alley. Sometimes the ball would end up on the main road and a car would bump it along, but, usually, it was traffic free.

*

At this point, I'll slightly digress to tell about our little football team. Soon after we had moved to St. Georges Place, it was agreed by several of the dads that our little group of scruffs could be formed into a proper football team, hence the many fund raising jumble sales, bingo nights and raffles to raise enough money to buy us some matching team shirts, so that we could compete (that's a joke), I mean, play in the local boys Seabrook league for teams under thirteen years old. Our top age was about ten at the time. Poor Robert was too old for the age group, but he still got as fully involved as he was permitted.

With funds raised, there was a vote taken among us players as to what colours we favoured to play in. It was split, mainly between Red for Liverpool and Manchester United, and Blue for Everton and Chelsea.

We got Green shirts!

So, looking like Northern Ireland's under Six, 2nd eleven, we had our team photograph taken in the Square.

We only had twelve shirts of varying sizes, so Brian and Lynton had to take it in turns to be in the photo, running indoors to swap shirts between pictures. In my photograph, I got Lynton.

I was the goalie, so not to clash with the team shirts, I wore my Green roll neck, hand knitted jumper of Aldington fame. For good measure, I had my dad's old driving, goalkeeping gloves on.

To make the photograph even more surreal, I was positioned next to the Curly Wurly Kid, who wasn't even in the team, but mum had insisted he be in the picture. He was even wearing his Grey shorts and Red plastic sandals!

And his sticky out ear was on full view!

So, we all lined up and smiled for the camera prior to our first ever game, down at St. Marys Bay against the might of the "Marshland Midgets".

I kid you not. That was their name.

Choosing our name prior to getting our kit was an ordeal on its own for us in the team. There was a meeting at Palmarsh hall, after the last jumble sale.

For the adults, dad was the main man in charge, the team manager. The other men all had different jobs within this massive organization, Chairman, Secretary, Treasurer etc. Our team had boys from St. Georges Place, Princess Terrace, Martello Cottages on the Dymchurch Road, and my two cousins, John and Paul Coombes from Palmarsh.

It was agreed that we would have the word "Palmarsh" in the name. Us boys put forward some names to emphasize the fierceness, combative spirit and competitive nature of the team.

Names were bandied about, such as "Panthers", "Rovers", "Pumas" and "Lightning". We all liked that one.

We were warriors!

The dads had the last say though. We were called…

"PALMARSH ANGELS!"

Unbelievable!

So, Palmarsh Angels all piled into various cars and vans, and we made our way to St. Marys Bay for our very first match. The first thing that we noticed was that we were playing on a full-size pitch, with goals to match. It would have taken two of me to reach the crossbar, and that was at full stretch.

Well, all that can be said is that our captain, Mick O'Brien, lost the toss, and it was cold, windy and raining on the day that the Marshland Midgets beat Palmarsh Angels in a very close, tight game by 16-0!

As we traipsed from the pitch and back onto our luxury coa… er, sorry, I meant, into the old vans and cars, it was the major topic of commiseration and conversation that the Midgets were all bigger and older than us. It was a fact of life.

PALMARSH ANGELS F.C.

Back row. L-R, Peter Munn, Gordon Scott, Mick O'Brien, Steve Miller, Steve Birch, Paul Coombes, Kim Maycock, John Coombes

Front row. L-R, Lynton Warne, Carl O'Brien, Kevin Pilcher, Barry Pilcher, Carl Harris

(Note the goalie's dads driving gloves)

To be perfectly honest, we were completely out of our depth in this league, against boys much older and bigger.

But we were nothing, if not persevering. Other teams were trying to outdo each other by scoring more goals against us.

It had to be clear to everyone watching that the team were all letting the goalie (me) down!

I was busier than the busiest bee, working overtime on a busy bee honey production line.

If the goals had nets on them, it made my back ache to keep bending down and picking the ball out of the net. If the goals didn't have nets, it knackered me, running after the ball when it went into the goal. Sometimes, with the wind behind it, it would go for, what felt like, miles!

If we managed to keep the score down to single figures, we all felt that we'd done well. Sometimes, very rarely, we even scored a goal ourselves, usually though, it would be in a 15-1 defeat, or similar score.

Our record defeat was 32-0, and we did incredibly well to get nil! I can't remember who inflicted that on us. I must have blanked that bit out.

It wasn't all doom and gloom for us Palmarsh Angels though. On one very memorable sunny Sunday afternoon, we ventured up to Horn Street, in Seabrook, to play the perennial Champions, and league leaders, Seabrook Athletic.

Most of our families came along to cheer us on, and some sad person actually counted the crowd as 139.

Obviously, they had a great deal of support there on their steeply sloping from side to side playing field.

Mick was going to go in goal for a change, but when he saw all of the people there, he totally bottled it, so on came the driving gloves (even though it was boiling hot), and goalies jersey (by now, I had got

a "Peter Bonetti" one), and between the sticks I went.
There was one other thing that went between the sticks on this ground, and that was a rope crossbar.
Yep, that's right.
The top team in the league, the Champions, had a string crossbar painted White.
Well, that day we didn't let anybody down.
Okay, we lost.
But John Coombes and Kim Maycock (to the ecstatic delight of his mum) both scored for us, and we only lost 3-2.
And I saved a penalty!
The entire crowd cheered us from the pitch and their manager, Mr. Bill Ward (a great man who I would later play for), came over to congratulate us on our performance.
We, although proud, were cheesed off that we didn't win.
That, I suppose, was our one major plus as Palmarsh Angels, in an existence that was largely on the receiving end of a massive thrashing.

*

There was one local team that we always had a crunch game against. They played on the big pitch at Reachfields, and they were called "Halterne".
They had an adult team in the Sunday Morning league, and they were known to sometimes be a tad violent.
Their Boys team were nowt like that though. Oh no, they could be very violent!
Managed by Jock Paton (He was Scottish, in case you wondered), the team was led by the three Paton boys. The youngest was Mick, then Tony (the same age as me, and in my class throughout our schooldays), and Dave, the eldest. Now, Mick would kick you a bit,

Tony would chase you and kick you a lot, and Dave, bless his little cotton socks, well, he'd just push your head into the ground!
I can say these things about the boys now, as we still all see each other and have a laugh about those old days, especially about their dad Jock, who when you got to know him (and if you could understand what, was a Scottish word, and what was a swearword!), was a great and loyal man and friend who wouldn't take a backward step to anyone.
Also, Dave and I worked together in our own little two- man road gang on the Council for a couple of years, and I go and visit him quite often now.
He's currently serving fifteen years in Parkhurst for G.B.H.
Only joshing!
He's a great friend and he lives in a bungalow in the village of Lyminge. (He'd still push your head into the ground, though!).
Anyway, at least our games against Halterne were a bit closer, despite most of their team being older than us.
Blimey, sometimes we even managed to beat them!
These more "unofficial" games against them though, were arranged on the spur of the moment, either at Reachfields or on our, make do patch of a pitch on the meadow. In these hastily arranged fixtures, there wouldn't be a referee or owt sensible like that, but there would be a lot of kicking and chasing after, or in our case, a lot of being kicked and running away.
As well as Halterne, we played "Burmarsh" on their Burmarsh Estate playing field, just a few hundred yards up the railway tracks from our meadow.
Their team consisted of, mainly mates of ours from school. Steve and Paul Watts and Jamie and George Mac Pherson were opponents, and good friends as well. Jamie and George were always arguing as brothers because, Jamie supported Rangers and George supported

Celtic but, as fighters, they were as timid as a shy kitten, put in a box full of Yorkshire terriers. They all got a kicking from the Halterne mob as well.

One day, Halterne played, and beat them in a game at Burmarsh playing field to win a small plastic cup (I think it was a Subbuteo trophy), and as the triumphant assault force made their way, with bloodied knuckles, back along the train tracks to their own terrain, they had to pass us, all playing on the meadow. As they waved the, now broken and blood- stained trophy, in the air as they sang on their way, we called them and challenged them to a game on our pitch, for the cup they had just won.

With a great licking of lips, as they had already tasted the blood of one cowering bunch, they accepted.

It was agreed that it would only be fifteen minutes each way, as there are only so many times you can be shoulder barged into a gorse bush or kicked through a freshly laid pile of dog pooh (folk didn't pooper-scoop then). The shock outcome was that we won the day by 4-3.

The cup that they had only just won an hour previous was duly presented to us by Dave Paton throwing it at Steve's head, and then the rest of the Paton clan chasing us through our little paths through the gorse, to attempt to shake us by the neck... sorry, I mean hand, and congratulate us.

We waved the cup in their face…. After they had disappeared down the rails, back to their encampment at Reachfields.

They did have a re-match with us on their ground the next day (at their insistence), and they absolutely stuffed us to regain the bent trophy. We made our escape this time while they did their lap of honour with the cup.

Yep, we all pretended we were at Wembley !

Chapter Ten – Diagnosis "Hippy Shoes"

Back at school, after my first summer holiday in Hythe, mainly spent playing on the meadow, and out on our bikes, I joined the Third year. We even had our own football pitch in the playground, playing with a tennis ball as about three million (slight exaggeration for effect) other excitable kids ran around you, getting in the way or getting knocked over. Sometimes, girls would set up their hopscotch or skipping rope right in the middle of the pitch (Did they not know?). They were soon chivvied off though, with a tennis ball whipping around their ears (no sticky out ones on display, to my recollection). I liked to play in goal, despite the occupational hazard of ripping the knees out of my trousers, with the inevitable, almost invisible repair by mum.
At least in the warmer months we could wear our short trousers. That way, I only ever took several layers of skin from my knees.
I can still feel the pain and the stinging now, just thinking about it, as the teacher would wet a coarse paper hand towel from the toilets and attempt to wipe the grit and stones from my bloodied, grazed knee, prior to dabbing a very liberal amount of TCP onto it.
COR!
At least that didn't sting too much, did it?
When they had finally prised my finger nails from the thickly plastered walls, I would be sent back out to play with a warning not to dive about, and to be more careful.
Off I would limp, with a large yellowing stain of TCP on the affected area.
When I got home after school, I would get the usual tongue lashing from mum, who would then attempt to get rid of the TCP stain by

getting a warm flannel, and then roughly rub it across my now visibly sore and throbbing graze.

It would be...

RUB, RUB, DAB, DAB, DAB,

"Ow! Mum, it hurts!"

DAB, DAB, DAB, RUB, RUB,

"And you want new trousers for school? I'll give you new trousers!"

RUB, RUB, DAB, DAB,

"Ow! Mum, use a softer flannel!"

RUB, DAB, RUB,

"I'll give you, softer flannel"

DAB, DAB, RUB, RUB,

"That's what I want, mu..."

RUB, RUB, RUB, DAB, DAB,

"It is soft"

RUB, RUB, no DAB

"No, it's not mum, it's like a Brillo pad, Ow!"

DAB, DAB, DAB, no RUB.

"I'll give you Brillo pad, cheeky sod!"

RUB, DAB, RUB, DAB, soak.

"I don't know how you keep getting hurt".

RUB, DAB,

"I don't mum, it's just, Ow! playing football"

"You're always saying your leg hurts, so you shouldn't do it"

DAB, soak, DAB, soak.

"It does hurt, but I want to play. Ow!"

"Well, you're seeing that Mr. Baird soon, so he'll sort it".

DAB, RUB, DAB, soak.

"Now dry it off, and TRY to keep it clean"

"Thanks mum, we're going over the meadow"

"Well, if you break your bloody leg, don't come running home to me crying"
I was out of the door before you could skin a weasel!

*

As the Bee Gees sang about "Massachusetts", or as we all sang "Massive Two Tits" (We were cheeky little chappies), I had my very first appointment with the Consultant responsible for legs and joints or whatever.
All we knew was that he was regarded as "The Top Man", although I expect that all Consultants were regarded the same.
Why mum had made me bath and wear my best togs for this I wasn't sure. Then she made me put on clean pants…
"Just in case you have an accident, or get run over by a bus!"
If I had an accident and got run over by a bus, clean pants would be the last thing I'd have!
Also, wearing all this clobber made me feel even more nervous and uncomfortable than I wanted to be.
The little Baboon was left at home with nan Coombes. She wouldn't take any strife from him. I was positive about that.
After the bus journey, via my beloved Court at Street (I didn't see anyone, they were all at school), we sat at the Ashford Hospital in Mr. Baird's waiting room, and mum then decided, for no apparent reason, to wet her hanky from her mouth and daub my face with it.
"Mum!"
"What are you doing?"
"Mum… I don…"
SPLURGGG!
"I'm just cleaning your face, you're filthy"
"I'm not, and you spitting on your hanky's not helping"
More spit followed.

"Mum, stop it!"
"Just a mark on your cheek, there!"
"Mum, leave me alo…"
"Kevin Pilcher please".
"Come on Todd", said mum, dragging me into the Consulting room. I sat there facing this little man in glasses and a Three-piece suit (Him, not me), with mum's wet saliva still glistening on my face, listening as my mum in her best posh voice, tried to explain my problem.
After he heard mum's very poor Queen Mother impersonation, Mr. Baird turned to me, and after asking me if it was raining outside because of my wet face, he told me to tell him, in my own words, and without the posh voice, what kind of pains I get and how I feel. I tried my best. Mum kept interrupting me though, until he asked her not to. That shut her up for a bit.
He did a lot of "Umming" and "Ahhing", and then he sent us both off to the X-ray department to get a picture of the offending joint. This took an age, because after having a couple of X-rays taken, we had to sit and wait for over half an hour so that the X-rayologist person (I know, it's "Radiologist") could check that the images had come out properly.
She then handed them to mum in a folder to take back to Mr. Baird. He put them up to the light and "Ummed" and "Ahhed" some more.
"Umm, not good".
What happened to "Ahh", I thought.
"Umm, not good at all, just as I thought".
Well, I admit, I've seen better pictures of me.
"What?"
"WHAT?", I was shouting inside.
"It appears to me that you may have Perthes Disease, young man"

"What is that?" said the Queen Mother (mum, really).
"It means, Mrs. Pilcher, that there is no fluid around Kevin's hip joint, see here".
He showed us the image. I could have been looking at a jelly baby at a road junction, for all I knew.
"See the area around the ball joint?"
"At the moment, he has bone rubbing on bone. No wonder he's in severe pain".
"Can you do anything?" said the Queen Mother (mum, again)
"Well, yes but it's a long process and I need further tests doing"
"What will happen then?" said the Queen Mother, who was starting to talk more like mum now, as the shock of the findings had come as ... well, a shock, really.
"Well, it may not be for another twelve months yet, you see, despite his short, puny, almost pathetic size (he didn't use those exact words), he's still growing".
He looked again at my lower region.
"Well, most of him is!"
Hmmm.
"He'll have to wear a calliper device for a while".
"For how long?"
"About two years!"
I sat, bolt upright at that statement.
"A what...?"
"Don't worry, Kevin, you'll be fine, and it will make you better".
Yeah, right.
"You'll still be able to do things".
"I want to play football, I don't want owt on my leg!"
I started to blubber a bit now. There must have been onions in the room.

"Well, it might stop that, I'm afraid"
"I don't want it then"
"Kevin, you won't have a choice if you want to get better"
At this point, he didn't mention the name calling, abuse, bullying and ridicule that I would have to endure…. But then, he didn't have to!
"I'll see you again a couple of times before he's fitted for it, Mrs. Pilcher".
"Thank you, Doctor" said the Queen Mother type mum, in a fawning voice, almost curtsying as she pulled me towards the door.
"Oh, I almost forgot, he'll have to go into Hospital for six weeks first, for traction. Goodbye".
I let myself be dragged along the corridor, in total shock.
"Mum, I don't want that" I said, pleading.
"You've got no choice Todd, if you want your leg to get better"
"Mum, he said I've got to wear a calliper!"
"You'll soon get used to it".
"I won't mum, I don't want it!"
"You'll do as you're told!"
And that, as they say, was that.
Flashing teeth of brass! How do I deal with this?
Oh well!
Red sky at night, shepherd's delight. Blue sky at night, …er…Day!
See, I'm delirious!

*

It was back home on the bus, after mum had taken me into the toy shop in the town, to get me another Subbuteo team. For some unfathomable reason, I chose No. 32. Alloa Athletic in Black and Yellow hooped shirts. They would become one of my favourites. At home, mum explained what Mr. Baird had said to dad, nan and grandad. Lurch looked up from his game of marbles with a big grin…

"Ha, you'll have a metal leg" He chortled to everyone.
"Metal leg, Metal leg!"
Yep, it had started, and I hadn't even got it yet.
And to think, I never called him any names, the little bag of pooh!
Grandad put his hand on my sobbing shoulder.
"Come with me"
We went out to his shed, where he started fiddling about with his tools. After a bit of an awkward silence whilst he was composing what he was going to say, he just came out with…
"You'll cope, mucker".
"But grandad, I won't be able to play football!"
"Where there's a will, Kev. You'll find a way".
"What about my bike?"
"We'll get around that as well. I'll build summat if I have to. Don't ee worry mate".
He put his tough weather, beaten arm around me and gave a squeeze.
"Now, what do you think? Shall we go shrimping?"
"Too right, grandad".
He called dad…
"Tide's right, Dave!"
"Okay Alf, let's load up".
We tied the shrimp net to the roof, loaded grandad's big basket, sieve and waders into the boot. Steve (who I'd called out to) and me jumped into the back with our ball and Sherry, the dog, and off we went to the Redoubt corner, on the way to Dymchurch. This was where we always shrimped.
We unloaded the old A35, and dad donned the chest high waders. Grandad used to be the one to push the net over the sandy sea bed, several yards out to sea, but he had now passed on that responsibility to dad. I could just watch and kick a football around,

but in years to come, I would take over the net from dad, with grandad still standing on the shore, shouting to us where to head towards, whilst he was sorting the crabs and small fish from the shrimps. His main nemesis was the Weever fish, which bury themselves in the sand and when dredged up, they can give a very nasty, venomous sting from spines on their fins.

I've seen grandad get stung and, with blood spurting up from his finger, he'd just say, in a slightly pained voice...

"AH! You bugger!"

And he'd fling the "little offender" out of the basket, to bury itself back into the sand. He would shake his hand to try to get rid of the sting, and just carry on sorting.

He was a tough old bird, was my grandad. I reckon that he had hands and arms of leather.

He once lifted his long john leg up to show me where a German Officer in the First World War had stuck a bayonet right into his calf. He then just rolled his long john leg back down, took a puff of his pipe, and said...

"It didn't do ee no good though".

And that was it!

He would hardly mention that war at all. Men like him must have seen so much pain and horror.

He had medals, but as I found out, he'd just chucked them in an old drawer in the shed, covered with old nails, screws and general junk and detritus that had gathered over the years.

And we all had men like that in our families. Brave men. Men with nowt else to offer but themselves in the line of duty to their King.

He once told me that when he was wounded (by that bayonet), he was laying on a Train Station platform, on a stretcher, with hundreds of other wounded soldiers, waiting to be ferried to the various Hospitals, when civilian folk would be rifling through their pockets

and kit bags for anything of value.
And that was in this country!
Unbelievable!

*

Back to the beach at the Redoubt.
I told Steve about what the Doctor chappie had said, but he didn't really know what to say to that, how to respond. How could he respond? How would I respond if somebody, a best mate, had told me that they were going to be a cripple?
Yep, that's how it was termed, and by golly, didn't I get called that on many occasions? And, obviously never in a nice way.
Steve, on the other hand, was very supportive, as would be my other good friends in the Square. Some might holler at me in the future, calling me every name under the Sun if I kicked them (accidently, of course) with my metal bit, but I had some good folk to play with.
Steve and I would run around with Sherry, kicking and chasing the football as it got blown along the beach unto it bounced into a groyne and halted. We occasionally got called over by grandad, who would point out something unusual in the basket, like a prawn, weever fish, large crab or submarine.
Okay, one of them I made up. Can you guess which one though?
After dad had had enough of wading through the incoming tide in waders that leaked and filled with sea water (trust me, I came to know this sensation myself), or grandad had got so many shrimps that it was difficult to carry them, we would load the car back up and all pile in. Sherry, the dog, would always be wet and covered in sand, which mum appreciated when she went indoors and shook herself all over the front room carpet (that's the dog, not mum). Nan would have a great big "copper", bubbling away on the cooker with salted water, ready for the shrimps to be poured in.

Grandad had the knack, gained over many years, of knowing exactly when the shrimps were ready to be tipped out onto the front room table. Still hot, they would be gathered up into a pint pot and put into paper bags. Then it was up to us kids to run them around to the many customers in the Square. Some folk bought more than one pint and I don't blame them, I could eat them till Mr. Duthoit's cows came home.

We used to catch them by the gallon, sometimes, up to three or four gallons and they were sold, at first, I remember for 6d a pint, then they doubled up to the princely sum of one bob, or shilling. What value!

Now, when I last checked, they were around £5 a pint. Unbelievable! And now, folk that I know going out shrimping hardly catch a couple of pints, if they're lucky.

I must confess that I loved the shrimps, especially how grandad cooked them, somehow, they don't taste quite the same these days. That's progress for you.

*

There was a surprise at school for me and Andrew Maytum. We were both selected to play for the school football team. The big surprise was that I was picked as a left winger and Andy was to be the goalie. No Third- year boys had ever played in the team before, we were told. What made it better for me though, was that John Coombes, Steve Miller and Mick O'Brien were in the side. Andy's friend and next- door neighbour, Graham Pearce was in the team as well. They were all in year Four, their final year. Steve Birch, a fellow Palmarsh Angel would soon join us as well, and it wouldn't be the last time that Steve and I would be together in a team either, possibly fighting against the tide against bigger boys.

My schoolboy football seemed to be solely played in Green and White, as St. Leonards Primary school, or Hythe school as everyone knew it, played in old style Rugby type shirts of Green and White hoops, Glasgow Celtic colours. Number 25 on the Subbuteo chart.

*

Christmas would pass with the usual fare within the family. A large Boxing Day get together at Aunt Daisy and Uncle Bill's house was always something that we all looked forward to. Uncle Bill always had lots of different drinks in, even for us little folk, as grandad called all kids. Mind you, Uncle Bill could have been one of the "Little Folk" as he was a small, slightly built man of Irish breeding and British Army discipline. A nicer, kinder man, you wouldn't find. Everyone was always made so welcome at their house and I've only got such happy memories of both, Aunt Daisy and Uncle Bill.

*

Chapter Eleven – A sentence, a stadium and a slipper!

The new year, 1968, dawned and my Tenth birthday (and Balloon boy's sixth) passed with The Beatles confusing us by singing "Hello, Goodbye" at the top of the hit parade.
I was starting to collect a few more bits for my Subbuteo by now. For my birthday I had even been given Floodlights.
Mum said that they named the chocolate bar "Bar Six" after her little "Baa", they didn't, but it didn't stop him noshing on a few though. I got my snout in his nose-bag when he wasn't looking, or if I fooled him by sending him out of the room to get me some left- handed marbles from mum. At times he weren't the sharpest pencil in the bag. Mum would send him back in and give me my usual rebuke. I'd also get a smack if she caught me with a wafery chunk of chocolate in my gob.
I would sometimes try and be sneaky by chomping his choccy bar, whilst holding my half eaten one in my hand.
The times that I fooled them. Blimey, I could count on the fingers of one of my mittens!
It was as if I had the word "Guilty" tattooed on my forehead.
Easter passed by in a wave of chocolate egg wrappers. They were about the only thing that a certain Charlie Choops left. You could trace his route around the house by the trail of little silver papery bits. To be honest, I think the dog nicked her fair share. Any exposed chocolatey brown was guzzled down by our big black pooch before you could chase a cat up a drainpipe.

*

Mr. Louis Armstrong, although he sounded like he had a sore throat, was telling us that it was a "Wonderful World", not for me it weren't. Oh no, that was a very different saucepan of fish!
I was virtually crying every night now because of the aching and the shooting pains going constantly down my leg. I hadn't, wouldn't give up playing my favourite games though, especially football and riding my bike.
Grandad had got me a bigger bike now as I'd just about knacked the little old trusty Blue one. This one was dark Green (Green again!), and it was a good reliable runabout with Three speed gears. Of course, it was all checked over and oiled before he handed it over to me. I think my old Blue one went to one of the smaller ones in the Warne clan. That's how we did things. You all helped each other. Grandad would sort out several of the kid's bikes if they had a problem. He was the "Go to" man.
I went for my second appointment with Mr. Baird, this time dad came along as well. "Baa" was left with nan again after he'd been seen home from school by the other kids from the Square.
At least, this time we got to go by car, albeit a tiny little Austin. We had the usual wait in the Waiting room. At least we were in the correct room to wait as it said "Waiting Room" on the Waiting room door.
As soon as I saw mum delve into her bag for her hanky, I was on my toes to the other side of the room where there were some old Readers Digest magazines on a low table (I think all the comics had been nicked by devious, thieving little children that had got there before I'd had a chance, myself).
Despite mum calling me over, I feigned the partial deafness that I'd get for real in later years. At last we were summoned into the "Great man's" office. There were only two chairs, so I had to shuffle about as I didn't want to sit on anybody's lap. I was Ten, after all.

Mr. Baird confirmed the results from the tests I'd had, and he laid out the procedure...

"There's about a Six month wait, then Kevin will be admitted here, to the children's ward, for Six weeks of traction".

Six weeks!

"What does "traction" mean?" asked dad (in his normal voice).

I wanted to know as well.

"It means, he'll have his leg stretched with weights. They'll be attached from plaster down each side of his leg. His leg will be up in this position".

He then proceeded to show us what he meant by getting me to lay flat on his examination bed, and then he pulled me about.

"He'll also have a surgical stocking on".

At that, I looked up.

"I don't want to wear stockings!"

"No, it's just one surgical stocking, Kevin. Like this".

He showed me a gauze type tubular thing.

"He will have to remain in bed for the whole time he's in traction, no getting up at all, for anything".

"What about the toilet?" said mum, trying to look at me reassuringly. And failing!

"He'll use a bottle and a bed pan".

"A BED PAN?" Says I.

"I can't go to toilet in bed!"

"Yes, you can, Todd" said mum, slightly putting her Queen Mother voice again.

"I can't pooh laying down, mum!"

I was ignored.

"Then, at the end of the Six weeks, Kevin will have his calliper. It will have already been measured and fitted for him while he's here"

We all just looked at him and listened. Mum and dad were just nodding, and I was feeling terrified.

"We'll then get him up and walking, and then he'll be home again in no time".

"Why does he need the calliper?" Asked dad.

Good question dad, I thought.

"That's to keep the weight completely off his right hip. He mustn't put his foot on the floor at all. This will give the hip a chance to regenerate the fluid around it. Don't worry, it's a tried and trusted method".

Yeah, right.

If only I knew then!

"How can he get around without it?" Good question again, dad.

"He can take it off indoors, as long as he doesn't put any weight on it".

We all looked at him, a bit confused.

"He can hop on his left leg or slide on his bottom for going upstairs. He'll find what's best for him!"

We all looked at him again.

"I've got to HOP everywhere?"

"Only when you haven't got your calliper on, Kevin".

"I'll be like "Hoppity", everyone will laugh at me"

"Nobody will see you indoors, Todd" said mum, failing in the reassurance stakes, once again.

"Hang on, TWO YEARS, you said".

"That's right, Kevin".

"That means I'll be wearing it to big school!"

"That won't be a problem, they'll be aware and be able to help".

"I'll get picked on and bullied!"

"No, you won't Todd, the school would watch out and make sure".

What planet were these folk living on?

"I'll get bullied, it's not fair".

"You may find that you're more popular because of your disability" said Mr. Baird, trying to end the conversation.

"You wear it then!" I said, now starting to get very upset.

"Kevin" chastised my dad.

Where had "Todd" disappeared to?

"Sorry, but I don't want this, dad".

"It'll make you better, Todd, and it'll stop it hurting".

"I'll be picked on" I whimpered.

"Thank you, Doctor" said mum, trying to get her Queen Mother voice back on, but failing.

"I'll see you and Kevin, just prior to his admittance to Hospital".

"Thank you, Doctor" said dad, in a subservient manner.

"Goodbye".

I just looked down at the floor as I was led out of the Consulting room, in a daze. It was getting to be a reality now, and I didn't like it one iota.

Two and a bit, years of my life, a prison sentence of sorts, except for the fact that I would be on public display, open to all forms of ridicule and abuse.

"Why me?"

This time, mum let me pick two teams at the toy shop as I was in a state of shock and upset.

Big, bulging packets of Bovril crisps, was I upset!

I picked out numbers 3 & 4, West Bromwich Albion and Stoke City, but even that didn't cheer me up.

Dad tried his best on the way home...

"Come on, Todd. Try to forget it for a bit now and look on the bright side. You're going to Wembley in a couple of days, you know you've been looking forward to it".

But I couldn't yet, get excited about our school trip to the National stadium for the first time, to see Oxford play Cambridge in the annual Varsity match. I expect I would on the day, at this moment in time though, my life seemed ruined. I wanted to do so much, out playing mainly, and very soon I was going to be called a "Cripple" and worse, much worse, by all and Sundry.
I knew that I hadn't got a choice in the matter, and that I'd have to face up to it, but it still hurt.
I knew that, very soon, I was going to be different to all the other boys. I didn't know anyone that was disabled, nor had I ever seen anybody with a disability, never mind anyone with a metal leg thing to clomp about in.
I knew that things in my life were about to change, and certainly not for the better. I was going to have to cope in life with one hell of a disadvantage to other kids. Big school was terrifying enough as it was, now I would stand out like a boy with two heads when the head count was being done. I'd get twice the attention and, I guarantee, most of it wouldn't be good.
Oh well. Hey ho!
When I slip in a pile of pooh, I can be sure to put my hands in it, getting up!

*

Still, I still had Wembley to look forward to. We were all so excited as we made our way by coach, from Hythe school up to the stadium. Imagine the feeling that a load of football mad Ten and Eleven, year old boys would get as those famous twin towers came into view. We were here. We were at Wembley.

Along with a few thousand other schoolboys and University students (well, it was their game), we huddled along and, by the steps to the

turnstiles, we all stopped to buy a programme and rosette.
Now, who's rosette do I get?
For me, it was the Light Blue of Cambridge. The rosette looked nicer. Forward, from that day to now, I have always willed Cambridge to win, whether it be in the Boat race, Rugby, Football, whatever. Once you pick one, you stick with one.
Hey, that catchy sentence could catch on!
To finally shuffle along with the crowd, and up the steps until...
In front of you is the pitch. THE PITCH!
THIS IS WEMBLEY!
We all just gaped around, eyes out on stalks, excitedly pointing things out to each other. The obvious talking point was England's win, Two years previous.
There was the goal where Geoff Hurst got his third, right in front of us.
"Some people are on the pitch, they think it's all over. It is now. It's Four".
Unbelievable!
We were here at Wembley. Who cares that it's only a Varsity match. We were at Wembley!
Playing football on Five Acres, the meadow, anywhere and everywhere, we would pretend to be at Wembley, and here we were.
I don't know if I've emphasized enough where we were.
WE WERE AT WEMBLEY!
I know that we weren't actually down on the pitch, playing, but in our little schoolboy minds, we were kicking the winning goal into the bulging Wembley net.
I would make many trips to this iconic stadium in the future, mainly with Mick O'Brien, following Liverpool, but nowt would or could compare with this first time.

I suppose they say that it's the same as remembering the first time that you have sex. I look forward to that moment as well!
That was a joke... I think.
Anyway up, Cambridge, in the Light Blue and White quartered shirts, triumphed over Oxford, in Dark Blue and White quartered shirts, by 3-1. It's strange how, years on, I can remember the result but the game itself is lost in the tangled undergrowth of my memory.
A special day though for everybody there for the first time.

*

Life at Hythe school progressed, like a meandering stream, gurgling along, like life itself on its wending course.
I can recall some of the staff at the time who I came into some form of contact with. A lovely couple, Mr. and Mrs. Macklin, he was a very popular teacher as I remember, and very funny at times. My own teacher was a lady called Mrs. or Miss Lukehurst (I'm not sure which), and they were exceedingly happy times there for me, well, they were, apart from one incident when I was accused of partially flooding the toilet area, not by peeing, but by leaving taps on and blocking the plug hole, in case you're in any doubt.
I was summoned to the Headmaster's office.
Shaking like a...er... like a shakey thing, I entered the room, after knocking on the stout oak door, obviously.
I stood, head bowed, whilst Mr. Fred Skinner, the Headmaster, a colossal man of over Nine feet (so it seemed to me) and as bald as a badger that had just been shaved (how else can a badger be bald?), pointed out to me, exactly where I was going wrong at school, and how I should alter that trend.
He then did something, the memory of which has stayed with me to this day...

He opened his drawer and pulled out a slipper!
I bet you wondered what I was going to say then!
He just held it in one hand (the slipper), and then slapped it across the palm of his other hand. He said...
"Do you know what this is, Kevin?"
It was a slipper, but I didn't want to tell him!
Tears started to well up.
"Yes sir".
"Well, do you want it?"
A daft question, really. Why would I want one slipper?
I was, by now, well gone in the waterworks department, and, quite possibly, a teensy bit of wee may have come out.
"No sir".
"Well, off you go then... and Kevin, be warned".
I was warned, alright!
"Yes sir" I sobbed.
I was out of that office like a ferret with its bum on fire!
Well, that really told him.
What an escape. Thank you, Mr. Skinner. That was as close to any form of physical punishment that I ever came to, in all my years at school.
One lesson well and truly learned, I hoped.
Some hope!

*

The Summer school sports day was next upon us, on the Green, opposite the school. There was the whole school and the Infants school out watching, along with quite a crowd of parents, each eager for their own child to be the best, despite them showing any outward impartiality, cheering on other children whilst at the same time, willing them to stumble or fall, leaving their own offspring as

the victor.
Come on, we've all done it!
Each child had practiced for their specialist event, their forte'.
Mine was the Bean Bag race.
Although, not at the time, an Olympic event, and at the time of writing this, for some reason, still not.
We all stood on the starting (chalk) line, waiting for Mr. Bishop, the music teacher, to blow his whistle. He did, in fact, also have a piano but that was considered too big to lug out to the Green and was still in his classroom.
(And who has ever heard of an important race being started by a tinkling of the ivories?)
Back to reality once more.
I wore the Yellow sash of "Keller", my house. The others were "Wilberforce" (Green), "Nightingale" (Blue) and "Shaftesbury" (Red). What a lovely cacophony of coloured sashes to adorn the Green on that day.
The whistle blew, and whilst Chris Duncombe of Wilberforce stood, rooted to the spot, waiting for the piano to start, the rest of us all dashed for our own individual bags of beans.
There were Three in total, at about Five- yard intervals, and you could gather them, one at a time, in any order and chuck them into your litter bin, then leg it to the finishing chalk line, approximately Twenty yards away.
With my very low centre of gravity, I was nowt but a blur to my fellow Bean Baggers. I won with a couple of yards to spare.
I'd actually won at something!
This was despite an appeal by Chris Duncombe's legal team, claiming that we had all told him to wait until the piano played. (It was overruled, obviously.) I think that he was very unfortunate, and I did ask for the race to be re-run.

(I didn't really, but today, he owns Palmarsh Garage and I like little bills for my car!)

Anyway, I got awarded a certificate...

"Kevin Pilcher, 3RD Year Bean Bag Race, 1ST Place" at the next school assembly. As my name was called out, I leapt up like a Dover Sole (I'm on the coast, remember? not many Salmon here), and strutted my way to the front to get my Olympic Gol... er...scrub that... piece of paper.

Mr. nine feet tall Skinner stooped down, smiled and said...

"Well done, Kevin" as he gave me my certificate. It was most certainly better than getting the slipper!

This victory in the little-known sport of Bean Bag racing put me in the school team for the District sports on Folkestone sports ground. There were screaming, cheering kids from all over the area. I never knew there were so many schools. Even little village schools like my old one at Aldington had some competitors.

Well, after waiting for what felt like all afternoon, my race was called. As I looked up at my opponents in the race, I noticed that I was the smallest. That didn't bother me though. Nerves aside, I felt reasonably confident. Had I not just won my own school sports race at a canter?

I felt invincible as I stared down the course at my bags of beans.

I came third!

"Ah well, ne'er mind" Mr. Macklin said to me at the end of the race. "You did your best Kevin, it's the taking part that counts".

"Is it, Pony pooh!" I may have replied, or something like that.

Third place certificates don't count, a monkey's squirt!

*

Chapter Twelve – Testing my luck, same again!

The summer holidays were very hot, especially for playing football on the meadow. Barney Rubble and his side kicks, David, Lynton and Brett spent most of their time "Lizarding", catching the myriad creatures as they basked on the rocks in the sunshine, it wasn't difficult. There were many lizards roaming around the meadow with their tails missing as the "hunters" had pulled them off whilst trying to catch them. Luckily for the lizards, they soon tired of their sport and went back to the strenuous task of moving marbles about.
We would make our goals out of anything we could find. We used empty old oil drums for ages, with some old corrugated Nissan hut sheets for the nets.
We hadn't yet, got sophisticated in our goal design, but we would. Late summer passed, with bike rides, football, cricket and shrimping, then it was back to school. I was now starting Fourth year, my last one in Primary school, and I knew, dreaded, that sometime soon, the letter would come about my admittance to Hospital. I was still in so much pain, but I would only let the tears come when I was indoors. At other times, I was "Jack the lad", making folk laugh, joking about and playing with my mates, oh, and getting thrashed with Palmarsh Angels.
I was covering up how things really were for me, I suppose.

*

The early weeks of being back at school were soon behind me. There were some new and exciting TV programmes to enjoy around this time.

London Weekend Television brought out a Sunday afternoon football programme called "The Big Match" with Brian Moore. Now we had "Match of the Day" on Saturday night and this as well.

"Sportsnight" with David Coleman also started on a weekday night in September. I also liked Please Sir, Z-Cars, The Saint, Take Your Pick, Double Your Money, Dads Army (which had just started), and It's a Knockout. That was a brilliant Saturday evening show with lots of laughter and very silly games (we'll gloss over the antics of a certain Mr Stuart Hall, the host, who went to prison for being a naughty boy in later years!).

It was during a wet, early evening at home that a minor, teeny weeny, hardly worth mentioning incident occurred. I had just finished playing soldiers on the floor, behind the sofa. Soldiers United had just beaten Daggington Hotspur 21-4, to go top of the league so I was feeling quite chuffed.

I placed my heroes back into their home (it was actually an old lady's large handbag with a solid base and three separate compartments for the team's and the goal, but I won't linger over that bit).

It was a nice bag, though.

Anyway, mum was in the kitchen, about to do us some boiled eggs (yes, and soldiers), and Lurchio was under her feet, whining about something or other.

Into the kitchen I went, straight into our own version of "Mr Pastry", he swung out at me, to push me, but I was far too smart for him, ducking out of the way.

With his momentum, he fell into mum, who… and now here's the important bit… knocked the sticking out handle of the saucepan (not his "sticky out ear"), causing the pan of, now boiling, water to splash and fall right onto the little fella's arm.

Good Golly Miss Molly!

Did he yelp?
Yep, indeedy do, he did. In fact, he was screaming, the poor lad. I didn't know what to do. Mum didn't know what to do. He was screaming in pain so much that nan, next door, heard him and came hurtling in. She wrapped his upper arm in a towel, just as dad got home from work. He was straight back out to the car, and him, mum and "Lobster Boy" were off to Folkestone Hospital.
I stayed at home with nan and grandad. I never did get my boiled egg, but grandad did me some toast, over the fire with his toasting fork, and we had some good strong cheddar, and a great cup of tea. Oh, yeah sorry, I almost forgot. They came home about three hours later. Barney had a large bandage and padding around his arm and he was grizzling. Mum and dad came straight in, and guess who got all the blame?
It's obvious really. Dad tried to chase me, to possibly give me a slap or two, but I ran as fast as I could, straight back around to next door, and nan prevented any cursory punishment forthcoming. She pointed out that I hadn't, in fact, done owt other than get out of his way and I was no way, anywhere near the saucepan that shouldn't have had a handle sticking out, anyway.
I still got blamed and smacked later though because "it was all my fault", and the little blister bum was still grizzling!
I just shut myself in my room and had a little grizzle myself. At least the sting from the smack took my mind off my hip pain for a while. To this day, Charlie Choops still bears the scar on his upper arm, and yes, I still get the blame.
What with that and the broken neck incident and my Perthes disease, anyone would think I was a "Jonah".

*

On that "Lucky" note, it was around this time, from playing for Hythe school in the local district "Herald cup", that Steve Birch and myself both got selected to play for the District team "Folkestone Boys".
Quite an honour and a proud achievement really, as it was a representative side from all the schools in the area.
We played in the National schools Trophy against Hastings Boys on a Saturday morning. This first leg being at Hastings. The large school that we played at was packed with youngsters, cheering on their local team.
We got trounced 4-0 in that first leg, and then, mainly due to my chronic hip pains and impending Hospitalization, I missed the second leg at Folkestone Town's ground, in which Folkestone Boys came back to win 5-0 to go through.
With my little Leprechaun of doom called "Jonah" upon my shoulder, I never played for them again.
Steve did very well though!

*

I continued to play with my Subbuteo on the table in the front room. The one thing that I needed was a fence to surround the pitch as I kept flicking the players straight off the table and onto the floor, whereupon they were quite often trodden on and in need of repair. There was only one way to achieve this repair (and I use that word very loosely), and that was by heating up a poker in the fire, waiting till the end was red hot, then attempt to weld their little thin plastic legs back together with the base.
The main thing that this achieved though, was to melt away their tiny legs in the intense heat of the poker, creating little legless players, their shorts almost moulded to the base. How I never badly burned my hands, I don't know.
I bet, if I did, I wouldn't have got much sympathy!

I had several dwarf players until I finally got a fence.
In case you're wondering why I used a red-hot poker, I would like to point out that there was nothing like "Superglue" in those days, and any normal glue wouldn't stick an envelope, never mind an International plastic miniature football figure.

*

Just before Christmas, the dreaded letter arrived. I was to go into Hospital one week before my Eleventh birthday.
Oh, Whoopy Doo!
I would have my birthday in a Hospital bed, with no friends or party. To be honest, I had never had a party anyway, so I wouldn't miss it.
I did have one special treat over the Festering period. Nan Pilcher's sister, Aunt Nell to me, and her husband, my Uncle Jim, were going to take me to Hastings to see the pantomime "Aladdin".
That's me, not me and Barry!
"Oh yes, they were!"
We got on a coach at the Hythe Albion Social Club, just opposite from their bungalow in Elizabeth Gardens, along with many others. I loved being with Aunt Nell and Uncle Jim. Aunt Nell was just like nan Pilcher, in that she absolutely doted on me.
Poor old Uncle Jim had lost a finger in the War, and he was always teasing me about where it had gone.
Anyway, all I can remember about the pantomime were the costumes and the lamp, but I was there, honest.
"Oh no, you weren't!"
"Oh yes, I was".
It was the whole shebang though that stands out. The afternoon coach journey to Hastings, fish and chips and pop. The theatre, the crisps, sweets, candy floss and ice cream, and then the late-night journey back to the Albion club, with more chips and pop.

And, no, I wasn't sick at all!

*

Christmas day dawned with a large pillow case of presents at the bottom of my bed.

Well, to tell the truth, the presents had been there all night since dad went to bed. I know this as I was pretending to be asleep, but I was peeping, and I could just about make out dad's figure as he sneaked them into my room. Father Christmas must have dropped them off to him and asked him to deliver them as he was quite busy.

I also know it was dad because I heard him talking to mum. I'm sure that Father Christmas isn't called "Dave".

I would try not to read my annuals too much as I could read them in Hospital, although mum had said that she'd bring me in comics to read. Among my other presents was No. 43, Coventry City and No. 17, Sheffield Wednesday Subbuteo teams. The games compendium was always present, and I got the "Bobby Charlton" Casdon Soccer game, which I loved playing with Steve Miller. There were selection boxes from both, Uncle John and Uncle Ron, so I quickly found a place on top of my wardrobe to hide my chocs.

I may not be bright, I may not be clever, but at least I'm stupid! Hang on, I think I'm missing a "not" there!

I tried to keep out of the way at the family Boxing day bash at Aunt Daisy and Uncle Bill's. The grown ups all wanted to talk to me, to reassure me that it would all be fine, but what did they know? They weren't having to go into Hospital for something they didn't want. I just wanted to be at home, playing with my soldiers.

My younger days, chasing the Aldington Boxing day hunt seemed light years ago (and I didn't even know what a light year was, still don't).

The only other thing of note in the family, this Christmas, was the news that Bett and Pete were going to have a second child in a few months (well, Bett was going to, not Pete, obviously), so I would have another cousin knocking around. I obviously didn't know it at the time but this cousin, along with her brother, Stephen, would be very special and close to me as I grew up, so would Bett and Pete.

*

Back at school, after the new year was very strange, as I only had a few days before I was condemned to six weeks flat out on my back. "OB-LA-DI-OB-LA-DA" by Marmalade was a New Year number one, after the Christmas "Lily the Pink" number one by the Scaffold. Both records were designed to cheer you up, when my mood was more matched by Fleetwood Mac's "Albatross". I was in a very sombre (sulky) mood at the time.

It didn't make matters any better when Mr Skinner made me stand in assembly, while he regaled the whole school about me having to spend my birthday in Hospital to have my poorly leg fixed, and that everybody was to help me and be nice to me when I got back to school. I expect that he told them all again, prior to my return.

I know that it was all done with the best intentions but imagine if you were that person and how it would make you feel. I was put in the spotlight for all the wrong reasons as far as I was concerned.

If anyone had taken the trouble to ask me how I felt about being singled out like this, then they wouldn't have done owt.

I felt as big as a gnat's nadger.

Still, ne'er mind eh!

It was only me that had to deal with it.

I was due to go to Hospital on Monday morning, so on Sunday afternoon, mum said that I could go to the Palmarsh Angels versus Martello game on Hythe Green, but only to watch, as I was already in a lot of pain, but at least I was clean. My dad had specific instructions and they involved nil participation on my part.

Mum knew that I was unhappy about this as I'd never missed a game and I didn't fancy just standing there, on the side lines, watching my mates, especially as it was plooting down with rain.

We all piled into the car as mum waved us off with her last-minute reminder to me, and threat to dad.

On arrival at the Green, we all disembarked onto the squelchiness of a football pitch. It was fortunate that the Green was built on the same shingle seabed as our meadow, otherwise there would have been no game at all.

There was a problem for the Angels though. A couple or three had cried off, possibly because of the weather or, more likely, because we took a battering most of the time. The Martello manager even allowed us to play Robert, despite him being older than officially permitted. That still left the problem of nobody wanting to play in goal. The reason for this was again, possibly because we took a battering most weeks, but almost certainly, because each goalmouth had a large basin like dip, around three inches lower than the rest of the pitch, stretching the whole width of each goal, and at least four feet out towards the penalty spot, this was caused by constant playing on by kids (us, mainly), wearing down the goalmouth area, hence making the crossbar even harder to reach, despite them being child-size goalposts.

There was also one other problem.

It appeared that possibly, after several gentlemen from Bengal had dined out at the local Indian restaurant, on a Phaal Bombay Goose curry with an accompanying very hot Mutton Vindaloo, Madras sauce with chillied chapatis and a Biryani side dish.... They discovered that the Goose was off!

After discovering this tummy churning moment, it was then possible that, in the darkness, they used the dipped goalmouth area as a communal toilet.
This assumption may have come about because the aforesaid mentioned "low area" of the goalmouths was filled with "Liquid Brown".
Nobody in their right mind would entertain the Idea of going in goal.
"I'll go in goal, dad" Cried out the big nosed midget, sensing that it could be a while before the opportunity arose again.
"Yeah, let him, Mr Pilcher" Cried out the Angels in support, but even more in desperation.
Standing in the pouring rain, looking down at his sopping wet, limping about, pain ridden son, I could see that dad wasn't about to be swayed.
"Okay!" he said.
"But don't tell your mother, for Christ's sake".
"Thanks dad".
I had no actual kit on me as I wasn't allowed to bring any. Mum thought ...
"That'll stop him from even thinking about it!"
Wrong!
"I'll play in my jeans and woolly top".
"Don't go near that big brown puddle though" said dad, now regretting giving his consent.
The game kicked off, and immediately Martello were through on goal, until...
I dived head first at the centre forward's feet, just as he was about to fire in his shot.
A mass of Brown water spouted up into the air, showering the Green shirts of the defenders and the Red shirts of the attackers alike then, out of the Brown gooey gunge, appeared, what looked like an early

miniature version of the Honey Monster, dripping all over the place, but holding the ball!

"Great save, Kev... I think" shouted a Green and Brown speckled Steve.

"Urguthosplat slurgsh umkosh" I replied.

I had saved the day, in the first minute, although I'd forgotten my instructions from dad.

I wiped the lumpy bits from around my eyes (probably Goose!), then I looked over for his approval.

He had his head in his hands, appearing to do a "Basil Fawlty" before he even existed. Could dad see into the future?

Probably. That's why he had his head in his hands.

How, in the name of Charles Dickens, would he explain this to mum? Me, on the other hand, thought...

"In for a penny... er... do as the Romans do!"

I was covered in "curry leftovers" from head to foot, so any more wouldn't make no never mind. I forgot my pains and impending incarceration and jumped and dived all over the place.

This was where I was happiest, playing football with my mates, covered in Gawd knows what, having the time of my life. I was like a pig in... whatever pigs roll around in.

The rain continued throughout the game and, at the final whistle, after Palmarsh Angels had fought to a very creditable 8-1 defeat, I was actually cheered off the pitch. I was unidentifiable as a person. Just a dripping blob of Brown ooze with a slightly protruding nose sticking out, but people were shouting "Well done" to me, and clapping. I think they knew!

Dad wouldn't let me sit in the car. I had to stand, and try not to drip all over the seats, or Kim Maycock!

I'll never forget that bit. It stands out. I had to have Steve and Mick hold me upright as we drove home, around the bendy bits in the road (and they pushed me onto Kim's lap once or twice, just to wind him up).

When we got home, mum had a face like a Bulldog chewing stinging nettles. Boy, oh boy, did she chuck her toys out of the pram?

She didn't have toys or a pram really, it's just a saying.

Oh, you knew that!

Most of the abuse, I think, was this time directed at dad, although it was hard to define what was being shouted as my ears were clogged with "Vindaloo sauce".

I was made to stand in the bath whilst I had my clothes unceremoniously pulled from my Browny coloured body. The worst bits were when my top and tee shirt were tugged over my head. There was no care nor subtlety in mum's approach to cleansing me of the goo. Nope, I got it in the neck as well, once dad had disappeared out of her range.

For some reason I got a couple of whacks as well when I couldn't stand still as instructed, because she was trying to pull my ears off, along with my top. You try standing still when a soaking wet gungy Brown neck hole won't go over your head, despite it, and you, being yanked upwards with accompanying chanting...

"I told you" Yank!

"Not to bloody play" Yank!

"But did you listen?" Tug!

"Did you, buggery" Yank!

"Stand still" Tug!

"Mum, it's hurting" Yank!

"Stand still" Tug!

"Mum, you've got my ears" Yank!

"It's your own fault, I told you" Tug!

"Ow, mum, you're hurting!"
"Stand" Whack! "Bloody" Whack! "Still!"
"Ow, what's that for?"
"That's for getting plastered in mud" Whack! Tug!
"You're going to have a good bath now, and I've got to scrub those ears" Yank!
"I won't have any ears if you don't stop. Ow!" Yank!
Off it finally popped.
"There, now look at you. Stand there while I run the bath."
"I'm standing in it, mum".
"I know, now get the rest of that clobber off and start washing!"
It took three reloads of the bath and a good scrubbing with one of mum's "Brillo pad" flannels to get the mud out from my ears and neck. She wanted me to be clean for tomorrow. I was made to go to bed early, but could I get to sleep not knowing what was going to happen to me? Could I, Partridges!
I spent the evening up and down the stairs to the toilet, out in the back porch, and laying in my bed reading comics.
I didn't want Monday morning to arrive.

*

Monday morning arrived.
With great apprehension, I packed and repacked my old battered case. I had a new pair of Sky-Blue pyjamas. I didn't wear pyjamas, but I was told that I would have to have them in Hospital. A toothbrush, toothpaste, flannel (Brillo pad variety) and soap. Some comics and books, and that was it.
There I stood, looking as nervous as a turkey, standing outside the butcher's front door at Christmas time. I would rather have been at school than waiting to go to the Hospital, which was a bit ironic really, as the school had very kindly given mum some school work for

me to do whilst I was laying, flat on my back in Hospital.
Wasn't that nice of them?
They had said that it was, so I didn't fall too far behind with my work. There was to be no Eleven plus exams for us this year for some unknown reason, and senior school selection would be done on our school work during the year and on recommendation.
I knew that mum and dad didn't want me to go to Harvey Grammar school in Folkestone as it was… well, in Folkestone, and the school uniform and kit required was quite expensive.
I was sure that I wouldn't let them down or disappoint their academical aspirations of me.
I still didn't fancy working out sums or writing about hundreds of years ago in History or owt, whilst laying horizontal in bed though!
Dad had got some time off work to take us to Ashford, so I said my cheerio's to nan and grandad. Nan spilt cigarette ash down me and grandad just ruffled my hair and walked off to his shed. I think that he really felt my pain and anguish. I got into the back seat of the little A35, knowing that I wasn't going to see my home again for another six weeks, and gulped back the tears that I felt welling up inside.
I just gazed out of the window at the fields as we chugged along the A20, through Newingreen and Sellinge. Oh, I wished that I could turn back the clock and be out playing in those fields again. I tried to picture me, with all my friends, from Court at Street and St. Georges, but all I could imagine was, me clumping around after them with this great big iron encased leg.
I felt about as low as a lizard's lunch box.
We passed Sellinge Stores, and then the turning for Harringe Lane. "Straight up there, dad and we'll be home in no time!" I thought to myself as we trundled on past to Ashford.

*

Chapter Thirteen – Caribbean Angels

Soon, the depressing sight of the Hospital entrance was in front of me. It was an old brick building, in the middle of the town, so mum said that it would be easy for her to get the bus each day, to come up and see me (and she did, bless her).
I stood there.
"I don't want to go in, mum" I pleaded for one last futile time.
"Come on, Todd" was all I got as a response, plus a very gentle nudge in the back. I think that they were going through their own little mini hell, as well.
I was checked in at the main reception and shown the way to the children's ward. It had the smell that only an old Hospital can have. It's hard to describe, but for anyone that's sampled it, you'll know what I mean.
We waited at the ward desk. Mum was pointing out toys and stuff in the play area, hoping to cheer me up, and failing. I think that she'd forgotten that I would be chained (virtually) to a bed. Anyway, the toys were for younger kids, not for a mature, almost Eleven, year old Adonis with a manky leg.
As I shuffled around, looking like an evacuee from the blitz, clutching my old suitcase, the ward Sister came along and introduced herself...
"Hello Kevin, I'm Sister Caine" she said.
She looked quite stern desplte her smile, but that, I found out as time went on, was just her outward "I'm in charge" appearance. She was a very nice person, a good "firm but fair" voice of authority, who would only administer a severe beating every second Tuesday.
Only joshing!
She always instructed the biggest nurse to do it!

Well, that was what was going around in my head that morning. I was living in perpetual fear of everything.

Sister Caine could obviously sense my terror, so she said that while she spoke to mum and dad, I would be taken off, by a guard... I mean nurse, to have a bath and get into my jim jams...

"Whaat?"

"Hold on, I had a bath, two baths, yesterday!"

"All children have to have a bath when they come in, Kevin. Don't worry".

The nurse led me off, away from mum and dad, to the bathroom, and let me undress whilst she ran a lukewarm bath with some smelly disinfectant stuff in it.

I tried to cover my dangly bits as I got into the bath. I didn't need a very big sponge!

I sat there for several minutes in the tepid water, until the nurse returned with a large, coarse towel for me to dry myself with.

As she helped me to dry and get into my night attire (at Eleven Thirty in the morning), I could almost sense her thinking...

"Where's his little willy gone?"

Please don't forget it was a very cold, early January day.

I was taken from the bathroom, in my natty brand- new pyjamas, to the ward. Why do they always make pyjama bottoms so long-legged? I could have got mum to put a Four Inch turn-up in them, but I'd learnt my lesson there. I'd just drag them along the linoleum floor to my bed in the corner, looking directly out into the playroom area. What was this? Mental torture as well?

There were Eight beds in the ward, but only half were occupied at present.

Possibly, some were away digging an escape tunnel!

The chief jailer, or nurse that had led me to my bed then disappeared, leaving me to say goodbye to mum and dad. I was fighting very hard to keep the tears in, but I failed. I was going to be left alone here, I didn't want to be left alone here. I had known for months that this moment would come, and now it had. I didn't like it at all. Mum and dad thought it would be best to leave me in the Hospital's capable hands, so with a...
"See you tomorrow, Todd" from mum, and a...
"You'll be fine, Todd. Come on, Marge" from dad, they both turned and were off. Mum had a quick look back and waved at the ward door. She didn't actually wave "at" the ward door. She waved to me when she was at the ward door. I hope that I've cleared that up. One other little point here. We don't do kisses in our family (apparently).
That was it. I really was on my Todd now.
I could cry and cry for England, but it wouldn't make no never mind, so I tried to just accept my fate, whatever that may be.
After mum and dad had gone, Sister Caine and a new face, Staff nurse Harris, appeared at my bedside...
"Hello, Kevin" said staff nurse Harris, with a smile. I would get to like her a lot.
"Hello" I mumbled, still trying to take in my new surroundings.
"Right, we'll need those pyjama bottoms off, Kevin" interrupted Sister Caine.
"What?"
"My trousers?" I spluttered out.
"Yes, Kevin, we need to tape up around your leg for the traction. Don't look so worried, it won't hurt".
No more to be said on the matter.
I slipped off my bottoms, onto the ward floor. I wouldn't need those again here. I wasn't aware of that at the time though.

Underneath, I was sporting a nice pair of Yellow Y-fronts with Blue edges. If nowt else, I was a trend setter in the underpants department.

"They're a nice colour, you can keep those on" said the nice staff nurse Harris, with a big smile.

Next, from a trolley of medical supplies that they'd towed in with them, came a big roll of, at least Three-Inch wide Elastoplast, which Sister Caine started to unravel.

"Okay Kevin, this plaster will start at the top of your leg and go all the way down, under your foot and back up the other side to the top, by your pants".

Before I could say owt or, better still, make an escape bid, I was being bandaged and elastoplasted up. There was a springy like contraption attached around the ankle area that went up, over the top of another contraption that was fitted to the bottom of the bed frame, and then downwards, suspended by weights.

Then the surgical stocking was applied!

Oh, I almost forgot the metal brace that was involved in all of this, that also went up both sides of my leg, to end in a sort of padded hoop around my Ging Gang region.

That was it. I was trapped!

I was stretched out over the bed, like a bearskin, minus the bear, fastened by my now, incarcerated right leg. I could have extra pillows to prop me up and a sheet and blanket to cover my snazzy pants and little spindly legs, but that was it.

My World for the next six weeks!

With my right foot suspended almost Two feet higher than my left one, creating a tent-like effect, I felt, and I suspect, looked a right dollop. Then Sister Caine asked me...

"Is that comfortable for you?"

I thought that I would end up like "Twizzle" (you must surely remember him from "Watch with Mother"), being able to extend my legs.
"Do I look comfortable?" I thought, but...
"Yeah, I think so" was all I said.
As they took the trolley away, I just lay there thinking...
"I've got six weeks of this".
Everything that I would have to do, would be done from this semi-prone position, and the one thought that kept spinning through my bewildered brain was...
"I can't pooh like this!".
As the day wore on, some other children came in, or back, to the ward and their beds from the tunnel. There wasn't very much conversation in the ward though. Mostly, they looked as scared and confused as I was to be there. Some had their parents come in to visit them. I sneakily noticed a few of them glance over towards me, and mutter to each other. I got some sympathetic smiles and a couple of nods, but mainly, I was left alone to just get on with it.
A freak in a freak show, with my bright Yellow and Blue undergarments on display at my tent entrance. Anybody viewing from the opposite side of the ward had a view to savour and marvel at!
My first day in Hospital ended, with me just laying there, at a strange angle, listening out to every sound as the ward lights were dimmed down, then turned out early in the evening (well, early for me, anyway), as there were some very young toddler types in here.
From my vantage point, at the far end of the ward, I could survey all around me and I wasn't at all impressed with the vista. To my left was the window to the playroom, now in darkness, and to my right and in front were the other seven beds. At the far end, by the door, was the ward desk where the nurses would sit. There was an office

for Sister Caine just outside the ward, opposite the dreaded bathroom area. I don't know why I thought of the bathroom that way now as, from then until I was freed, I was informed that I'd be having "Bed baths".

When I pointed out that the sheets would get soaked, staff nurse Harris laughed. I had a lot to learn!

It was a lonely, fretful night for me. I was, in effect, chained to the bed and I wondered what would happen should there be a fire, and the Hospital burn down.

Cheerful little thoughts like that, and wondering if chickens used fowl language kept me, both awake, and a little amused.

*

Reveille' or breakfast was between Seven and Seven Thirty in the morning (well, it would be daft if it was at night!). I was given toast and I asked for, and got, a cup of tea. I did ask for Marmite for my toast, and they said that mum could bring some in.

Mr Baird always did his rounds on Monday mornings, so I had missed him this week. Still, some of the nurses were changing over so I would have new ones to get used to.

Up until now, I had only seen two nurses. They were okay. They both said that they came from Ashford, so they were local.

As I watched the nurses change over, I couldn't help but notice that the two new nurses weren't from around these parts. For a start, they didn't have the pallid skin complexion that one would attain from being from this area.

Nope, these nurses were of the darker coloured variety!

I had never come into any contact with any different coloured skinned folk before, I came from on the top of Romney Marsh, for Gerald's sake!

I was intrigued and, I suppose, a bit bewitched by them. From what I could hear at the other end of the ward, they laughed a lot. I watched as they made their round of the beds, spending a little bit of time at each one. I knew that it would be my turn soon. They both reached the foot of my bed, and in an accent that I'd never heard before, not even on the T.V., the first one said...
"Hello Kevin, I'm..."
I can't remember either of their true names now, fifty years on. There is reason for this, which I'll get to.
The one thing that I do vividly remember though is their smiles. Flashing White teeth against a dark, open smiling background. If I was frightened of being in this place (which I was), then these two beautiful nurses had suddenly brought the ward to life, and they had made everything so much better.
They were both so bright and bubbly. It was as if I'd been given two new "big sisters" to look after me.
Yep, my first ever encounter of anyone different to me, and I fell in love with these two nurses, as only an almost Eleven year- old could do.
I know that I struggled with their names at the time, but when they told me where they came from, and showed me in an atlas, that's what I called them from that moment onwards.
They both thought it hilarious, so did staff nurse Harris. Sister Caine wasn't too impressed though, but Hey Ho!
From that initial introduction, I was looked after better than anybody could ever imagine by my two special friends and nurses.
"Barbados", who was my favourite, if I had to have just the one, and "Trinidad" were, in my personal Hell, a gift from Heaven.
My "Caribbean Angels".

*

Mum came in to see me at afternoon visiting time and was a tad shocked to see me all "Tractioned up", but she was also pleased and surprised to find me so chipper. When I introduced her to Barbados and Trinidad, I think she knew that I'd be okay.

Mum would stay for a couple of hours, then get the bus back to Hythe. Over the time that I was there, she really did put in the "bus miles". Good old mum!

Over the weekends, she would occasionally come in with dad, and sometimes bring the little urchin with them, although he preferred the freedom of being left at home with nan Coombes, to hunt out any stash of goodies that I may have had.

He didn't find any though as grandad had let me hide my stuff in his shed, and "Sugar puff face" wasn't allowed in there!

Apart from being able to laugh along with my two "Angels" and staff nurse Harris, life for me, on the ward was reasonably dull and boring. I was having no actual treatment, other than my "Twizzle" mechanism so I just had to lay there, watching the other kids come and go, in quick succession. I never got to know any other kid on the ward at all. I was just the "Dummy", stuck in the far-off bed, who sometimes got nodded to by visitors.

When my Caribbean Angels were there, the time would always pass by quicker with lots of cheery smiles, jokes and laughter, but when their shift ended, it was back to the boredom of staring at the same scene, watching the large wall clock move it's hands ever so slowly, and dread any time when I may require a bottle, or worse still, a bedpan!

I'll gloss over the second option there, but suffice to say…

It is just about possible to pooh laying down, but it's not pleasant, nor is it to be recommended.

Try to imagine doing it standing upright. Now, imagine that, horizontal! Enough said.

And the food, well, that was nowt to write home about, which was just as well really as I didn't have any writing paper…or envelopes…or pen…or stamps, come to think of it. Anyway, with mum there every day to see my teatime meal, I had no need to write home. Mum could tell everyone.

There was one lunchtime when Sister Caine had a pop at me. She said…

"Now, come on Kevin, eat your cabbage, it'll put colour in your cheeks!"

"But I don't want Green cheeks" says I.

The ward staff fell about laughing, but Sister Caine gave me one of those looks that could kill.

Which wasn't a very good advert for herself, or the N.H.S.

*

My birthday passed on a Friday. Eleven days after being sentenced. I got a small cake and Barbados and Trinidad sang a sort of "Happy Birthday" calypso to me, which I, and everyone else there applauded and thought was brilliant. Calypso music originated in Trinidad and Tobago, so if anyone had the right to sing one, then they did.

They made an otherwise non-event Eleventh birthday just that little bit special.

I had asked mum to bring my Soldiers United in, as there were some toy soldiers here and I wanted my team to play them. Obviously, I couldn't use a ball, and I couldn't play on the floor. I couldn't reach, for a start. So, I devised a small playing area on my slide across table and used a dice as a ball. It was a bit embarrassing taking my team of World beaters out of their granny's handbag for their first real, official tour match, but I coped.

In some close games, Soldiers United triumphed, as I knew they would.

I do have to come clean here, a few of the Hospital players did so well, that I gave them a "Free transfer" to one of my home teams. What I mean is, I put them into the handbag along with Soldiers United, and I snaffled them!
I'm not proud of it, but at least I'm owning up to my misdemeanour, albeit fifty years on.

*

As well as my comics, I had really got into reading the little Commando War books, along with Battle, War, Air Ace. In fact, it's a habit that I've never kicked. To date, I own over two thousand of them, and I still read them!
Mr Baird's Monday ritual visit was about as exciting as chewing cardboard flavoured cardboard. He would saunter in, surrounded by several trainees, stand by my bed, read my notes, ask Sister Caine some questions about the springiness of my spring, or whatever, then he would just saunter off, usually without even acknowledging my presence in the bed in front of him.
I certainly never got a kiss!
Mum would always try to get in for his rounds, to perhaps ask a pertinent question, I don't know. The only time she did manage to arrive before him, she just said...
"How is he doing, Doctor?" in her best Queen Mother's voice.
Blimey, she should've known how I was doing better than him, she saw me every day. He only ever appeared to see through me once a week.
"Oh, fine, fine" was all he'd say, then he would get back to impressing his students.
Sister Caine was duty bound to fawn after him with the patients notes. Staff nurse Harris would just roll her eyes at the sheer charade of it all, and Barbados and Trinidad would get back to cheering us all

up when he had gone. Staff nurse Harris told mum more of what was happening with me than any of the so called "experts".

The one thing that we were permitted to have in the ward (when Mr Baird weren't there) was the radio. It was always tuned to Radio One, and we loved listening to the charts. There was a TV in the playroom, but it was only turned on in the daytime for things like "Watch with Mother" or any other children's programmes. I found out, very early in my enforced stay, that there would be no "Match of the day" or "The Big Match" for me. They didn't even have it on for "Grandstand" or "World of Sport" on a Saturday, so no Teleprinter results service for me, then.

It was pointless me moaning about it anyway, because although I could just about see the screen, I couldn't hear owt as there was a large window between me and the box, so that little avenue of enjoyment was closed to me for the duration of my stay.

But, as I said, the radio was there, and as a special surprise for me, mum had written in to the "Breakfast Show" with a request for me. So, on the 7th February 1969, as I lay recumbent on my bed, with my two favourite nurses, Barbados and Trinidad puffing up my pillows and emptying my wee wee bottle, the voice of Tony Blackburn announced my predicament to the Nation in full and graphic detail, I think that his dog "Arnold" may have even given me a bark. This teensy, weensy moment of National fame was followed by "Blackberry Way" by The Move, the new number one record, just for me (although I suspect others may have eavesdropped).

Roy Wood, the singer with The Move, would feature in my musical World, further down the road with Wizard in the 1970s. He also had a hit single himself, with "Going down the road". I know, because I've still got it. I suppose, now looking back, it was nice, and a relief, to have my request read out by somebody not, in years to come, involved in "Operation Yew Tree!". Thank Lord Snooty that it wasn't Jimmy Savile!

*

A person from the physiotherapy department came around with a tape to measure me up for my "Metal leg" or calliper, as it was known. Mum had been told to buy me a pair of shoes, made from good leather with a thick sole and heel. This was for the leather straps and spring to be attached on the right leg, and for a built-up bit, like a flat iron, to be attached by screws under the left foot.
I knew two things here, one was that these shoes weren't going to be cheap, and two, that I was going to look a right clown, fit for mocking!
The weeks passed by and I was getting more and more institutionalized in the ways of the Hospital. The only thing to break the boredom for me were mum's daily visits, with a few sweets and, maybe a new comic to read.
The Beano, Dandy, Buster, Beezer, Victor, Valiant, Hornet, Hotspur, Tiger, Topper, Sparky, Lion, Eagle, TV Comic, Whizzer & Chips, I had the lot, not to forget my Commando, Air Ace, Battle, War picture Library little comic War books.
I devoured them all, like a rabid squirrel with a stash of nuts!
A couple of times, when her mind was elsewhere, mum would also bring me the Bunty, Jackie or Mandy in amongst my manly collection. There would always be...
"Mum, these are girl's comics, I don't want these"
But instead of insisting that she took them away, I would sneakily file them under the pile, and then read them when nobody was around or looking.
Well, I did say that it was boring, just lolloped about on a bed!

Once, Barbados came over and caught me trying to hide my Bunty under the sheet.

"What you got there, young man?"

"Nowt, Barbados. Honest".

I could never manage a look of glib innocence.

"Staff nurse Harris, come and look" laughed Barbados.

By now, anyone within earshot was staring over as Barbados quickly pulled back the sheet to catch me grasping my Bunty!

"What's dis, Kevin?" (Sorry, I can't do Caribbean accents).

"It's my Bunty!"

"I've run out of my comics to read".

"Can I read it after you?" chuckled staff nurse Harris.

"Then we'll let all the other girls have a good look at your Bunty, if that's okay with you"

"Yeah, okay" says I, laughing along with them, knowing that I'd been hung out to dry.

We didn't do "innuendo" or "Double entendre" in 1969!

These little episodes, especially at my expense, kept everybody smiling, and the nursing staff always took great pleasure in bringing the subject up, especially in front of any visitors.

I quickly became the joker in the ward, the "go to" person to have a chuckle with or to cheer any of the younger kids up. To be honest, I wasn't going anywhere. I was the eldest inmate...er...patient in the ward, the other five or six always appeared to be much younger than me, and we never had all the beds occupied (still tunnel digging, I presumed).

Also, I was the only bedridden one there, never mind being confined to quarters, I was confined to bed. I was given some exercises to do in bed, and I had some cream to prevent bed sores, and to rub on where mum's "Brillo pad" flannel had scratched my delicate soft skin. It certainly wasn't "Nivea", more like a dollop of White "Swarfega".

*

There was one serious moment amongst all the revelry on the ward. It was a few days after my Radio One request slot, even Sister Caine became embroiled in the debate.
"Was Auntie Jean, Tingha & Tucker's real Auntie?" asked Trinidad on this particular day.
She had absolutely no Idea who Tingha & Tucker were, as I suspect, you possibly don't either.
If you don't, look them up on the computer. Winklepedia it, or YouFaceTube them!
To Sister Caine, it was an open and shut case...
"Auntie Jean is human and they're both Koalas, so she can't be".
"Ah, but she may have adopted them" said staff nurse Harris.
"What about Willie Wombat?" I interjected.
"He's a wombat" said Barbados, almost as bemused as her Caribbean companion.
"Ah, but is he related to Tingha & Tucker?"
"Don't be daft Kevin, he can't be. He's a wombat" retorted Sister Caine, trying to put on her stern face, but allowing her grin to permeate through.
Well, this debate went on for ages, even involving Andy Pandy, Teddy, Looby Lou, the Woodentops, Sarah Brown and Hoppity. The cutting edge of politics it wasn't, it was far more entertaining. We all ended up singing "The Wibbly Wobbly way", can you remember that? I can still remember the tune now, although, as then, the words are a bit vague.

At time though, I considered myself to be more of an expert than the nursing staff, because at one point in my younger days, I had been a member of the "Tingha & Tucker" club, so there. "Na na na na na" with brass knobs on!
I even had the badge.
I lost that as well.
Thinking about "Sara Brown and Hoppity", as I just have been, I can even remember some of their songs.
Mrs Brown was always...
"Sewing, sewing, sewing", perhaps she could have given mum some tips! And Mr Brown was singing...
"Plink plonk, a nail goes in. Then I add a nut, then I add a screw.
Plink plonk, the soldier stands, and walks around as good as new.
I'm always mending soldiers, that can't stand up no more.
I stand them up and they fall down, upon the kitchen floor".
They just don't write gripping lyrics like that anymore, and it's our loss!
I think that it may have been one of Lennon and McCartney's lesser known songs!
Sorry about that, I was digressing back to my earlier, happier years, before "Jonah" the God of misfortune, kicked me up the backside and left me in searing pain, horizontal in a Hospital bed, prior to two years of perceived, unbridled misery.

*

Still, it could have been worse...
Sister Caine, in her sternest of faces, told us of an elderly skiing relative of hers, who, about a month before he died, had his entire back covered in lard... after that, he went downhill fast!
As a certain Mr B. Brush may say "BOOM BOOM"

The tedium of daily life on the ward was broken by those daft exchanges as the clock of impending disability ticked slowly onwards. I had several "measurings", but I hadn't yet seen the contraption that I'd have to wear.
That was all about to change.
Staff nurse Harris had pre-warned me that it was going to be brought up to the ward this day, and they would do a trial fitting. Whilst I was on the bed, they could just unclip the traction spring as they had done in the past, several times before.
Well, how else do you think that they could change my trendy Y-fronts?
I wasn't still wearing the same bright Yellow and Blue ones, five weeks on. I'd had at least two changes since then!
I knew that they had to do this fitting soon as I'd only got another week to go before, with full remission for good(ish) behaviour, I'd be home again, albeit in very odd and different circumstances, but when the Physiotherapist came through the door, holding this overgrown Meccano creation, my jaw dropped lower than a Gecko's gonads and my heart sank to the depths of despair.
"Right Kevin, let's just slip this on your leg".
"I can't wear that!"
"You'll be fine, once you've got used to it!"
"I won't get used to that. It's horrible!"
It really did resemble, in almost every way, a calliper that a poor Polio victim would wear, except mine had the extra bit with the spring attachment on top of the shoe, connected to the sides of the calliper, to keep my foot off the floor.
It was slipped up my surgical stockinged leg, right up to the top, where the leather- bound hooped bit rested tightly against the inside of my leg.

The physiotherapist then buckled the leather restraining strap around my knee. My leg was now in an almost rigid position. There was some slight leeway and I'd get more, the more it was worn, I was assured.
I couldn't yet get off the bed and stand on it as the shoes hadn't, at the time, been completed, but they said it was a good fit. I could think of a word that rhymed with that but, obviously I kept that to myself.
When mum came in that day at 2pm, on the dot as usual, she could tell by my face that I was the opposite of happy, but what could she say? It was going to happen, and I would just have to make the best of it. Again, I thought...
"Why me?" A small tear fell from my overfull eye and trickled down my cheek.
"Mum, I can't wear that calliper, I'll be picked on and bullied rotten".
"No, you won't Todd, you'll get through it and you'll get that hip better, just you see".
She would be right with her first prediction, but way off the mark with the second one, but that's to come, later in my life.
"Steve's coming in to see you tomorrow".
Steve was only one of two friends that wanted to come to the Hospital, the other was Mick. In fact, they came in together once with mum and dad on a Saturday afternoon. To be fair, I hadn't wanted anybody else to see me, all trussed up like a Christmas bird. Whenever they came in, with tales of football and whatever, we all laughed and joked about a lot, and to be honest, it took me out of my grim situation for a while. Talking with either of them, I felt that I couldn't wait to get back out there, kicking a ball about and riding my bike. In my head though, I was sure that it wasn't even a possibility. In my heart though, with their encouragement, support and positive attitude, anything was possible.

One of us must have had a Crystal ball, it certainly wasn't me though. Whatever anyone else would do, or shout at me, I knew that I'd got some special mates around me. Without their support and friendship then, and in the coming couple of years, my life as a shortish disabled lad would have been much, much grimmer.
When Steve did visit, the next day, I tried to describe the calliper and how I would have to get about. Seeing how down I was, he tried to make me see the funny side to it all. Those visits would also, almost certainly, involve an in-depth discussion about our Subbuteo, and I do confess that, when I was left back on my own again in the far corner of the ward, I shed several quiet tears, feeling very sorry for myself.

*

To make me feel even better about my situation (not), both Barbados and Trinidad were taking their annual leave. They were both venturing home for a few weeks, back to the Caribbean, and I would miss them both greatly.
When they left, they both came over and gave me a big hug, saying that they would keep in touch with me, but it did leave a great hole. I wouldn't see their smiling faces, nor hear their laughing anymore. I just wanted to get home, myself.
A few weeks after I got home, I did receive a lovely letter from Barbados, to cheer me up.
Mr Baird did his usual Monday morning visit. This was the one where he would discharge me as I'd done the full six weeks.
He must have had an argument with Mrs Baird over his breakfast boiled egg or something, because I couldn't believe it when he said to Sister Caine to...
"Give it till Friday, then he can go home".

Now hold your blooming horses, buddy!
"That's more than six weeks!" I cried out.
"You'll be home on Friday, Kevin" said Sister Caine, in her best official tone, as Mr Baird was still hovering, checking my notes.
"That's six and a half weeks, not six!"
He just peered at me briefly, over the top of his half moon spectacles, then handed Sister Caine the notes and flounced off like a…like a…er…big flouncy thing, with his entourage grovelling in his wake.
I hoped his boiled egg was incredibly snotty and his little toast soldiers all defected!
"That's nearly seven weeks" I mumbled to Staff nurse Harris, she could only give me her sympathetic "I know" smile, and get me to do my bed exercises, ready for the big day, now on Friday 21st February, six and a half weeks after my admittance.

*

During my time, laying horizontal on the bed, the tops of the Elastoplast plasters had started to curl up and come away from my skin. Any slight tug of the end of the plaster though, would cause me to wince, as the rest of it was stuck firmly on, all the way down the outside of my leg and back up the inside. This area near the top of my inner thigh was particularly sore and sticky when I pulled it slightly, as my skin was more tender in that region.
I hope that I'm painting a good, almost sensual image of my predicament here. You see, my theory was that, if it hurt this much when I gave it a gentle, slow tweak, what would the pain be like when the nurse removed it completely?
I was dreading that moment as I was convinced, I'd scream the place down.

Well, Friday came along, as I knew it would. All my stuff (and some of the Hospital's) had been packed away, awaiting my impending departure. I'd had several calliper fittings but hadn't, so far, stood or tried to walk with it on. This was something that I wasn't looking forward to.

I knew that mum and dad had been told to be up for me at around lunchtime, so I'd had my last tasty Hospital dinner.

The dreaded moment had arrived.

Staff nurse Harris and Sister Caine were going to carry out my final piece of torture. They unhooked my retaining spring, or perhaps that should be "restraining spring".

Next, they rolled down, and pulled off my smelly surgical stocking to fully reveal…Da Da Da!

The offending length of sticky Elastoplast!

"Please don't hurt me" I pleaded through fearful eyes.

"It'll be fine, don't worry" stated Sister Caine, sensing her final chance to inflict sadistic pain upon me (I thought).

"I'll do it, so you'll only feel a slight sting, Kevin" laughed staff nurse Harris.

"Please do it slowly" I asked with a trembling voice. I was ready to run for it, but I remembered that my foot wasn't meant to touch terra firma, and I hadn't yet learned how to fly.

Is that what they mean when they say, "Hop it"?

Anyway, staff nurse Harris grabbed the outside top end (the easier bit) and said…

"I'll count to three, then just pull it off".

"But please do it slo…!"

"Ready? One, Two…!"

YANK!

"Aaaarrrggh!!!! that wasn't three, that really stu…!"

YANK!

"Aaaarrrggh!!!!"
She'd quickly ripped the inner side away while my thoughts were elsewhere.
"All done, well done" she laughed.
"You cheated, you didn't count to three".
"Ah, I fooled you, didn't I?"
"Yeah, thanks" I said, whilst rubbing my leg and trying to pick the little dirty sticky bits off that were left.
"Next Kevin, we're going to wheel you down to physio, to get you walking in your calliper" said Sister Caine.
"Oh, deep joy!"
Once I'd made the very short journey in the wheelchair, staff nurse Harris turned to go back to the ward.
"Come and say "bye" before you go, won't you?"
"Will do" I said, now realizing that I was at last on my way home.

*

The physio fitted the calliper to my right leg, I had a pair of football shorts on by now. On my left foot, the shoe was placed, and I was instructed to stand up, between a pair of parallel bars, with the bars taking my weight.
This was a strange feeling, I was at least two to three inches taller than I was when I came in, and my right leg was stiff, secured within the metal framework.
"Go on Kevin, try to take a few steps".
I fell over!
"Try again, this time try to stay upright" joked the physio.
Believe it or not, this helped relax me.
The first thing that I discovered, was that I could only move my right leg forward by swinging it out sideways a bit, as the knee wouldn't bend.

So, I would swing out my right leg, in a sort of arc, and then lift my, now heavier, left foot, and clomp it forwards.
It was the only way that I could propel myself. I was doing okay with this awkward movement, so I had a go without the protection of the bars.
There I went. Lift, clomp, swing, clomp, lift, clomp, swing, clomp... then...
"Aarrggh!"
I had trapped one of my Brussel sprout type appendages between the padded hoop and my inner leg.
"Oooh!"
First the pain, then the sick feeling descended quickly. I had trouble focussing as my eyes seemed to be leaking.
My initial attempt at walking unaided had ended with me being doubled up in agony with a "pinched" Ging Gang!
"Oh yeah" I spluttered
"I won't get called "Lift one, Swing one", will I?"
That was obviously a rhetorical question.
Of course, I would, among many other things.
Anyway, once that part of my nether region had reduced back to the size of a pickled walnut, I carried on with my crusade to master this and propel myself as much as I could without falling off my left shoe, causing a twisted ankle or worse, and trying to muster as little "swing" as possible with my rigid right leg, or else I would become a self-propelling scythe as I moved along.
After a fair amount of time, my left ankle and lower leg around my calf were really aching and I'd managed to catch my bits twice more. Mum and dad had turned up by now, so with a lift and a clomp and a swing and a clomp, I made my way back to the ward, to bid farewell to, and to thank Sister Caine and staff nurse Harris. In a strange way, I knew that I would miss them both. I was sad that Barbados and

Trinidad weren't there that day, but perhaps it was best that way, although they could have popped back from the Caribbean for an hour!

I would never forget my Caribbean Angels.

With a final glance towards my bed for the past six and a half weeks, I waved and made my way, clomping down the corridor, to the Hospital exit. I think that by now, we can take the lifting and swinging bit as read.

Chapter Fourteen – Clomp, Kick, Snap!

The journey back home in the car was a weird one, I had to sit on the back seat with my "bad leg" sticking out along the seat. I was looking out at the familiar scenery and half listening to mum and dad, whilst at the same time, wondering what sort of reaction I'd get from the others in the Square. Like me, they'd never seen owt like this before. They had certainly never seen me like this, like a penguin on stilts. I hoped it would all be okay.

When the little Austin pulled up outside the house, sitting on the wall, waiting for me were Steve, Mick, Kim, Carl, Robert, Brian and little Carl Harris, our newcomer to the gang.

As soon as I floundered out of the car door, they all descended like vultures over a tortoise carcass. They all wanted to have a look, asking me all sorts of questions about my calliper, my long spell of incarceration and what were the nurses like!

Mum told me not to be long out there, and her and dad both went in for a cuppa.

When mum looked out of the front room window two minutes later, there wasn't a Palmarsh Angel to be seen!

Mick had just innocently asked me if I would still be able to kick a ball with "that thing" on.

Robert had just said...

"Come on Kev, let's find out!"

So, we all clomped off to the Square. Well, I did.

The others ambled and ran in their usual way.

We immediately fell back into our usual teams and started a game. It was a bit awkward at first, trying to kick the ball.

Alright, it was flipping nigh impossible!

I had to pivot on the calliper with my right leg. The hoop was as far up my leg as was possible.

Then I had to attempt to kick with my raised left shoe.
I know that this is hard to believe, but it's completely true. I did manage a way to balance and kick a ball in very quick time. I also found out that, due to the rigidity of my right leg, I could only dive to the left.
I surprisingly mastered a sort of technique in a very short space of time, and I was soon flinging myself all over the place. Mum and dad and a couple of the other parents came out to see. They were all just shaking their heads in disbelief. Only a few hours earlier, I was horizontal in a Hospital bed.
I think that it was poor old Brian Warne who became the first recipient of a misplaced kick with the metal "flat iron" on the bottom of my left shoe. In time, all the kids would have that "special" bruise to show that they to, had been caught by it.
After a while watching, dad called me in. It was starting to get dark by how anyway, and mum had promised me a fry up. Nan Coombes tut tutted, tipped her fag ash down her apron and said...
"He's only been home five minutes, and he's straight back out there kicking a ball about"
Grandad gave me his knowing grin, lighting up his pipe, blowing smoke into the room, he just said...
"He's a Kev".
He called me over, ruffled my hair that he'd cut six and a half weeks ago, and just said...
"Told you so, didn't I? I said you'd cope".
"You did, grandad".
It was good to be home. Even Barry was being nice to me.
"I got you a bar of chocolate and a comic" he said as he handed over

some Cadburys Dairy Milk and the "Victor".
"There's some squares missing" I said as I felt the bar.

He just grinned the grin he always did when he'd got one over me.
"Thanks" I smiled back.
It was a happy house, that evening as we all sat down to a plate of artery blocking fat and chips!
The hardest thing to get used to that night was taking the calliper off and hopping around the house. I so nearly put my right foot down on the floor on numerous occasions, but I did manage to keep it airborne. This task would become easier to perform as time went on (I hoped). At least I would have a week to get used to it before going back to school as it was half term week.
It was great to be able to sit on the floor behind the sofa again, as Soldiers United had some important league fixtures to catch up on. The Hospital recruits were installed into their new teams in various handbag compartments.
It was brilliant to be able to watch the weekend football programmes again. To be perfectly honest, it was great just to be able to watch any TV again, but that was only when I was indoors.
Outside, it was a time to see what I could and couldn't now do. Grandad called me over to the shed. He had my bike out.
"That's something I can't do, grandad" I said, looking gloomily at my bike.
"'Ere, just get yer good leg over and sit on" he instructed. He put his pipe down on his workbench and held the bike steady. Once I was astride, he said...
"Right, now put the pedal through that bit under yer shoe".
I did.
"There ee goes, you can pedal it with that 'un", he pointed out.
He then pushed the bike up the alley, and I clomped along behind

him.

Once out on the path along the road, we went through the same procedure.

"Now Kev, when you get going, you push this 'ere pedal round and down, then you pull him up again"

He demonstrated this by rotating my foot around on the pedal. It meant that I'd have to keep my right leg out of the way, lifting it up and forwards, a bit like a Knight with a jousting lance, but it could work.

He pushed me off and I had a go. I fell over twice, but then started to get the hang of it. I pedalled, one footed, up to the Prince of Wales pub, then back again. It was hard going on one leg, but it worked. I could propel myself forwards on my bike. I would topple off and have many mishaps, but it worked. Grandad had thought about it and made me have a go.

I suppose, in a way, my great big, flat iron bottomed, old fashioned, built up leather shoe with a gap in the middle, could have been a forerunner of today's new-fangled pedal clips on those posh racing, or road bikes!

"It works grandad, thanks!"

"I told yer, you'd cope. Now try not to fall off".

"No problem grandad, I've got the ha….!"

Over I toppled, like a tree being felled.

If I leaned to the right, I had no chance. I would just go. At least, if I could manage to lean to the left, I had a chance to save myself, if I could free my shoe from the pedal in time, that is.

Steve and Mick then appeared on their bikes, so we went for a short ride around Palmarsh to check out my balance. They had to "tread water" a bit as it was difficult at first to keep up with them, whilst remaining completely upright. I only had half of the pedal power that they did, but they couldn't spear a hedge like I could!

Soon, it was back to the Square as the others were now about, so it was time for a game. I was getting used to only diving or falling left.

Sometimes, I could stick out my "bad leg", as it became known, and I could stop a goal with my calliper. At the end of a good football session, I would clomp off home, wincing as I clomped as I had constantly rubbed an area at the top of my inside leg red raw, due to the hooped bit and friction. I would have to smother the area with soothing cream (or salad cream, if no soothing cream was available), making sure that none got onto, or into my trendy Y-fronts!

When indoors, especially after very sore times like that, it was such a relief to take the calliper off and either hop, or shuffle about by half crawling on one knee. I don't know how I managed to always keep my right foot aloft. It must have been a combination of willpower and fear, as I knew, I think I had been told, that any lapse could result in going back to "Square one", and I didn't want that.

It was difficult, I admit, for a young Eleven year- old boy, with ants in his snazzy pants, to comprehend how this treatment would result in a completely cured hip. I mean, how could just not using my right leg in any way lead to a recovery?

There was no provision for preventing or dealing with any muscle wastage in my leg. It was meant to just "hang" there, out of commission, out of order, useless and even spindlier than before. Oh, the other point that I haven't yet mentioned is that I was still in agony!

The spring on my calliper may have prevented any foot to floor impact, but by basically clomping about, there was still some friction or movement in the joint (a joint without fluid, remember?), so it was hard to understand the point of the exercise (or lack of it). My hip ball joint had already started to wear away and wasn't a smooth boney bit anymore. I think that the medical folk, in their wisdom, believed that it would all grow back and return to normal, fully lubricated.

You'll have to wait till the end for the outcome. Meanwhile, I'd just got to grin and bear it.

*

A thing happened whilst I was playing football in the Square that would turn out to be a regular occurrence.
My calliper broke!
What I mean is, that the rod down the side actually snapped!
What could I do?
What would happen when I told dad?
Well, I didn't need to worry on that score because grandad was the first one to see it. He just had a look and said…
"Slip it off Kev, me and your dad will take it to get welded".
And they did.
There were a lot of factory units behind Princess Terrace and the laundry, so dad and grandad took it there and found a chap to weld it. He would weld that calliper on so many occasions, once even three times in the same day. That was his record, and all on different parts of the ironwork on the calliper or on one of the two metal struts that attached the shoe to its base.
And do you know what?
He never took a brass farthing for his efforts. He said to dad and grandad that he was so impressed that I still wanted to do what everybody else could do. He was such a nice chap. They even took me there once, as he'd asked to meet me. I had to hop about while he went about his task, but that was okay.
His boss even came out to meet us, and jokingly said…

"Ah, so you're the young fella that's giving us all this work. Good for you, son".
"Sorry" I said.
"Don't apologize, anytime it breaks, you just bring it here"

Dad and grandad were so relieved that they had found somewhere to get it repaired so quickly. Getting it done for free was the icing on the pie, as my ironwork would require several welds as the two years progressed. Dad made sure they got a nice "drink" at Christmas. They were such nice people, and I couldn't thank them enough. Because of their help and generosity, I was able to stay mobile.

*

Mind you, Mr Baird wasn't too pleased to see the state of my calliper and shoe when I went for my first appointment with him, fully callipered up.
I had clomped down to the X-ray department to get my (in my mind) pointless X-rays, showing exactly, the same images as before. My leg on view with a knacked hip joint!
How many pictures of this did he want?
Was he collecting them?
Into his office we went, when called in.
He watched me lift one, swing one, as I clomped in.
"What's happened to his calliper?" he asked mum, and not me.
"Oh, we had to get it welded, Doctor" said the Queen Mother… sorry, I mean mum.
"Get it welded? Why?"
"He broke it playing football, Doctor".
"Playing football? Playing football?"
He liked to repeat words.
"Er, yes" said a now shrinking mum.

I, meanwhile, just sat there with my leg sticking out for anyone to trip over and smiled to the nurse.
"He's not meant to be playing football in it, Mrs Pilcher"
I spoke up

"You said I could do most things with it, so I play football with my friends!"
"It's not intended for sports, Kevin" he finally directed his thoughts to me.
"I play in goal, mostly" I said, rather proudly.
"But you must keep your foot off the ground, Kevin. You must not exert pressure on your hip, or strain or stretch it. You must take things steady".
"I can ride my bike too!"
The rest of the conversation went over my head, as he addressed any further comments to mum. He wasn't going to stop me doing stuff though.
"Kevin, I know that you love playing football and doing things other boys can, but you must try not to keep breaking your calliper".
I just nodded.
"I'll see him again in six months. Goodbye".
And that was it.
He didn't want to hear about any saves I'd made or how I'd managed to ride my bike. All he was interested in was his blooming horrible calliper that was now sporting several "War wounds".
"I thought he'd be happy that I was doing stuff, mum" I said, as we walked and clomped back to the bus stop, via the toy shop to buy Derby County (No. 10) and Wolverhampton Wanderers (No. 49) Subbuteo teams, to join my ever-growing League.
Mum came out with one of her classic's....
"You'll just have to make sure that the metal doesn't snap!"

"How do I do that, then?"
"I don't know. Don't kick the ball so hard!"
"What? I don't kick it with my bad leg, mum. If it breaks, then dad and grandad will get it fixed".
"Other children don't break their callipers!"
"What other children? I've not seen any".
"There must be others, Todd. You'll just have to be more careful".
"You could keep me at home to play with my soldiers, then I won't have to go to school. That way, I wouldn't have to wear the flipping thing" I laughed.
"Then you wouldn't be able to play out with the others though"
"That's a point. Hey, don't walk so fast mum".
I was having to adopt my new running "lift one, swing one" clomp to just keep up. I was adapting as best I could to life like this, and it seemed that Mr Baird wanted me to just sit and do nowt. He had more chance teaching a budgie to fart!

*

There were three things of mention, since my release from Hospital. Firstly, on the music front Peter Sarstedt reached number one on 5th March with "Where do you go to, my lovely", and the Beatles had "Get back" there on 30th April.
Then, on 6th May 1969, my little cousin Karen was born to Bett and Pete. This tiny bundle would grow up to be, along with her older brother Stephen, my favourite other family members. I would, over the coming years, spend a lot of time at their house, and I even babysat them at a young age. I developed a very close bond with them and Bett and Pete from those youthful days.
The final thing was that my time at Hythe Primary school was ticking away. I had returned to school after the half term to lots of stares

and sniggers.
The children weren't much better, either!
I could cope with the comments from the younger kids as I was about to embark on a journey that would be much harder. Most of the little snide remarks would be dealt with by my friends in the class, such as Andrew, Geoff, Steve Birch or Chota (His real name was, and is, David. I have never found out why we called him that, but we did).
It was a smallish school, so any adverse remarks or whatever from the other kids could be instantly dealt with by Mr Skinner or Mr Macklin if Miss Lukehurst was otherwise engaged, looking after the girls.
Outside of school, it was a very different matter. If I could get hold of the culprit who may have called me a name, I would possibly give them a little tap with my left foot. That quite often sent them limping away, calling me all sorts of names, some not even associated with my bad leg!
Then, if the little tyke's parents were about, I would usually get even more, caustic abuse and even threats from them. I'd get...
"'Ere, you little cripple, you touch my frying son again with that frying peg leg, I'll wrap the frying thing round your frying neck, you spastic, frying cripple!"
I may have inserted my own descriptive word in there in some places, but you get the frying gist!
And that would be some of the posher ones. Honestly, some journeys to and from school could be like walking through a corridor of vicious and hostile abuse, a fair bit of it from adults that didn't know what they were doing, nor did they care.
As I've said before. Different times indeedy!
There wasn't any point in telling anybody, either at home, or at school about some of the verbal, and at times, physical abuse that I

had to endure, especially when it was carried out by folk that should have been old enough or intelligent enough to have known better. Some of it, I spoke to close friends like Steve and Mick about. Other bits, I've just dealt with in my own way.
I know that there's a rhyme about "Sticks and stones", but to a vulnerable Eleven-year-old boy, in quite a lot of pain from a "bad leg", and clomping around in a calliper...
The names hurt!
Betcha by golly wow, they hurt!
Still, mustn't grumble, eh!
And to think, I was the holder of a "Bean Bag Race, Winner" certificate!

*

The year's F.A. cup Final was won by Manchester City, in their away kit of dark Grey and Black striped shirts and Black shorts, who beat Leicester City, in almost Black shirts and White shorts 1-0, with a goal by Neil Young. We still only had an old Black and White TV, but dad assured us that we'd have a coloured set before next years World cup in Mexico. Whoopee Doo!
Finally, my time as a Primary school pupil had come to its conclusion. To this day, my early school years at both, Hythe and Aldington, have given me only happy memories, despite "pooh parcels" and "peg leg Pilcher" calls, but onwards and upwards. It was now time to progress into the World of the "Big school".
I really tried my best not to let mum and dad's expectations down regarding the final school exams and possible selection to Grammar school.
I managed to achieve and even exceed their expectations. We were informed that I would start at Brockhill Secondary school for boys in September.

In some folk's eyes, it could have been seen, as an abysmal failure, but not in the Pilcher household. Our bar had been set quite low (well, I was disabled and couldn't get my bad leg over a tall bar). Out of my close friends, only Steve Birch went to Grammar school, but we'd tie up again on the football pitch in Seabrook in the future.

Chapter Fifteen – Big Boys, Bad Words.

Summer holidays were spent in the usual fashion. Nobody that we knew ever went away on holiday in those days. Why would anybody want to go away anywhere when we lived by the sea all year round, with beautiful countryside, a steam railway and a lovely scenic canal? We had it all!
France was only a short, Twenty-Four mile ferry trip from Folkestone Harbour to either Boulogne or Calais on the French coast, but I can't recall anybody ever making the voyage, not even for the day.
In those less enlightened, much less troubled times, even someone from London or "up North" was alien to us South-East Kentish country folk. Scots, Irish and Welsh all appeared okay, but they spoke different to us, and as for "Johnny Foreigner" across the Channel, well, they ate snails and frog's legs and horses, so they definitely weren't the same as us. I mean, our dads would bet on horses, but eat them? Not on your nelly!
They didn't eat owt covered in lard, swimming in greasy fat or anything like that, and I bet that they'd never even heard of a bread and dripping, never mind eaten one.
That was one of the delights that I'd enjoy for supper in later times with grandad, sitting by his fireside.
Our summer holiday jaunts were Sunday drives to Aunt Kate's to see her and nan Pilcher. As I've stated before at a younger age, these days out to East Langdon never changed one iota, apart from the fact that as Barry and myself got older, we would explore further and

climb higher in the trees (although that bit was curtailed for me for two years).

There would always be family around, especially as nan and grandad were next door. Nan Coombes Bingo nights at Palmarsh hall were always packed out with ladies of all ages (it was mainly ladies), with their perms and curlers and big old handbags, although I can't really comment on those.
Mum and Aunt Daisy became Bingo fanatics, in fact, mum still is now. I think that its because of this fanaticism that they all had for the game, that I absolutely hate it. Perhaps it's the same with dad's love of horse racing. I grew up detesting that as well. It could just be that I'm adverse to gambling, I don't know, but I wouldn't bet against it!

*

Anyway, during the summer, there was one thing that everybody was watching, and that was the Apollo 11 moon landing between 16th and 21st July. The grainy images on the TV were consumed by millions of people all over the World, and in Scotland!
As Neil Armstrong said...
"One small step for man, one giant clomp for Kevin" or something like that, we all watched, eyes agog. In fact, I don't think my eyes had ever been so agog as this.
I thought that, as a factual programme, it was alright but, if I'm being perfectly honest, I preferred to watch the more down to Earth Jack Hargreaves, with his countryside programme "Out of Town", on Southern Television. In it, he showed how things were done, and used to be done in olden times, in the Southern English countryside.

Again, Winklepedia him on the interweb, if you don't already know of him. A truly fascinating, knowledgeable man. Old school.

*

During the summer months, Kent County Council had been in touch with mum and dad to say that they were going to supply a private taxi to transport me to and from my new school as I was disabled. I would be the only disabled boy in the entire school, and I would be arriving in my own transport, with a chauffeur, no less.

Well, I certainly wouldn't be singled out there, would I?

"Mum, I don't want a taxi, I want to get the bus with everyone else".

"They say you've got to have it, Todd".

"Mum, nobody's allowed in it with me, I'll be on my own. Why can't I get the bus with the others?"

"Because you can't. You'll do as you're told".

"I'm not going to school in a taxi!"

"You are, now get outside and play".

"I'm not, it's not fai...!"

SMACK!

"You'll do as you're told!"

"Ow, that hurt!" I clomped off to the door.

"And don't break that calliper again!"

As I went out of the back door, still smarting from the smack on my bare arm, grandad looked out from his shed, he was sharpening a bagging hook.

"Alright, young Kev. You in grief again?"

"Looks like it, grandad, I've got a taxi for school now, did you hear?"

"Yup, looks like you've gotta use it, mate. It'll get better, you'll see".

With that, he told me to bring my bike over so that he could give it a quick service (a few squirts of oil).

"Don't want ee rusting away, D'you want me to oil your leg iron?" He gave me a big grin.

"No thanks, I get in enough trouble when I break it, I don't want it dripping all over" I laughed.

He always seemed to be able to cheer me up, and we got on so well.

I climbed over his back fence, by his old crab apple tree (Yes, I could manage that), and headed for the Square, passing "Marble man" and Brett, playing their usual energy sapping game.

Once the few of us regulars had got together, it was over to the meadow for a game of "Two and in". We'd made a bit of a proper goal in Rob's back garden. Two goalposts with a crossbar nailed on with a couple of bent, rusty six- inch nails. We didn't even have a hammer. Rocks or a bit of angle iron usually did the trick.

We had already gouged out two holes in the shingly ground. They never seemed to be the correct distance apart, so we had to stretch the posts sometimes to reach, resulting in the nails coming out of the crossbar, causing it to fall onto somebody's head (normally Kim's) From somewhere on the caravan site, over the railway track, we'd found two metal stanchions which, when nailed to the back of the goal, made it look like one of the goals at Derby County's Baseball Ground.

We all thought it looked great, until the whole structure would collapse (usually on Kim, again) and we'd have to rebuild it, which we always did, several times.

Those happy, carefree days of playing in the meadow, riding a one-legged bike and generally larking around as a junior kid came to an end.

*

Big school beckoned!

For a start, it was long trousers all the way, and yes, mum had turned

them up in her own inimitable style, giving me a two-inch border around the bottom of my callipered leg (at least she'd used Black cotton!).
A thick cotton, almost felt-like, blazer with a Grey or White shirt, dark Green or Grey jumper and a Brockhill school tie made up the debonair ensemble.
The posher boys had much nicer blazers, trousers and shirts, and there wasn't a hand-knitted jumper to be seen on them.
A satchel (briefcase for the posher boys), with an assortment of fountain or cartridge pens, pencils, rubbers, rulers etc. completed the look.
As well as all that gear, a sports or Duffle bag containing, football boots, shirts, shorts, socks and plimsoles, White tee-shirt or vest and White socks was required by every single boy in the school…
Except one!
Yep, I wouldn't be needing any sports or P.E. gear at all.
And it made me cry!
I wouldn't get a "Crackerjack" pencil for that.

*

My school taxi was a Maroon Austin Maxi, driven by a lovely elderly chap called "Mr Cooper". He only lived just along the road from us, at Palmarsh Crescent, so I could see him reverse out each morning and be ready at the roadside. He even wore a suit and a chauffeur's cap. Bless his little cotton dungarees!
As Zager and Evans sang about "The year 2525" at number one, there I was, dressed up like a tailor's dummy with the trots, ready for my new life at Brockhill Secondary school for bullies and abusers… er..I mean, boys.
By the time, on my first day, that I got picked up, everyone else had gone, either on the bus, or walked. Steve Miller and Mick O'Brien's

families had both, by now, moved. Steve's, to Princess Terrace, and Mick's, to Martello cottages, both along the main road, but nearer to the school.

I would have loved to have walked, but there I was, arriving by my own personal taxi, in amongst all the buses and coaches in the main playground. Cars weren't normally allowed there but an exception had been made for me. Another thing to make me stand out from everyone else.

Mr Cooper even got out to open the passenger door for me on that first day, to the interest of all the boys gathered there. I vowed, there and then, that I would open my own door from that day onwards.

As I clomped out of the car, thankfully some of my friends from Hythe came over to greet me. At least, for a moment, I wasn't the only frog out of water, as this environment was new to all of us. The bell tolled, and we followed the throng into the large Assembly hall, through the Crush hall, where us "Newbies" were told to go to the front rows. The sound of me clomping over the parquet flooring, as well as the sight of my lift one swing one motion, drew quite a few sniggers as I clomped towards the front, after the others, to take my place on one of the metal-framed, canvas seats.

After the welcoming speech from Headmaster, Mr Jack Setterfield, we were allocated our classes, or forms, as they were now called. I was grateful not to have any special mention in assembly as I didn't need the attention. It was bad enough as it was, being the only disabled boy among over five hundred others.

I was placed in Mr Phillip Bond's form. I pretty much knew that I would be as he vaguely knew dad, and he had told him that he'd watch out for me, after dad told him about my slight handicap. So, I was to be in 1B, if you get my drift.

Mr Bond, I have to say, was not only a great form teacher, but also a very nice person who did his best to make sure that I was okay. He certainly kept his word to dad on that score.

Apart from the obvious differences in schools for us, like the uniforms, discipline, and fact that we were now the small fish in a big bath, there was the immense size of the place.
It was massive, mainly consisting of the old main building, the new large building and the outer classrooms, called huts. I was in a hut. H5, to be precise, and we had to find our way around the entire complex, as now our lessons would be held in lots of different rooms, in different buildings, with different teachers.
I could wear the rubber off my calliper bottom in no time at all as I had to clomp everywhere, trying to keep up with my new classmates. I was never the first to arrive anywhere.

*

There was so much to take in during the first few days at Brockhill, so many new and different subjects.
There was Maths and English with Mr Bond. Geography with old Mr Craker in room 3 in the Old building, History with Mr "Taffy" Lewis in room 5. Religious Education with someone or other. Art with Mr "Baby" Martin in the Art room in the New building. Science with Mr Pearson in H1. Rural Science down at the farm with Mr Johnson and Mr Adams. Music with Mr Dowsett in room 2 in the Old building. Technical drawing with Mr "Wally" Walton in H3. French with Mr Bamber in H5. Metalwork with Mr Robins in the Metalwork hut (it figures). Woodwork with Mr "Ernie" Goodhew in the Woodwork hut (that figures too), and P.E. with Mr Kennedy in the main hall. That last one didn't affect me, I just had to sit on a bench and watch as the lucky ones got to climb wall bars, play sporty games and

generally get all sweaty.
Another little piece of mental torture for me there.

When it was Games afternoon, Mr Bond normally got involved in taking some of the boys for football. There were four separate football pitches, three hockey pitches and a rugby pitch, along with three cricket pitches, so quite a large area of grass to mow.
The four football pitches were called, "The Athletics pitch", "The Cricket pitch", "The Rugby pitch", and "The Hump" (it wasn't flat), so that wouldn't be at all confusing!
At first, I had to stand on the touchline, wishing that I was in goal, watching all my friends running about, doing what I wanted to, but couldn't.
At break times (not playtime now, as we were bigger boys), we would congregate on the upper playground (or tennis courts in the summer) and play football. This time, I could play in goal, and I (accidently) kicked many boys whilst competing for the ball.
It was during these games that the name calling began…
"Come on, Peg Leg!"
"Kick it, you cripple!"
"Come on, you spastic!"
"Oy, Ironside, you cripple!"
"Spastic!, Spastic!, Spastic!"
Yep, I had all of those, and many worse ones. I've missed out all the disgusting foul-mouthed expletives that went alongside these little examples, but I'm sure that you get the gist.
I had to have a spirit and resolve, as hard as "Newby's knocker". (That's a local adaptation that folk here use instead of "Newgate's knocker").
I'd heard a few directed at me before, since I had to first start wearing the calliper, but nowhere like the scale I had to face now. I

would be grabbed and pushed by some boys, usually the mouthy, bully type. If I lashed out with my left foot and caught any of them, they'd know about it, but I very rarely got the chance.

They would hurl abuse in my face and be away, out of kicking range, long before I could react. If any teacher, such as Mr Bond, got to hear owt, he would grab the little (or big) offender by his lapels or even, by his ear, and he would then put him right on a few issues. I think that Mr Bond felt an empathy towards me as he had his own slight disability. He only had one eye. I believe that other one was glass. Mr Setterfield, the Headmaster, also understood my problem. He had chatted to mum and dad about it and how I would cope, on a couple of occasions, and he also walked with a considerable limp, so perhaps his and Mr Bond's understanding was better than some of the other teachers, who couldn't really be bothered about my handicap, in some cases.

I would never let any abuser know how hurtful to me their comments or actions were though. There was no mileage in that, but of course it was upsetting and spiteful. I would take it all home with me and deal with it in private, in my bedroom, and nobody would know, not even mum or dad.

I knew that all the bullying, physical and mental abuse would carry on all the time I had my calliper, as it showed off my disability as a weakness in me, yeah it would continue, but I would get better one day, and then I'd show 'em.

I suppose the way that I was treated in those formative years has shaped how I feel today, and felt growing up, towards anybody with any form of disability or handicap. It's as if I can look them in the eye and let them know that I know what it's like.

I've been there!

Thankfully, these days there isn't the same level of what I had to

endure, hopefully there's none, but back then, in the 1960s and 1970s, it was rife, as was any form of discrimination.
As I've said. I've been there!

*

Anyway, enough depression. It wasn't all bad for me at school.
French, for example, now that was very strange. Our teacher, Mr Bamber, was a Scotsman with a very strong Glaswegian brogue!
So, picking up on the lives of the "Dubois" family was always going to be a challenge. There has always been one sentence, quoted to us at the time, that has remained, embedded in the spongey wall of my brain.
In this one French lesson, Mr Bamber bellowed out to me, in his gruff Scottish lilt...
"Loook at the boook and repeat after me, in a Ferench arccent laddie!"
"John acute la radio!"
It was like listening to Billy Connolly on speed (whatever that may be!).
We spent the entire first year believing that all French people came from the Gorbals!
It was hard enough understanding him trying to speak English, but when he spoke French, well...
"BonJour mes enfants, see you Jimmy!"
I was slightly concerned that this could hamper my chances of making it to University in the years to come.
Music was another new subject for all of us. Basically, it involved sitting near, or in the back row in the Music room, whilst Mr Dowsett pummelled away on the piano. We would be expected to belt out

such classics as "Kumbaya", "Michael rowed the boat ashore", "Morning has broken" and "Dirty old town" (to which all sang "Dirty old man"), plus many other foot stompers, whilst all we would be interested in musically, was what was where in the Top Twenty.

"He ain't heavy, he's my brother" by the Hollies was at number three in October. They obviously weren't referring to my brother. He was heavy. It was all that chocolate and chips.

*

After so long, watching the other boys playing football and the like, during the Games period at school, Mr Bond realized that it was a tad unfair to me, when I, myself was itching to be involved, so he let me stay in the form room to either catch up on my homework (another new thing for us), or to generally do as I pleased. I chose to do as I pleased.

I was permitted to raid the large classroom cupboard for any paper that I required, and I noticed a lot of old, partially used exercise books, gathering dust in the bottom of the cupboard, so I liberated enough to become my own Soldiers United fixtures logbooks. This helped to pass the time for me, writing out match details for later in the week, at home behind the sofa, while everybody else was out doing what I'd rather be doing.

As the final bell of the day sounded, shrieking, joking, laughing boys would all bundle out of the buildings to jump up onto their buses and coaches, or in the case of my friends, would all file off down the driveway together, homeward bound, whilst I clomped out to my taxi to make my journey home in silence.

Mr Cooper, nice man that he was, wasn't much of a conversationalist. I would sometimes spot one of my mates and give an embarrassed, subdued wave, but more often, than not, I would just keep my head lowered towards the foot well of the car, cursing my misfortune.

*

Once home though, after tea was gulped down, in our house, usually at around half past four, once dad was back home from the Council yard, I would be able to clomp out to the Square, with all manner of fried delights slopping around inside me. On some calm evenings during September and October, we would go off to the Redoubt, shrimping.

This was now a bit more interesting, or fraught, for me with my calliper on. For a start, I found it very hard to get down the sloping sea wall to the sandy beach. It was only about a thirty-degree slope, but it was festooned with green algae slime and the seaweed (that sounds like some Country and Western band).

Try to remember that I was attempting this with one "blocked up" shoe and a steel rodded rigid contraption on the other leg.

Many was the time that I'd complete the journey to the bottom… er…on my bottom, and a very wet slimey green bottom it was when it reached the bottom!

Then, for obvious rust reasons, I couldn't go anywhere near the shoreline, so I would mainly stay with grandad, chatting and watching as he took on the Weever fish.

Cor blimey, could you imagine me clomping back to Mr Baird with a calliper covered in welded bits and rust!

He would expel enough hot air to stem the tears of a weasel!

*

As the nights of winter closed in, more time was spent in the evenings, either at the table, perched on one leg (that's me perched on one leg, not the table. It would just fall over), or on the floor, commentating on a Soldiers United match, in a shrill voice, whilst being told to keep the noise down by mum as she tried to make any sense of the plot in "Crossroads".

Did you ever notice the scenery move about on Crossroads?
One minute you would be watching Benny talking to Miss Dianne, and the next, you'd see the wall swaying behind his woolly hat!
My cute faced little brother with the sticky out ear would still be playing with his marbles, but he also had a collection of teddies to play with now, as well. As I recall, he had Big Ted, Little Ted, Blue Ted, Woolly, and his favourite teddy called Freddy.
He didn't have a vast imagination.
I, of course, still had Michael, but we didn't play. Oh no, we would just indulge in intellectual chats as we snuggled up on those cold, winter nights. I was nearly Twelve, you know.

*

Christmas consisted of the same routine, or tradition, as I believe some households now describe their Christmas routine.
Once again, I spied Father Christmas delivering my presents, only this time, as well as not wearing his usual bright Red outfit, he had a Woodbine sticking out of his mouth!
Just like dad smoked!
Oh, what a great time for parents to be able to kit out their young male offspring in attire that should never see the light of day, never mind be worn.
It was the time of the flowery matching shirt and tie, in some of the most gaudy, sickly colours you could ever imagine.
Just try to picture the look on some poor child's face as he tore away the Christmas wrapping paper to find that he'd been bought a lime Green flowery shirt with matching tie!

So, as I opened my matching lime Green flowery shirt and tie combo, mum looked across at me with her proud...
"I got you that" look, my first thought was...well, my only thought was...

"Nora Bone! Where the heck, does she expect me to where this?"
Luckily, I got a couple more Subbuteo teams and some accessories, plus the usual comic annuals. Victor, Tiger and some of the more "grown up" annuals were replacing the Dandy and Beano, which Barry now got instead (I still read them, though). I got a Charles Buchan football annual as well.
Unbelievably, I still got a Games compendium. This now seemed "routine" or "tradition".
Hopefully this would be our final Christmas having to watch "Morecambe and Wise", The Benny Hill Show", Billy Smarts Circus, Top of the Pops, Christmas night with the Stars" and the rest in Black and White.
Boxing Day, as is "tradition" or "routine" followed. Again, no Aldington Hunt for us. Our lives had changed now in so many ways, but I still missed the old ways.
I still miss them now, after all this time. That's the sort of sad character that I am.
An early lunch, as usual, of cold meats and gristle, was followed by the short trip up to Aunt Daisy and Uncle Bill's House.
Into the house I clomped, adorned in my lime Green flowery shirt and matching tie. Ah ha! With unmatching light Blue trousers with matching calliper.
There was the usual embarrassed mirth and comments at my expense...
"Oh, don't kick me with that, will you, Kevin?"
"Oops, mind how you go. Can you get past there with that?"

"Can you drive that thing?" etc. etc.
It wasn't their fault. Who knows what to say when faced with an unfamiliar sight?

It would have been nice to have been treated as a normal person, but not with my calliper on, it seemed.
I was glad when we got back home though.
No, not because of any comments, but just to get out of that lime Green flowery shirt and matching tie!
I looked like a camp tree frog!
Ooh. Get you!

*

Now, here's a good one... The Christmas number one of 1969 was still at number one on my Twelfth birthday, some weeks later.
It was Rolf Harris, singing about "Two little Boys".
Wasn't it a bit ironic that, many years later, in 2014, he'd have to be explaining to a Crown Court Judge about "Several little Girls!"
You couldn't make it up!
Was there nobody that we could trust in the Pop music or T.V. World from this era? (apart from good old Tony Blackburn, of course).
Let us hope that better, safer times would be ahead in the 1970s when we reached the Glam Rock era, with respectable performers, DJ's and presenters!
There was one major item of note for me in January 1970. There was a new comic out called "Scorcher", featuring brilliant stories about "Billy's Boots", "Bobby of the Blues", Lags Eleven", "Nipper", and others. Obviously, this became a weekly order for me. It would, in July 1971, become "Scorcher & Score", which was even better (if that could have been possible).

*

Chapter Sixteen – Who's dishing up my dinner? You must be joshing!

So, my Twelfth birthday clomped on by, with Rolf telling us that he had "Room on his horse for two". I bet he did!
I was Twelve and Butch "the Ball bearing Kid", was Eight.
Ha! He was still three years and three hundred and sixty-four days behind me.
The appointment letter for Mr Baird had dropped through the letterbox so, off we trundled yet again, to go through exactly, the same palaver. Another two identical X-rays were added to Mr Baird's collection of identical X-rays, and we waited in the Waiting room to be summoned in. I noticed mum dip her hand into her handbag…
"Don't you dare" I said, trying to give her one of my sternest looks.
"Do you need the toilet?" she said.
"No. Why?"
"That look on your face. I thought you were straining"
"No mum, I was trying to look…Oh, never mind"
"You sure you don't need the loo?"
"Mum!"
At last, in I clomped, following mum who was almost curtseying to the man.
Mr Baird made me strip down to my best clean pants. Luckily, I hadn't had any accident with a bus on the way.
I had to hop up onto the bed (literally), whereupon he proceeded to poke and prod around my hip area.
When I say, "my Hip area", I don't mean a trendy or chic region. I mean, "my Hip area". The area around my hip. I want no confusion there.

He told me to slip my calliper, with numerous welds, off and then he started yanking and pulling my poor leg all over the place. It wasn't a comfortable nor pleasant experience, and I knew that I would really suffer in the aching and shooting pains department later.

I was then instructed to get dressed again and take a seat. I got dressed again but I didn't know where he wanted me to take a seat to, so I just sat on one, next to mum.

"I see that his calliper has had further welding done, Mrs Pilcher".

"Yes Doctor, the welder's very good".

"That's not the point though, is it?"

"Pardon?"

"There shouldn't be any breaks on it at all. It's not made for playing football in".

"I can play Rugby as well, but only if I tackle on one side, so it's not as good" I chipped in.

He let out a sigh.

"Kevin" He said, in his best condescending voice.

"I've told you before. You can't keep playing football or any rough sports and keep breaking it. There is now almost as much welding as there is calliper".

"They do a good repair though, and they won't charge for it" said I, defending my right to have some sort of life.

"Look! Look!" He raised his voice and pointed to a welded area near the top of the calliper.

"And how, may I ask, did that happen? Were you diving in a quarry?"

"Oh, no, that one was when I fell off my bike and went over old Mrs Scott's wall!"

"Oh, I despair" He said, holding his head in his hands in mock disbelief (I think).

"Please, please, take it easy Kevin. See you again in six months, with no more welds. Goodbye".

"Goodbye Doctor" said mum, reversing out and pulling me along with her. In troubled times, times of panic or chastisement, her Queen Mother voice deserted her.

For some reason, she wasn't very pleased with my last answer about falling off my bike. She was so displeased, I never got to visit the toyshop. It was just a rapid lift one, swing one clomp to get the bus home.

*

School continued with the usual hurtful and spiteful comments from boys who, perhaps didn't know any better. There were some teachers though, who took every opportunity to make a sly, snide remark on my disability, who most definitely should have known better. These were the folk that I was supposed to turn to when I was suffering from any form of abuse. It was only a couple or three that made the remarks, but you only need one rotten apple to bugger the whole basket up.

I have to say though that the Headmaster, Mr Setterfield, and my form teacher, Mr Bond were great allies for me, and they gave me immense support. Strange that, is it not? Them both having disabilities themselves. They understood possibly, what I was going through, and they tried to help.

As I found, my so-called fellow schoolboys could be vicious with their abuse when they wanted to be. My best reaction was to laugh and joke my way through it.

What do they say about "The tears of a clown?"

Oh well, pooh pooh happens!

*

The highlight during the early months of 1970 was the arrival from Southern Rentals of our first colour TV set.

WOW!

With the 1970 World cup on the horizon, it was perfect timing. Whilst talking about the World cup, Subbuteo had organized their own World cup tournament, with the winners in each country, allegedly, competing in Mexico.

Well, I entered, much to the annoyance of dad, who had to drive me up to Maidstone for the Regional Qualifiers. It was only Forty miles up the track from our house, but in a little old Austin it took three days…or was it just over an hour?

It felt like three days!

Anyway, I took Alloa Athletic No. 32 and Chelsea No. 42, as you had to take two teams in case of any colour clash.

I clomped around the table and won two absolutely, riveting games (for those of us playing) 2-1 and 1-0, before losing, I believe in a Quarter Final 1-0. I didn't do too badly. There were grown men competing as well, in fact I lost my last game to one of them. There weren't any concessions for my one-legged handicap, and nor did I expect any. I was quite chuffed to get that far. Dad was quite chuffed to get home again.

*

I had started to get a bad toothache just before the F.A. cup Final between Chelsea, in all Blue (Ah Ha!), and Leeds United in all White (Oh). It was the first proper, full game that we would watch in colour. When I say "we", obviously I hadn't forgotten or forgiven dad's desertion for the 1966 World cup Final. My "we" didn't include him. The Judas!

I didn't call him that whilst we were sitting together, eating shrimps and watching the game though. That would have been silly, and perhaps painful for me (and I could have lost out on the shrimps).

The game itself, on a muddy pitch, ended 2-2, which meant a Wednesday night replay at Old Trafford, Manchester United's ground. This was the first Wembley Final to be replayed.

As Wednesday evening loomed, I was taken (kicking and screaming) to a Dentist in Hythe High Street to have the offending tooth removed. For the time of year, it was a dirty, wet early evening as I sat, trembling with fear, in the Dentist's waiting room.

"It's better, mum" I pleaded, through the jaw throbbing pain.

"We're here now, so stop whining" said mum, with all the compassion of a wine gum.

We were called, I was dragged in, with my calliper trying to attach itself to any object, like a grappling hook. I would have gouged my fingernails into the Lino, if I hadn't bitten my fingernails.

I was physically strapped into the Execution chair (I was frightened, okay?), and then the Dentist tried to place a gas mask over my face.

"What the ...!"

I fought it and fought it, so he had to hit me, several times, over the head with a gas bottle!

I may have made that last bit up, but it was very scary, and I did fight the gas. I think, in the end he had to give me a gum numbing injection. I fought that as well. I may have even kicked out with my good leg, although I don't believe that I connected with owt other than his equipment trolley.

I do remember (with horror) some form of clamp over my jaw, to stop me biting him like a rabid budgie, I imagine. There was a crunching noise, and a lot of blood, most of it mine (are you enjoying this bit?). I wasn't.

Then I was released from any restraints and led, gurgling, spitting and spluttering from the torture chamber, or Dentist's surgery, to give it it's other title.

There seemed to be a large gap where once there was a gnasher. I couldn't be sure how big the gap was because, although my tongue now felt as large as a house brick, I'd lost all feeling in my face.
"All done, Todd. Let's get home now for your football".
"Mmnsflughspluffousher!"
"What was that?"
"Miggleshlufflughser wiskhshgiffis!"
"Try not to dribble on your jumper, Todd".
"Msnufflush ikshum!"
"Do you want some chips on the way home?"
I tried to point to my face.
"Arghshfuffshk!"
"Here's dad and Baa now, you'll soon be home".
Dad pulled up in the car. Barney Rubble appeared to enjoy my discomfort.
"He don't want chips Dave, do you two want some?"
"Murgshumflth" I said, I just wanted to get home.
"Can I have a sausage, mum?" pleaded the little fat gatherer.
"Course you can, Baa" said mum, as I curled up on the back seat, waiting while mum went into Park Road chip shop.
Once home, mum, dad and Charlie Choops tucked into their chip suppers whilst I stood over the kitchen sink, spitting blood and remaining bits of tooth towards the plughole. The feeling was slowly starting to return to my jaw, and with it came the throbbing pain. I still had toothache, despite the tooth no longer being there, plus my entire face was in agony due to the GBH inflicted upon me.
We all eventually sat around the TV to watch the match. Well, we didn't physically sit all around the TV, because anyone sitting around the back of the set wouldn't see the game, plus they would have electric cables and cobwebs all over and under them!

I want to cheer and shout along with the rest but, despite the numbness fading, the throbbing prevented me from enjoying it too much.

Chelsea won by 2-1 in extra time, in a proper old school, physical encounter, nowt like the girly, namby pamby, cheating, no-contact trash that's on offer today. Well? Tell me different, then!

*

I was halfway through my calliper days by now, and I felt that I was coping quite well. My first year of everything being different for me was trundling on, and I felt that I was being accepted by most of the boys in my year now for who I was, and not for what I was. There were obvious exceptions, but I thought that I could either handle them or, better still, ignore them.

As Spring ended and Summer burst forth, our time playing on the meadow increased.

The Summer flowers, sweet smelling grass and the sound of birdsong…would have been nice, but as I've described before, we had shingle, gorse, glass, nettles and lizards. Did we care though? No. Not a jot!

We'd play out after school, in our old football gear, one of us inwardly praying not to tear any clothing, to incur the wrath of one of mum's needles, or to snap anything made of metal, thus, to incur the wrath of dad, as no welding could be done until early on the morrow.

Kim, me and Rob sitting on Kim's garden wall in the Square. This is the only photo I've got with my calliper in view (I wonder why?)

We would amble home, when called, but never until then, covered in sweat grimed dirt, and one of us (Guess who?) would become victim to one of mum's "Brillo Pad" flannels.
Apparently, I could never manage to wash my own face or neck, as mum would grab the "Brillo Pad" from me and slap it into my face, as if it was a custard pie. She would then proceed to rub it rapidly, all over my face and neck, spreading any grime as she went.

"Here, give me that flannel" she would demand, whilst snatching it out of my grasp.
"You never wash yourself properly!"
She then plunged it straight into my mush!
"Arghh! Mum, don't...!"
Splat! Rub!
"Gungle spliegal gumf my nose, mumfff!"
"What?"
"Stand still".
"Splungle duffsh my ears alone plea...unffmf!"
"There, now dry yourself".
She then handed me what she obviously assumed was a large fluffy towel, but it was obviously a large, coarse graded sandpaper cloth! You didn't so much dry, as scrape yourself with it. I can't recall whether softener was about then for washing purposes, but if it was, then mum couldn't spell it.
It would then be, calliper off, Soldiers United out, until bedtime, then it was a short hop and a long shuffle up the wooden hill to my bed. I always said that I had done all my homework, so I had more time for the important European Cup fixtures of the team. Most of it was done at school anyway, copied out of Reference books in the school library, especially Science projects. What was all that about? Could you burn anything other than "Bunsen"?

*

My First- Year school outing was so impressive and memorable that I've totally forgotten where we went. Canterbury Cathedral or somewhere, I think.
Next year's one would be memorable, but for all the wrong reasons!

The school year ended. My first at "Big school". I had survived (just) with my obvious disability, although it had been very traumatic at times. Next year, I thought, I won't be one of the "Newbies". I'll be a Second-Year boy. I had got through school, like this, all by myself. At Primary school, mum was always around to help me if she was called in because of a problem with my calliper or whatever, but here, up out of the way, in deepest, darkest Saltwood, I was on my own. On my Todd. I liked it that way as well. I didn't want to be singled out or molly-coddled. I wanted to be just one of the boys, like the others, keeping parental involvement to a minimum, hiding problems or discipline issues completely, having no parent within hollering distance.
I was no "mummy's boy".
If only I'd known!

*

The Summer holiday was mainly taken up with the World cup in Mexico. The England squad, who were World cup holders, as if you could forget, produced a chart hit record, entitled "Back Home", which incidentally, was somewhere that they would be before the Semi Finals took place.
I think their problem was that they didn't have "World cup Willie" with them, this time! He was still in custody after being arrested along with Bobby Moore, in Bogota', Colombia. Apparently, he's still there to this day, although he's now the Prison Governor!
Again, the last paragraph hasn't been fully researched by myself, I rely on a team of small pixies to do the more mundane jobs.
This was the first World cup that I would take a full interest in because I was only Eight in 1966. I was a more mature, grown up Twelve, now. I had a wall chart and I got dad to collect the Esso coins for me as well.

For non-football fans, I thought the best two games were the Italy 4 West Germany 3 Semi Final, and of course, the Brazil 4 Italy 1 Final. Brazil were now everyone's favourite team. I expect that all non-football fans are now converted!

We tried to re-enact most of the tournament out on the meadow, although our Aztec Stadium had more gorse bushes and shingle than the one in Mexico!

Of course, I played the part of Edson Arantes Do Nascimento, or Pele', as he's better known. Bamboozling and amazing his opponents whilst wearing a built-up shoe and calliper.

It was soon school time again, after six and a half weeks of being outside, clomping about over the meadow or out on my one-legged bike.

We did try to take a bike ride up to Court at Street, but I couldn't push my bike up Lympne hill. Well, you try walking up a steep hill for at least a quarter of a mile, whilst on stilts, with one completely rigid leg, and pushing a bike!

It's not easy, I can tell you.

That meant that our cycling was restricted to the flat of the surrounding Romney Marsh and canal area. Not a bad option for being out on your bike with your friends.

No. Not a bad place at all.

And the time would soon come when I'd be able to cycle back to my beloved Court at Street, of that, I was sure.

*

There were a couple of surprises in store for me, especially on the return to school.

Our Scottish French Language destroyer, Mr Bamber, had left to destroy the French Language in another school, and he was replaced by Mr Peter Riley. The new teacher was an inspiration for me in my quest to conquer the World's languages. He made French so enjoyable.

In fact, apart from sport, it was the only subject that would have kept me at school. I loved it.

The second surprise was on a much more personal level, and it wasn't a pleasant surprise when I found out, not at all pleasant.

Mum would be joining the kitchen staff as one of the Cooks!

Crikey!

Mum even burnt cabbage at home!

I wondered just how this new appointment would turn out, and how it could affect me, now having mum in such close contact on a day to day basis.

I was about to find out!

The new term started, much as the last one had ended, except that I was one of the slightly bigger boys now. Not in stature, even with the added height from my leg apparatus. No, this was because there were now younger boys for the school bullies to pick on, so they could leave me alone.

But they didn't leave me alone at all.

"Oy, spasmo, you cripple!"

"Get out of the way, Peg Leg!"

"Sorry Sir" I would reply!

Only joshing, it wasn't quite that bad (mostly), and the other quotes, all similar with a few expletives thrown in for good measure. There wasn't an awful lot of variation in the moronic abuse.

In fact, when a group of them gathered around me, all chanting stuff like...

"Cripple!, Cripple!, Cripple!", it sounded much like the Neanderthal football supporters, chanting...

"Ingerlund!, Ingerlund!, Ingerlund!",

Where is that place, anyway?
And to think that my grandad fought two Wars to give them a chance!
Oh well.

*

Back to a more tuneful happening. There was a new sound around. A brother and sister duo, and she had the voice of an Angel gently blowing in your ear. Her name was Karen Carpenter. Even today, I have never heard a voice to compare with hers. It was stunningly beautiful.
My mum, on the other end of the scale, had a voice like Hilda Ogden. When mum sang, the birds all left the trees and migrated!
It was very similar to the sound of fingernails being dragged over a blackboard by a tone-deaf Rook!
Mum and Karen Carpenter.
The chalkiest chalk and the cheesiest cheese!
The album, "The Carpenters 1969-73" is still one of my favourite LPs. The music of the time was gradually changing. There were lovely ballads by The Carpenters, Gene Pitney, Elvis Presley, Gilbert O'Sullivan, Elton John and the like, through to T.Rex, Status Quo, Pink Floyd etc. It was certainly an exciting time to be a kid, regarding the music in the 60s and 70s.

*

Back in school, we were now to be in Mr Craker's Form. He was an old man of about 103, who smelt of stale cigarette smoke, but that wasn't the worst bit. That came when I discovered that our new Form room would be Room 2, in the Old building. That wasn't an issue for any of the other boys, but for me, it meant that I would have to clomp up to the first floor several times a day, and of course,

that also meant that I'd have to clomp back down again as well.
I could have been "The Grand Old Duke of York", except I didn't have any men that I could clomp up and down with. I just had a calliper that I had to lift one, swing one, up and down the old wooden staircase many times during the school day, as we had our lessons all over the place.
Today, of course, it wouldn't meet stupid Health and Safety guidelines. It certainly didn't give any disabled access, other than jumping out of the window, but back then, we all just got on with it, and things still ran okay.
They hardened us up for real life at Brockhill school.
They also hardened up the Yorkshire puddings and sponges now that mum was employed in the kitchens, although I would like to make it clear at this point, that they didn't use one of her overdone batches of roast potatoes to demonstrate the art of Dry-stone walling down on the farm!
That is a myth that must be quashed here and now.
They were used in the foundations of a new car park!
I knew of no greater embarrassment than having mum standing at the serving hatch, as I clomped along with the other boys in the queue at lunchtime. Especially when, as I reached the ladies dolloping out the mash, veg, and what have you, mum would chirp in with…
"Go on Todd, you like that" as I tried to pull my plate away from a mound of soggy, lumpy swede.
"I don't" I said, trying to clomp away as quick as my calliper would let me.
This would occur several times over the first few days, then weeks, at the serving hatch.

I knew that I would have to have words with mum at home. It was bad enough having to attend school in a private taxi, clomp around in a leg iron and be the only disabled boy around for miles, without having my mum point out the food to me and inform the entire English-speaking population of my culinary preferences. Blimey, she'd be coming over to my table next, to cut it up and spoon feed me.
I didn't need this!
And she would have to stop calling me "Todd" at school. People were starting to notice.
On the plus side (yes, believe it or not, there was one), when mum knew that it was a dinner that I didn't like, she would pack me up extra Marmite sandwiches to see me through till teatime, and when it was something that I did like, such as Lemon Meringue pie or Gypsy tart, then I would always get a much bigger bit, with not so much crust on it.
This didn't only benefit me, but my entire table of friends gained as well. It would, on a good dinner day, be...
"Hello Mrs Pilcher".
"Hello Steve (or whoever)".
A large dollop of something tasty would be forthcoming, then...
"Oh! Thanks Mrs Pilcher".
It seemed that it was quite a good thing to be friends with me at lunchtime.
So, they were the two sides of having mum working there, in the kitchen.
There was one obvious disadvantage having her there though, and that was that, if there was a problem, disciplinary or whatever, Mr Setterfield could make a bee-line to the kitchen, and I wouldn't be able to hide any minor misdemeanours.

There would be one particular issue, heading my way very soon. School plodded on for me, especially on the stairs with a ...
"Clomp, Clomp, here!" and a "Clomp, Clomp, there!".
"Here a Clomp, there a Clomp!"
"Everywhere a Clomp, Clomp!".

*

"By golly, Gosh and Gumboots" What a handsome, Blue-eyed little chappie! Butter wouldn't melt in his mouth! (At least my calliper's not showing).

I was looking forward to being released from my handicap. Another appointment with Mr Baird followed. X-rays taken, we were, once again, summoned into his office.

"Ah, Kevin, Mrs Pilcher. How are you? How are you, Kevin?"
"Er...fine, thank you".
"Good. Good. Let's have a look at these then".
He held up the X-rays. They looked exactly, the same as every X-ray that had been taken of my hip.
"Mmm. Good. Good. All going okay."
"Is he doing alright, Doctor?" Hey up! The Queen Mother's back. Oh no, it's mum.
"Seems to be, Mrs Pilcher. It's hard to tell, exactly."
"When can I get rid of this?" I interrupted. I wanted to know when my sentence would end.
"You'll have a final appointment with me in March, when you should be back to normal...with a few restrictions".
"What restrictions?" I had taken over from mum as the main questioner.
"Nothing much. Just advice. We'll discuss that in March. Anything else, Mrs Pilcher?" He was back talking to mum.
"No, that's good news, thank you Doctor" Bow. Bow. Curtsey. Curtsey.
"Okay, see you in March then. Goodbye".
Out I clomped, knowing that I only had to do this once more. But what restrictions? What advice?
"What was all that about, mum?"
"I dunno, Todd" Mum knew as much as me.
"Can I have that one?" I pointed to a Subbuteo team in the toy shop. No. 15 Mexico, if you must know!
Please don't think that it was just me that had Nine and Eleven spent on him. The Curly Wurly Kid also got bought something, and it was usually something more expensive. I didn't mind. I knew what I wanted each time we went there, then I would check out the other

teams on display and I would never come out with the one that I was going to get.

*

Back at school, Christmas was looming out of the dull Grey skies, as it seemed to do every year around Christmas time!
At Brockhill, some of the Year six Prefects would put on a spoof show with a few of the teachers. Although, not being at all religious, I did enjoy the Christmas carols. I would be there, singing along with the rest, none of us really knowing what we were singing about, but there were some nice tunes.
I always thought that the little baby Jesus was unlucky to be born on Christmas day as he only ever got one lot of presents!
In the Music room, "Michael" was still rowing his boat ashore, Hallelujah!
His arms must have been aching.
My French was now coming on in leaps and bounds, or "Pas de ge'ant" as they may have said in Montpellier!
All my other schoolwork was "adequate".
I may have stood out in the "Clomping" stakes, but in schoolwork I just excelled in being average. I appeared to be in group Two for most subjects. Group One was for the brainy, swotty types, whereas group Four was for boys destined to sweep the streets or become psychopathic killers or worse still, members of Parliament!
I haven't actually researched that last bit, so please don't quote me!
After an "over the top" festering school Christmas dinner, followed by Marmite sandwiches in the playground (I don't like Christmas pudding), it was a final afternoon of quizzes and games in the classroom until the final bell of the school year tolled and we all piled out of the buildings, some boys to their buses and coaches, some running excitedly down the school drive, laughing and chasing each

other, and me, clomping towards my Austin Maxi taxi, with an elderly gentleman in a cap.
Oh, how I wanted to be normal.

*

The year's Christmas number One was "I hear you clomping", sorry, I mean "Knocking", by Dave Edmunds.
A very apt record about three wise men, banging on a stable door (I think).
If they were that wise, why didn't they use a Road Atlas or stop and ask those three shepherds who were washing their socks by night, the directions?
I'm not daft, I know Sat Nav's weren't about in those days! Mind you, they were navigating by a star!

*

The only change to our Yuletide frolics was our Christmas dinner.
This year, we all gorged on minced sparrow in fish sauce!
No, we didn't. I was just being a little tinker. There was no change at all, not a jot, unless you count watching the Christmas TV shows in colour, which I don't.
Our "Routine" or "Tradition" went as per usual. This year's gawdy outfit for me to wear consisted of a Pink shirt with Aeroplanes on it, and a matching tie accessory.
Either the fashion hadn't moved on, or there was a surplus of these unsightly Combo's. I'll opt for the latter!
For some reason only known to mum, to discourage me from diving about, playing football and breaking my calliper, she bought me a "Peter Bonetti" goalkeeper's shirt. I wasn't at all ungrateful and I'm sure that Mr Baird would have been as chuffed as nuts to know that I wasn't being encouraged to participate in anything too energetic!

It was Green, and it went well with my goalkeeper's jeans and calliper.

A Winter's visit to Aunt Kate's and nan Pilcher's in East Langdon followed the new year, 1971. It was too cold to play out in the garden, so we all made do, sitting around Aunt Kate's large farmhouse kitchen table, eating homemade cakes, tarts and pies, and drinking tea and lemonade, whilst nan got out her old photographs and the adults all reminisced and laughed over them. There were quite a few of me as a baby, as well.

Photographs like that are quite treasured today, and they all tell a lot about the times, when taken.

The heat from the big old Aga ensured that we all stayed warm, until the Sun went down over the Westward hills, and it was time for dad to defrost the little Austin for the journey back home through the Alkham Valley.

They must have been such special times there at Aunt Kate and nan's, because they remain so vivid in a cobwebbed crevice, deep within a, frequently visited yet undisturbed, compartment of a brain, now battered by the encroachment of age!

Did I just write that?

What I think I'm trying to say is...I remember it well, despite the distance of time upon the faded withered edges of my mind!

It's at times like this, that I wonder how I never progressed further than C+ for English on any school report.

*

I became a teenager, listening to the dulcet tone of Clive Dunn at number One, singing about "Grandad". Ah!

They don't make 'em like that anymore. Elton John had reached number Four with one of my all-time favourites, "Your Song".

As kids, we all looked forward to Sunday nights and the new Top Twenty on the radio. It was just about the only thing to look forward to as, in our house like many others, it was bath night for us young 'uns, followed by an early night, after watching "Sunday Night at the Palladium", as it was school in the morning.

Just how did so much dirt and grime get behind your ears and between your toes? Also, as kids, we always seemed to have, what our mums described as, a "Tidemark" of dirt on our shirt collars. Mind you, the meadow was a filthy, muddy place to play on in the Winter, and a grimey, dusty place to play on in the Summer, so we couldn't really win, either way.

*

Chapter Seventeen – Standing on my own Two feet.

I carried on at school, clomping around whilst waiting for, hopefully, my final appointment with Mr Baird. The letter was taking an age to arrive. January and February passed, and it wasn't until the middle of March that we were summoned forth for the last time.
This time, as it was going to be the final appointment (fingers and toes crossed), and a momentous occasion for me, dad took us in the car.
For the last time, just before the Easter holiday was about to commence, I clomped down the old wooden staircase from our Form room. Friends that I wouldn't be seeing over the holiday wished me good luck with the appointment, and I playfully forewarned Martin "Higgy" Highland that I'd be challenging him for the school goalie's jersey after the break, although it would be Summer sports of Athletics, Tennis and Cricket then.
I would have to bide my time, but he knew!

*

The echoing sound of clomping reverberated down the corridor as I went "Lift one, swing one" from the X-ray department to Mr Baird's office, armed with a fierce determination, two X-rays and mum's wet hankie, hovering over my face!
"Please let me go home without the calliper" I pleaded, over, and over, again in my head.
I even crossed my teeth for added good luck!
Please don't believe that bit.
"Do you need a wee?" asked mum.

"No, I'm fine" I said. I was concentrating, trying to relay positive thoughts through the door, to Mr Baird's brain.

"You sure you're not holding it in?"

"No, mum. I'm fine".

"Why's your face all scrunched up then? And you've crossed your teeth!" (She didn't say the last bit, as I explained).

"I'm concentrating".

"On what?"

"What do you think? I'm trying to …Oh, never mind, it's…!"

"Kevin, please come in" called the nurse.

"Here goes" I thought. Look positive.

"Ah, Kevin. Good morning" said Mr Baird.

Blimey, he was smiling, and he talked to me.

"Good morning" I said, in my most positive voice.

He looked up at the 45th and 46th X-rays of my leg (I'm guessing, there).

"All looks good".

How could he tell? They all looked the same to me.

"Well Kevin, you've had your calliper on Two years now."

"Two years and Four weeks, Doctor" I corrected.

"Mmm. Yes, I see".

"And Six and a half weeks in Hospital!"

"Yes Kevin. A long time, and you've managed very well with it. You've even played football".

"And rode my bike!"

"Mmm, yes, and you've rode your bike".

"Yup" I replied with a beaming grin.

"You've also managed to break your calliper and shoe in more places than was thought possible!"

"And I've broken lots of springs as well" I was still beaming.

"Yes. I've noticed that. Tell me, how did you manage this break, just under the hoop?"

"We had a pile up on our bikes. My calliper went into Steve's chain and he fell onto Mick's bike. I hit a parked car and…!"

"Yes. Yes. Never mind that. I think you can lose the calliper now and so long as you take things steady…I don't know why I'm saying this bit to him, Mrs Pilcher. So long as he takes things steady, his hip should now be fine, and he should be pain free".

"Yes, thank you" I said, nearly wetting myself with both, excitement and fear. I had just realized what he had said.

"Now, you'll just have to get along to Physiotherapy, to start putting some weight back on your right leg. Just remember, don't try to run before you can walk!"

"No, Doctor".

"It may take a while to get used to moving about again on Two legs, so take one step at a time, if you know what I mean" He actually smiled!

"Yes, Doctor".

I got up with mum and turned to leave the room, whilst mum reversed out, curtseying.

"And Kevin".

"Yes Doctor".

"No football!"

I didn't answer that one, I just smiled.

I'd like to think that Mr Baird did too!

Along at Physio, they removed all my own personal scaffolding from the past Two years and Four weeks and made me stand between the parallel bars. I had all my weight on my left leg. Gradually, I lowered my right foot to the floor. Very gently at first. I was absolutely petrified. I placed a little bit of pressure on my toes and the ball of my foot, still with most of my weight on my left side and the bars.

Then...
"In for a penny...er... another door opens!" I thought.
My first step. Still supported but, my first step.
"Are you still holding the rails, Kevin?" asked the physio.
"Yeah, but I'm letting go now!"
"No, don't let go ye...!"
Too late!
"There, see. I'm going to walk now!"
And I did!
The physio, mum and dad (who had come in) just stood and watched as I hobbled, gingerly at first, then stumbled, then walked across the room. I still placed more emphasis on my left side (I still do, today), but I was walking, calliper free.
I wasn't going to cry. Mum did a bit though.
After a short while, the physio said that she thought I'd do fine, and that I was to remember that I must allow my muscles to gradually build up again.
I'm still waiting!
I got the usual "Take things steady" lecture. I was even offered a stick to help me. I could see the others having a field day with that one.
I took a final look at the calliper and shoe standing up against the wall, turned away, and we were off. Mum had brought my plimsolls, just in case, and ...
"Be Bop A Loo La" they felt so good!
Since February 1969 until now, March 1971, I had endured bullying, abuse, name calling, you name it, I was called it. I thought to myself...
"No more. No more will I have to hear that"
Now, here's a weird thing. Much further down the track, Geoff Underwood emigrated to Australia. I lost touch with him for several years but, in the early 2000's, I'd got his telephone number in Brisbane. I called him up, and his first words of greeting to me, in his

Aussie accent were...
"G'day Peg Leg, how are ya going, mate?"
Apparently, in some instances, you never lose it!
Back to March 1971...
The journey home was filled with warnings, reminders of what I'd been told I could do and shouldn't do. I just nodded, they knew.
As soon as I got home, nan and grandad came out to see how I was. Nan gave me a further lecture on do's and don'ts. Grandad just smiled, nodded and puffed on his pipe, then he went quietly back to his shed to clean his mower.
I quickly got changed as Steve knocked the door.
"Now, you remember what Mr Baird said, Todd. Take things stea...!"
"Mick's got a new ball" said Steve, excitedly.
I was gone!
I was straight back to the Square. No more metal induced bruises for the likes of Brian, Kim, Rob or the others. It was straight into a game. They hadn't treated me with "Kid gloves" when I first appeared in my calliper, and they weren't about to start now. I was grateful for that. I was just one of the boys again. I was still, for obvious reasons, totally left sided and I still only dived that way. It would be a trait that would never leave me in my future years as a goalie. It never held me back, nor did me or any of my team's any harm.
I had been home only a few minutes, and just as it was with the calliper, I was out with my friends, kicking a ball about.
The ins and outs, ways and why's, ifs and buts, regarding the future of my hip can come out later. As for now, I felt normal again.

*

It was very strange to be going back to school after Easter. I'd had to say "Cheerio" and "Thank you" to Mr Cooper, prior to the break. I would still see him as I passed his house, on my bike though.

Now, back at my true height and weight, I had to look up to most of the others in my class. It was almost the same scenario with my little brother, who I had left at home, gorging himself on any remaining Easter eggs, as Hythe Primary, which he was now a bright pupil at, didn't start back for another couple of days. I knew though, that left alone to search, he'd still never find any of my hidden stash as it was still in grandad's shed.

Nan would keep him fully fed though, so he wouldn't starve. The poor little chubby mite.

My good, true friends back at school were pleased to see me, as were some of the staff, who had a genuine interest in how I was coping now, without the calliper.

It should be remembered that nobody there, apart from the St. Georges mob, had seen me without an encased leg. There would be no more clomping up and down the stairs or across the parquet flooring in the main hall. I could now, almost run across it in my P.E. kit.

It's so difficult to put into words how I felt when I entered the changing room for the first time with my duffle bag, full of my P.E. stuff. I had the sense (justified) that almost everyone had a sneaky look as I changed. What they expected to see, I don't know. I had the same amount of legs as everyone else. I know my right one was slightly thinner than my left one, but that was because I hadn't used the darned thing for over Two years.

After the initial curiosity had subsided, it was accepted that I was almost as normal as they were, so I was able to concentrate fully on scaling those wall bars. I'd wondered what it was like to be at the top of them, looking down, since I'd started at Brockhill. Now, they were mine to conquer, and by heck, did I throw myself into all forms of P.E.

I think that Mr Kennedy latched onto my enthusiasm very quickly. I had so much time to make up for. I'd not only wondered what certain things in P.E. would be like, I'd dreamt about doing them, and doing them better than all the others, and now, there I was, running around like a duck with no head (chickens didn't have the Monopoly in Kent).

One of the things I was told by the Physiotherapist that would be good for my hip and leg muscles was swimming, it was fortunate that part of the school curriculum involved a swimming club. I got my name down for it as soon as I could.

There were Three very good reasons for doing this. The first one, I have just covered, secondly, I lived beside the seaside and I couldn't even swim, so here was my chance to learn, and thirdly, it got you out of lessons like Science!

I wasn't so confident with the swimming as I was with land-based exercise, so it was with trepidation that I boarded the coach to Folkestone Sports Centre for our first lesson. We would all be aboard, nervously singing...

"She ain't no Witch, and I love the way she twitch, Ah Ha Ah" from the T.Rex number One record "Hot Love", that stayed at the top during March, April and May.

I could tell that I wasn't the only one reluctant to bare all, as I changed into my Soviet era swimming trunks.

It was cold in the changing rooms! That's the excuse we all used. Once safely clad in our swimming attire, with what appeared to be, two marbles and a sweet cigarette shoved down the front, we made our way out to the pools. The first thing to negotiate was the small paddling pond of chlorine stuff. Well, it may have appeared like a small paddling pond of chlorine stuff to the more able swimmers, but to a landlubber such as me, it appeared to be a deep, disease infested chasm.

Yes, okay, I know you only had to step through it, but my alarm bells were already telling me that I wasn't yet ready for the depths of the baby learners pool. I skirted around the main pool, leaving at least a two-yard gap between me and the very deep water, and made my way, with the other "losers", to our pool of impending doom.

Mr Bond, dressed in his part woollen East German reinforced trunks, instructed our small group of ten terrified boys to descend into the sub -zero temperature water. Once there, almost up to our waists, for crying out loud, we were told to lower ourselves down, so that only our heads were above water.

Yeah! Right!

I forgot to mention that we were permitted to hold onto the edge, but that still didn't give me, nor some of the others, any crumb of comfort or confidence.

As we crouched there, in at least three feet of water, you could see the shockwaves and tremors on the surface, as we all shivered and trembled with fear. There was a loud gurgling noise as some bubbles arose from the rear of Geoff's trunks!

The next thing we all knew, after the laughter had settled back down, were these polystyrene floats, being hoyed down to us, as we splished and sploshed after them.

Mr Bond somehow got us all grasping the floats, then kicking off for the opposite side of the ocean...I mean, pool. It was only, I suppose looking back now, about four yards or metres across, but to those of us not blessed with either gills nor fins, it felt like a cross channel swim.

And then! And then! When he thought that we weren't scared enough, he told us to hold onto the floats and shove our heads under the water!

Yep, that's right. Under the water, then have a good look around!

And to think that I put my name forward for this!
Eventually, we all did as he instructed, almost.
Well, there was no way that I was going to open my eyes and let all that water in.
I wasn't stupid…or brave!
I forced myself, along with the other nine creatures of the land, to lower my head under the waves, which, by now I'm sure, contained other fluids than water!
Through clenched shut eyes I had a good gander around. I didn't like it.
Up I surged, gasping for air and spitting out possible urine!
"What did you see, Pilcher?" asked Comrade Bond.
"Oh, it was brilliant Sir, all sort of weird under water" I lied with consummate ease.
Most of us couldn't wait for the experience to end. Soaked to the skin, but dry inside thanks to my eyes being clenched tightly shut, I followed the other boys back through the smelly pool of infestation, and back to the changing area, whereupon we all proceeded to dry, or in my case, scrape myself, prior to getting our uniforms on and returning to the safety of the coach.
Well, we didn't need a shower, we'd all just had a bath in snot, spit and urine, before traipsing through a large tray of disinfected scabs, warts, verrucas and other various foot diseases!

*

It was soon after the start of the Summer term that the school's Doctor appeared, and every boy had to have a medical. This would involve the "Cup & Cough", and General Health examination, plus hearing and sight tests. Dental tortures were carried out at a different time by the school's Dentist, when he was out on day release from prison!

Now, at these medical's, you were permitted to have a parent present with you, but being young growing boys, obviously none of us wanted the embarrassment of having to be molly-coddled in front of his classmates, so everyone chose to have their mum's and dad's out of the equation. When I say "everyone", I think you can see where this is heading...

So, there we were, sitting in the Gym changing rooms in our vests and pants, all boys together...and one mum!

Yep, mum had decided that, as her job was only a few yards from the Gym, she would take some time out, to attend the medical with me. That should help me with the persecution and ridicule!

At least she kept her hankie in her bag this time.

I had all the medical tests on my body. Mum tried to explain about my little handicap in the hip area, I kept very quiet about my little handicap in the "Gentleman's area".

Then, after a successful hearing test, it came to the eye test. I was sat in front of a card with little coloured spots on it.

"Now Kevin, please tell me what you see" Said the Doctor.

"Lots of spots" Said I.

"Come on, Todd, don't mess about. You can see the number" Interrupted mum.

"What number?" Says I.

"Please Mrs. Pilcher. Don't tell him!"

"But it's as clear as can be! Come on, Todd!"

"What number?"

"That number 7, Todd. You can see that!"

"I can't!"

Mum started to outline it with her finger.

"Mrs Pilcher, please!" Pleaded the Doctor.

"Show him another one, Doctor".

"Now, come on Todd, try to look properly!"

"What? I am looking properly!"
"Try this one Kevin" Said the Doctor, now starting to lose his patience with mum.
Mum again, physically outlined the number.
"See Todd, it's a 4!"
"Mrs Pilcher, please stop helping him".
"But it's a 4! Anyone can see that. Come on, Todd. Look!"
"I can't see owt!"
"That's fine Kevin" Said the Doctor.
"It's all "Blibs and Blobs" to me, sorry".
The Doctor tried several different cards, with the same result. I even tried making up an answer and hope that it was correct. That didn't work either!
"You're not trying, Todd" Said mum, accusingly to me.
"I'm afraid that Kevin is colour blind with the colours, Red and Green, Mrs Pilcher".
"What does that mean, Doctor?" asked mum.
"Well, to put it as basically as I can, it means that he'll never become an Airline pilot, Mrs Pilcher".
That was that career possibility buggered, then!
"Mrs Pilcher, who is "Todd"?" He asked, as we left.
Mum just kept going on about how clear the numbers were, and that she was sure that I was doing it on purpose.
I didn't get much in the way of understanding, sympathy or praise when I got home either.
Guess what I did get? It stung, as well!
They were all just "Blibs and Blobs".

*

The Summer term lumbered on, and as it lumbered, it reached the date of the school outing.

Now, I know that it involved Pegwell Bay, near Sandwich, the Hovercraft terminal, a Viking Longship, a Kiosk, lots of over excited boys and some pilfered George Best stickers. We may have even visited Dover Castle on the way.

My memory fades but the scars still linger!

I think that it's safe to say that, prior to our arrival, there was a large box full of George Best stickers, each one costing Two and a half new pence (or sixpence, in proper money), and after our departure, there was a large box, devoid of George Best stickers!

Our school party had made it back to the coach and skedaddled before the Kiosk proprietor had a chance to report his (alleged) loss. The full effects of the actions of a few (most of) boys wouldn't be revealed until school Assembly, the following morning.

Our party was kept behind after Assembly, and every boy was told to empty his pockets, satchel or briefcase.

What did they expect to find?

Only a stupid Idiot would have carried his ill-gotten gains into school the following day!

So, about Twenty of us stood there, in the Crush hall with our George Best stickers lying on the floor at our feet, for all to see.

I had got three. Why? I don't know.

He was a Manchester United player and I supported Liverpool.

There was no excuse. I know.

Looking back, I could say that it was because I wanted to be "one of the boys" after being a bit of an outsider with the calliper for so long, but I don't think that's true. The real reason, I believe, is that it was just something that some of us, not all of us, did.

What excuse did any one of us have?

None, whatsoever!

George Best was there (in sticker form only), and some of our party took him. Some others took sweets, their evidence was long gone.

The upshot of this Plonkerish behaviour was that the parents of each guilty boy was sent a letter stating the facts, and we all received a ban from any further outside school activities.
So, the story that I've told ever since that day was that...
"I can't swim because of George Best!"
Obviously, that then requires an explanation, but it's a more "romantic" version of what happened, and I've stuck to it.
Of course, I wasn't required to take a letter home like the others, because Mr Setterfield chose to deliver mine by hand, directly to mum in the school kitchen.
That went down well!
Especially as he regaled the entire story in front of the other cooks, causing mum acute embarrassment.
I can report that several parts of my body hurt and stung for a long time, that evening.
We didn't even get to keep the stickers!

*

To attempt to get back into mum and dad's good books, I approached Mr Nicholson, who owned the local V.G. store and Post Office beside Palmarsh hall, to ask if he had any vacancies for a paper boy.
As it happened, he said that one of his paper boys had gone out in a strong wind and had blown away, so he had a vacancy!
Paper boy. Strong wind. Get it? Ne'er mind.
He did actually have a vacancy that had just come up though. It was to deliver papers to Palmarsh Crescent, along the main road, and then down Palmarsh Avenue, to the bottom end, beside the train tracks. The bonus for me was that it was an immediate start, and as decimal currency had just commenced, I recall that my wages were around £1.75p per week to start with.

A single record was 49p then and an LP was about £2.45p. There was also a lot of football gear that I could save up for as well. My paper round wages would almost double, in time.

Mr and Mrs Nicholson were such nice people to work for. Mr Nicholson would mark up the papers for us early each morning, for our 6.45am start. Most of my deliveries were for papers such as The Daily Express, The Daily Mail, The Telegraph, The Guardian and The Daily Mirror. The Sun newspaper wasn't a favourite in the leafy Avenues at the time. On Wednesday, there was also the local Gazette, and on Saturday morning there was the large Folkestone and Hythe Herald broadsheet paper. That certainly weighed down my paper bag.

I can recall that Mr Nicholson would wear a different coloured coat, depending on what he was doing in the shop. It was a Brown one if he was outside, at the garage dispensing paraffin and a White coat for the slicing of bacon, ham etc, and a Grey one for general shop work or down a little slope down to the Post office section, that was also where the sweets were kept. Chocolate, sucky sweets and chewy ones were at the front, and behind there were lots of sweetie jars, all full to the brim with an assortment of goodies to be bagged up in Quarter or half pound paper bags. Mum would always buy grandad's favourite extra strong mints from here.

There is another little point about working for Mr Nicholson, and that is that I never purloined so much as a Black Jack or Fruit Salad chew from him. It would never have even entered my brain to do such a thing. They were lovely folk to know.

There is one other peculiar thing to mention here before I return to 1971. Today, I actually reside in a house in Palmarsh Avenue that I used to deliver papers to, almost fifty years ago!

*

So, I had obtained my first paid employment (I couldn't include helping to bring the cows in, from my Court at Street days, as we didn't get owt for it). Having a paper round gave me some independence. It was odd because Steve had a paper round at Uden's Newsagent's at Pennypot, and his round covered Palmbeach Avenue. We would meet at the bottom, where the two roads formed a horse shoe by the train tracks, and we would cycle off home together. I would go in, get my breakfast (normally Ready Brek or toast and Marmite), then get my school stuff together and bike down to Steve's house.

I would put my bike in his dad's old tin shed along with all their old bikes, then once Mick had come along with Kim, we'd all walk up to school.

At the Light Railway Station, we would get our climbing gear out of our satchels and, attaching crampons, we would join the throng ascending Barrack hill, up to Saltwood and school. At least that's what it felt like because it was a stiff uphill climb all the way.

It was about three miles from Steve's house and that journey could be fraught with danger, as we had to pass the Paton's stronghold patch, as we neared the Laundry and Reachfields. Sometimes we would get through, suffering only a couple of rabbit punches to the back of the head, or a rough grab of the blazer lapels, followed by a sharp throw into a lump of dog pooh!

Yep, the "Halterne Gang", led by Dave, Tony, Mick and dad, Jock were possibly our own version of the Krays, except the Paton's were more frightening!

Oh, I know that the Paton boys would love to read that about themselves…if any of them were able to read!

Head honcho, Dave tried colouring in once, but he kept going over the lines. That was something that they never did though, back then. They could be fearsome at times, but they never crossed any lines, and they all, in time, became good friends (they told me to say that!). Their mum was such a lovely lady, as well.

The final leg of the journey up to school would be past St. Leonard's school for girls, then along Dark lane alongside the school playing fields.

There was always an awful amount of strutting, preening and posing going on by some of the bigger boys as they tried to impress the girls. The amount of hair brushing and general grooming going on as they approached the girl's school had to be seen to be believed.

Along with Steve, Mick and Kim, I didn't have to try to impress or attract any girls.

I didn't have to try because it was totally pointless. No girls were going to give any of us a first glance, never mind a second one. Steve, Mick and I put this down to the fact we had Kim with us!

He disagreed.

Anyway, none of the girls could play football (as far as we knew), so they were no good to us, other than as goalposts!

Sometimes, on the way back home, we would cut along the canal path or the railway tracks from the station, as far as Alton Wireworks factory on the small Pennypot Industrial Estate. All the way, we'd be scanning for any wood or item that would make our goals better on the meadow.

We were that obsessed by having a goal net that we'd use old sheets or blankets that our mums had chucked out for us. We would attempt to tie them together, although one shot from Robert would usually rip them to pieces. Our goal sizes came down to a more realistic size to fit our small pitch. As this happened, our "net" obsession grew even stronger.

There was one occasion when Steve, me, and a couple of the others, waited until it started to get dark as we had noticed some old netting, the type folk put over their strawberries. The only problem was that this particular netting stretched out over a garden pond that had a few fish swimming about in it.

Oh yeah, the other slight problem was that it was in someone's back garden in Palmbeach Avenue!

The garden backed onto the meadow, and the pond was just through a low gate, only a few paces away. We knew the lady whose garden this was, she was quite a large specimen, very vocal and quite handy swinging a broom about, so we were all taking on a challenge.

When I say "We", I noticed that it was only Steve and myself left as the others had scarpered, claiming that their dads had called them in, so...

"Fortune favours the...er...broken hearted!"

We slipped the latch on the gate and crawled in on our hands and knees. We were like the St. Georges S.A.S. (Search and Snaffle).

"You okay Steve?"

"Yeah, get the stones off, quick".

The netting was held around the pond by some small rocks. The job was going well. We could almost picture the ball bulging this net, then...

The back door opened!

"Kev, she's coming!"

"Oh Gawd, stay still".

"Well I'm not going to do a dance. She's coming to get her washing in!"

How we'd failed to notice several pairs of large bloomers, hanging from the washing line, just a few feet away, I don't know.

"My foot's in the water!" I whispered.

"Ssshhh" He sympathetically replied.

"My foot's in the water!"

I lay flat and still, I daren't move. She was only a couple of yards in front of me. Inwardly, I started to get the giggles!
"Not now, please not now" I tried to stifle any sound coming from my mouth, this caused me to get a snotty nose.
"Don't look round, don't look round" I said, in my head as I attempted to silently sniff the snot back up my nostril. My foot was "treading water".
All I could see of Steve was his eyes, staring up in partial fear, hardly daring to blink. He blended in with the Rhubarb patch, to his side. He was further away from her than I was. His dark clothing helped him stay hidden in the twilight.
She carried on folding her drawers and placing them in her wash basket. They certainly weren't "Smalls".
Steve was as cool as a Rhubarb stick, in his semi-concealed position. I, on the other hand, was poohing it!
I was laying, right beside the pond, with one foot submerged, and I was sure it was being nibbled by a Piranha!
Finally, with all washing gathered, the large, frightening lady with a penchant for whirling broom heads, disappeared back inside and closed the door.
"Blimey, that was close" Said Steve, not noticing a shiny slug had fallen onto his back.
"Quick Kev, let's get it off, and get gone!"
"I've got a wet foot".
"Never mind that, grab your end".
In our haste to complete the task, some rocks toppled into the pond. Grabbing the net, I went to stand up, in doing so, my dry foot pushed another small rock into the water, only this time, my foot followed it!
"My other foot's wet now!"
"Well, I'm okay. Quick, let's go" He said, with a grin.

With that, we turned and scuttled back through the gate opening, to the safety of the gloom and gorse. We'd hide the net and get it tomorrow when the coast was clear, and when my pumps had dried out!

Fortunately, no mention was ever made about the missing net, nor the fish suffering from headaches where the small rocks had fallen on them.

We did make a very small "Ice hockey" type of goal in the meadow, which our new netting almost fitted, until it got torn to bits by another of Rob's "too hard" shots.

That was our first foray into the World of net snaffling. It wouldn't be our last.

*

As an almost fully mobile thirteen-year old boy now, I was able to enjoy the Games afternoons without having to sit in the classroom, writing out Soldiers United fixtures. I loved playing Cricket, I wasn't bad at it either. Tennis was another ball game that came quite naturally to me. My hand to eye co-ordination was my advantage against quicker, more mobile boys. My agility and ability to throw myself all over the place also came in very useful (so long as it was to the left!).

Athletics though, now that was a different ball game, or not, as it turned out. In 100m races, I doubt that I would even be two thirds of the way down the track before Geoff had finished. I compensated for this spectacular failing by feigning a slip, or to say that my bad leg had given way (yes, it was still an issue).

Well, you try sprinting with hardly any right leg muscles!
You could end up running around in circles!

My constant flops on the starting line very quickly got sussed out by Mr Kennedy, but I think that he knew and understood what I was up to, turning a blind eye to it. Oh, hang on, it was Mr Bond who had a blind eye!

Also, I believe that he let it go because he saw that I put so much into most other sports. The exceptions being Hockey and Cross-Country running, which I'll come to in due course.

*

In June, the "Middle of the Road" had a number One hit to follow the previous number One by "Dawn". Now, if it was a year earlier, I could have said that "Clompy, Clompy, Clomp, Clomp", took over from "Clomp three times", but the calliper related songs had come to an end, and I was grateful for that.

In other matters, in the wider World (to me), my team Liverpool, had just been beaten in the F.A. Cup Final by Arsenal 2-1, giving them the "Double". The highlight of the competition though, was in the Fifth round on Match of the Day, when Colchester United beat Leeds United 3-2. We re-enacted that game, and others, many times on the meadow.

The Summer term reached a conclusion, with me still unable to swim, and now even more unlikely to represent the Great Britain swimming team at the Munich Olympics in 1972. To be perfectly honest, Montreal in 1976 was looking in doubt, as well.

There were decisions to be made at school at the end of Second year. Choices on future subjects had to be sorted out. For me, it was quite straight forward.

I would obviously carry on with French (potpourri, mes enfants!). I wanted to keep Woodwork, Art and Metalwork as well. The Farm and Rural Science didn't appeal as it wasn't Manor Farm at Court at Street, and I felt that I already knew more than they were teaching the class. Science certainly did not appeal. I never understood it and I didn't really want to. I had just completed a whole year's project (or homework), writing about "Plankton".

In fact, along with most of the other bored boys, I'd just copied it all from library books. The Science teacher of that year, Mr Fred Rierra, would just check your handwriting, and scribble "5" on the page.

Poor old Geoff would painstakingly write out his project each week in his best handwriting, but "Fred" would always say…

"Rubbish, do it again", without even looking at what Geoff had written. He would rip it up and Geoff would walk away, looking all forlorn. In the end though, Geoff would write any old garbage, even putting occasional swearwords in. Old Fred never spotted it once. Because he never even looked!

I don't think that he'd have challenged Geoff though, as he towered over our little vicious Science teacher. Geoff was the only boy who was told to shave before he became a teenager.

The other subject that I certainly didn't want to carry on with was Technical Drawing with Mr "Wally" Walton. This involved Geoff as well, as he did want to carry on with it. Mr Walton went around the class, pointing to each boy individually, and asking what he wanted to do. On my turn, he said…

"Pilcher, do you wish to carry on with Technical Drawing?"

"No Sir, I don't like it".

"Well, I think that you'll be good at it. You're staying!"

Gulp!

"But I don't want to Sir!"

"You're staying. Next. Underwood?"

"Yes Sir, I'd like to keep Technical Drawing next year. I like it a lot Sir"

"Well, I happen to think that you're useless at it, so the answer's "No". Next"

Geoff was totally devastated. The rest of us virtually wet ourselves laughing, until I realized that he thought that I'd be staying. No way, Pedro!"

Geoff and I approached Wally Walton at the end of the lesson, and reluctantly, very reluctantly, he agreed to swap us around, despite his lack of faith in Geoff's ability to draw straight lines.

*

Chapter Eighteen – Small Gains and a Big Loss!

The Summer holiday was spent, as was the norm now, playing on the meadow and bike riding. The War games were very similar to the ones played out as a younger soldier or cowboy at Court at Street, except that there was more gorse, glass and shingle, and a certain lacking in sheep and cow pooh. We would crawl on all fours, through the gorse bushes, to make camps and watch the trains steam by. They would always be packed out with sun coloured, red-faced holiday makers. Our little corner of the World seemed to be a very popular location for camping and caravanning, hence the large sites, over the railway lines from us, and the Prince of Wales and the Bluewater caravan parks. There were also lots of these sites along the coast to Dymchurch and St Marys Bay, plus a couple of holiday parks as well.

The folk who frequented these sites and parks, mainly stayed near the beach, leaving us locals to have the surrounding countryside, marsh and canal areas to ourselves.

There were two boating stations on the canal, in Hythe. One was at the Grove, in the middle of the town, and the other one was at the Light Railway station. When I eventually left school, I would spend a summer, working at the latter one with a lovely old chap called Reg. Happy days, indeed.

During the summer months, after we'd been out shrimping, some of the caravanners and campers would get to hear about the possibility of a pint of locally caught shrimps, and they would be knocking on nan and grandad's door, hoping to buy a pint or two. Grandad would always make sure his regulars were fed first though.

The "Corona" man would come around in his lorry, selling Lemonade, Cherryade, Limeade, Orangeade, Cream Soda and a couple of others that I obviously didn't like, as I can't remember them.

There were the Ice Cream vans as well. Mr Whippy was my favourite, although there was Walls and Rio's as well. Anytime, during the day, these vans would turn up, blocking our football pitch in the Square.

We didn't mind though because every child would disappear indoors and a few seconds later, reappear clutching some loose change. Half pennies, One penny, Two pence, Five or Ten pence. Blimey, that was Two bob in old money!

Gone now were the good old days when 3d or 6d would suffice, or a thrupenny bit or a tanner, to us more mature folk.

A strawberry or Pineapple Mivvi would be my lolly of choice. No Fab or Zoom for me. If it was Mr Whippy, then a 99 with a flake shoved in would be the order of the day, and we'd try to lick the ice cream before it ran down the cornet and all over our hands and arms. If we only had a few pence, then "Ice Pops" would be bought. I remember, many times squeezing my Ice pop, only to see the icey bit shoot up out of the top and land on the floor. Not to be wasted, this would always be picked up, licked clean, then popped in my mouth.

We all did it!

If you had an ice cream from the Walls van, it came as a wrapped block that neatly fitted into an oblong cone. No flake was going to penetrate that.

I always remember Rio's as the ice cream cornets with bits of ice in the ice cream. They weren't my favourite at the time, but they're still going strong now, and their ice creams are very good.

*

As this was my first chance for over Two years to have a proper two-legged bike ride, we picked a perfect sunny day. There were many to choose from, that summer.

Steve, Mick, Rob, Kim and I all gathered at the top of the Square, armed with nowt more than a couple of sandwiches each and a bottle of weak Orange squash to share between us. We would all share the burden of carrying it as well. We all knew where we were heading.

There could only really be one place (for me).

So, there I was again, at the bottom of Lympne hill. This time I had two legs (well, one and a half) to push my bike up to the top. We made it! At the top of the hill, we sat on the wall of the Shepway Cross War memorial. There was a great panoramic view, out over the marsh towards Dungeness Power Station, which still hadn't been completed. You can't rush the folk of Kent.

Then, after a quick guzzle of Orange from all of us, it was onwards, passing Lympne Airport just as a Skyways International flight landed from Paris. We all stopped to watch as it taxied to the small terminal, where a coach was waiting to carry the passengers on to London.

It was a sight and sound to behold for a young impressionable lad, as for several minutes, the silence of the countryside was tossed asunder by the noise of the propeller powered engines.

Once that excitement had passed it was, at times, five abreast as we travelled along the Aldington road to the hamlet that I knew and loved so much. As was normal here, there wasn't a soul about. By now, the Banyard clan had also descended, down the hill to live somewhere in Hythe. I didn't know of their whereabouts now. Robert harden and his mum were both out as well, although his grandad was there, pootling around his back garden. He didn't even say "Hello", though I can't ever recall him speaking when I lived there. I showed them all five Acres, and then I took them through the farmyard to show them the view from the old chapel and pillbox.

Kim got chased by a pig as we went through their little fenced off area, which was quite funny. Well, it was for us. I think that the wildest animal he'd seen before was a barking dog on the meadow.
"Go on Kim, stroke him" I said.
"Stroke him behind the ears, they love that. Look" I stroked a big old porker as it nuzzled up to me.
"I'm not going near it" He said.
"It'll bite me!"
"It won't bite. You Idiot. Go on, stroke it".
He leant down to stroke him behind the ears.
It bit him in the short's region!
"Arrgghh!"
We all fell about again, as Kim started to run for the gate, with the large pig snuffling along after him. It was a good few minutes before he stopped sulking and started laughing with the rest of us.
We left Court at Street behind and headed on to Aldington, as they had all asked about where I had started school. We passed the cottage of my birth, which I pointed out, despite the fact, that it still had no Blue plaque to commemorate the momentous event. It was looking very run down. I wasn't even sure if it was inhabited at the time, but I was too scared to go knocking on the door.
There was also nobody now living in my nan's old friend's corrugated cottage either. That also looked in an abandoned state. It was all rather sad to see.
We reached Aldington school and peered in through the windows. It all appeared so small to me now, but it wasn't that the school or any other things had changed or got smaller, it was just that I had grown and changed. I had got bigger!
My rate of growth wasn't very much though, especially in some areas.

I showed them all the front porch entrance where I used to have to stand with Percy the Pooh Machine and his newspaper bundle. Despite us all chuckling about it, I swore them all to secrecy. I didn't want it broadcasted to all and sundry that my little urchin brother had an "Open at will and Shoot" bum hole!
Heavens above, no! That could never be allowed to happen.
At least I could be counted on to keep the secret.
I would only tell my very close friends.
Oh, yeah, then I would write all about it in a book!
At Aldington, we retraced our tracks back to Court at Street, where we turned left, past the Welcome Stranger, down Harringe lane towards Sellinge stores, a couple or so miles on. There we replenished our stocks.
By that, I mean we all bought a can of Coke, some chocolate, sweets and crisps, then made our way back to the main line Railway bridge. It was a good spot to have our healthy lunch.
A packet or three of Mr Smith's finest Bovril crisps, the best crisps ever invented in my humble, but correct opinion, and a Mars bar for me to supplement my Marmite and cheese sandwiches, all washed down with a fizzy, gassy, burpy Coca Cola. Life was grand.
It felt so good to be back in my favourite place, that I never even noticed any leg ache or owt. During my time confined to my calliper, clomping about, I'd yearned for this time to come, and now it had.
At that special time, I wouldn't have wanted to be anywhere else, with any other mates. Oh, if only I could have bottled that time, and that feeling.
After luncheon was tidied away, a glass of Port taken, and all the washing up was done, it was time to play, what would become a favourite game of ours on this bridge.

As the diesel passenger trains would thump their way up and down, between London and Folkestone, Dover and beyond (by that, I mean Ramsgate, they didn't carry on to Copenhagen or anywhere else), we would all stand, leaning over the parapet on the bridge, and wave frantically at the driver, smiling all the time.

He'd almost always wave back. Once his driver's cab had passed under the bridge, we'd all then throw empty Coke tins at the carriage roofs, seeing who could get the best bounce off them (little things and little minds).

When the train had gone, we'd all slide down the embankment beside the bridge to replenish our supply of ammunition. There was always loads of empty cans around the track, I suspect, thrown out of the windows by litterbug passengers. This quite harmless, though utterly pointless bit of a lark could keep us amused for ages. As I said, Little things, little minds!

*

It was towards the end of Summer that nan Coombes sadly passed away. She had been suffering, unbeknown to us kids, for some time with her chest, and it was a major shock for the whole family and neighbourhood. She had lived there and been a stalwart of the local community for longer than most folk could remember.

I recall, on the day of her funeral, all of us youngsters keeping out of the way, all mooching around outside, on the street, up the alley and in the back gardens, as the older relatives and friends transported trays of sandwiches, cups of tea and other drinks between our two houses. Grandad tried to avoid as much of the scene as he could by going out to his shed, where us kids all gathered near him in support of his loss. Different folk deal with such things in different ways and this was just his way of coping. We all knew that we'd watch over him. The only thing was that, at that time, I didn't know just how much that would involve me.

We all missed nan immensely, especially mum, living next door, and her brothers and sisters. Everyone would keep a closer eye on grandad now, to make sure he was okay.

*

The time had come for a return to school. It was September, Diana Ross, with "I'm still waiting" had taken over from "Get it on" by T.Rex at number One in the charts, and it was time to "knuckle down" I was told, on the subjects that I'd chosen for Third year.

At least, I thought, I had got away from some of the subjects and teachers that I hated, and scared me, in that order.

How I'd wangled my way out of Technical Drawing, I didn't know. All I knew, as we trundled back up Dark lane for our first day in year Three was that I would never have to set foot in H5, the Technical Drawing room again, nor would I be frightened by the nasally twangy threats of Mr "Wally Concorde" Walton, a man obsessed by overpowering discipline, straight lines and sharpened pencils!

Yippee!

So, as we all gathered, trembling with fear, in our new Form room H5, our new Form teacher Mr "Wally" Walton or "Concorde" as he had now become known as, because of his extremely large, pointy conk, spat out the names on the register with a nasal snarl!

Oh deep, deep joy!

The only thing that gave us any hope was the knowledge that, after registration and Assembly, we could all leave his World of sharp angles, and even sharper noses (he even made mine look tiny). We could smile as we passed boys, queueing and quaking outside, waiting for their two hours of pencil sharpened purgatory!

I think that Geoff was now wishing that he hadn't been so keen to draw straight lines! Ne'er mind, eh!

*

It's hard to explain the excitement, for the first time since being at Brockhill, that I could wear my football gear for Games. My new goalie's jersey with a quilted, padded chest would adorn my putrid body as I stood between the sticks, resisting shots from all comers. Well, it was during football. In Rugby, I'd wear an old cotton Rugby shirt as I got battered by all comers! Playing Rugby, we'd just throw the ball to Geoff and he would trample over or through anyone who was stupid enough to get in his way!

Then there was Hockey. I would wait, again between the goalposts, whilst the other boys attempted to hit an old White cricket ball with a stick with a bent end, only succeeding in striking each other on the shins in the process. As a goalkeeper, I could have taken my Scorcher and Score annual out to read, as they had as much chance of hitting the ball in the goal as I did, farting an Opera!

I mean, what was the point?

I do admit that sometimes, either at school or at weekends when we'd cycle to South road Recreation Ground to watch Hythe Town play, we would play football in the Hockey goals, as they were more our size. Obviously, first we would remove the daft boarding inside the goal. You couldn't get the net to bulge otherwise!

I was starting to get a fetish about goal nets!

In fact, today Steve would inform anyone who would listen, or was too bored to walk away, that I could be shown a picture of any club's goal nets and stanchions from the late 1960s to the middle of the 1970s, and beyond in some cases, and I could say who the club was, and which ground it was at. Sadly enough, it's true!

I must have had a very shallow life, growing up.

At least folk can't say that I don't move with the times or fashion!

October arrived, with songs like "Johnny Reggae" by the Piglets, and the lovely Karen Carpenter singing a double A-side "Superstar" & "For all we know". There was a double A-side at number One as well, it was "Maggie May" & "Reason to believe" by Rod Stewart. I can't say that the man's music or appearance has had any effect on me, other than, along with David Bowie, I still play a lot of the music today, and I have sported a "Rod Stewartesque" spikey hair style to this day, forty-odd years on!
Once again, at least folk can't say that I don't move with the times or fashion!

*

School progressed in the boring way that school often does, but at home, there were going to be changes.
It was becoming apparent to all, bar himself, that grandad possibly needed a closer eye kept on him, just a bit of company, somebody to talk to at times and to also, give him back a bit of responsibility and purpose. A sort of two-way objective.
He was by himself, swimming around in a three bedroomed house, and now he slept downstairs, as the climb up the stairs could be a tad much for him at times. He was still very active and independent, but he wasn't, as the saying goes, getting any younger (or prettier!).
I was, by this stage, always around his house, either sitting at the table with him, watching Match of the Day, The Big Match or Southern Soccer, or I'd be watching him watching his favourite sport, Boxing, when he would sit there, ducking and diving along with the fighters, or else I would be on the rug in front of a roaring fire, seeing Soldiers United through their League or European programme.
It would be late in the evening that I would pack my soldiers away, say goodnight, and pootle back to next door, swinging my old granny's handbag as I went. I had to have my supper with him first

though. This was always at nine O'clock on the dot. There would always be a pot of tea, and he would have damson jam and I would have Marmite. Bread was toasted by using the toasting fork over the open fire, until almost blackened sometimes, then we'd sit at the table, watching his old Black and White TV, whilst filling our faces. He didn't get a colour set for donkey's years (whatever they are).

How was I to know then, that I would look back in fifty years, and remember those days, along with Court at Street, as the happiest times of my life.

*

It was one evening when Aunt Daisy, Uncle John and mum were there, talking to grandad about stuff in general when I rolled in.
"Hello young Kev" said Uncle John.
"Hi ya, Hi Aunt Daisy. Grandad, do you want the kettle on?"
"Good lad" He said, sticking his gnarly thumb up.
"There's your answer" Said Uncle John, obviously referring to an earlier conversation, prior to my arrival.
"What answer?" asked mum.
"Kev there. Why don't he stay here? He's here all the time, anyway"
"That's not a bad Idea. It would certainly solve a lot of problems"
Aunt Daisy nodded in agreement.
I wasn't aware at the time that they had been told by some busybody organization that grandad needed somebody there, a sort of unpaid carer, but not a "carer". A Night watchman. That's better.
"Dad, if you had to have anyone here, who would you want?" asked Aunt Daisy
"Buggered if I know" said grandad.
"You really need someone who knows you well, it would have to be someone you can trust, somebody that you know well. It would have to be somebody you got on with" said Uncle John.

I walked in with a full pot of tea.
"All done, grandad".
"Let her brew, Kev" He said, as he always did.
Aunt Daisy then spoke to me...
"Kevin, we need someone to live here with grandad".
She called me "Kevin". I hated serious talk, and I hated being called "Kevin".
"Why? I'm always here".
"That's what we're saying, Todd" said mum.
"But I like being here with grandad" said I, totally getting the wrong end of the sticky thing.
"How would you like to live here and have the big bedroom upstairs?" Said Uncle John, getting to the point, as usual.
"Me?" I looked at grandad for some guidance.
"If I've got to 'ave some 'un here, young Kev, you'll do!"
I think that was approval.
I looked at mum.
"It makes sense, Todd. You spend all your time here with grandad anyway, and you're always moaning about your small room (I wasn't). You've got all the upstairs here. You can still have your dinners cooked at home".
"I'll have to think about it" I said, smiling at grandad.
"I've thought about it. Grandad, you've got a new lodger!"
"You'll do me, matey" That definitely, was approval.
Everybody seemed happy. Aunt Daisy told me to go and have a look upstairs. I didn't need any second bidding. I was up those stairs like a ferret up a trouser leg. I opened the front bedroom door. The room was massive, with a large metal framed double bed in the middle of it. This was going to be my bed. There were two windows that gave me a view directly over the road, to the Ranges and a narrow ribbon of sea beyond.

I could see distant ship's smoke, on the horizon.
There was a large chest of drawers, a closed off fireplace, with an ornamental mantle over the top to put my bits and pieces on, a little bedside table, a wooden chair and an old comfy armchair. The other two smaller back bedrooms were all full of discarded furniture, so I could pick and choose whatever I wanted for my room.

*

I would spend one last night in my small box room at number 5, before moving all my stuff to my new abode at number 6. If Lurch was sad to see me move next door with grandad (which I'm sure he was), he hid it very well behind a sticky out eared grin.
I think that mum was also pleased, because they had bought me a Transistor radio so that I could listen to European football matches in distant countries, during the late evenings, and along with all the interference and static, whilst trying to hear the games at fullish volume, I think I may have been slightly spoiling their enjoyment downstairs of whatever they were watching on TV.
They weren't too keen on some of my choices of television programmes either. I, along with thousands of others, had discovered the wit of "Monty Python's Flying Circus", as well as stuff like "The Goodies" and "The Two Ronnies".
Well, obviously a show featuring two blokes called Ronnie wasn't going to last, now was it?
I think that it can be seen from some of my inane rambling that I loved the show, and their type of humour. Four candles, anyone? Hang on, was that Four candles or Fork handles?
Sadly, at the same time as those shows started, another favourite of mine had run its course after nine years. "The Beverly Hillbillies" with Jed and grandma Clampitt had come to an end. I can still clearly remember its theme tune!

I was lucky, because as well as all the sport, grandad also enjoyed "The Two Ronnies" on Saturday nights, so we'd sit and chuckle along together, even though grandad was hard of hearing.
I said, "HE WAS HARD OF HEARING!"
Does me writing it in capital letters make it sound any louder?
There was another aspect of grandad that some folk weren't aware of. Just in case he was ever in the bathroom and he felt like chewing on a large hard lump of toffee or a chunk of rather tough coal, he kept his teeth in a pot on the window sill!
I could never remember him having teeth in his mouth. He had developed gums like a metal crusher in a scrapyard because of it. His lack of gnashers never stopped him chomping down on any food. Even Christmas nuts would get pulverised to a pulp between those jaws of steel.
Moving into grandad's front bedroom was such a joy. I could have my radio up loud, and because of his deafness, it never bothered him at all. Not that I did that a lot, only when the top Twenty was on usually, because the rest of the time, during the hours of darkness, I'd be downstairs with him, in front of the fire, squealing like a stuck pig, as I commentated on the exploits of Soldiers United.

*

It was around this time, as I was now a mature, almost, Fourteen year old boy with a paper round and lodgings, that I was allowed to cycle down to Steve's house on some evenings, so that we could play Subbuteo on his mum's kitchen table, after they had finished their (late for me) Six O'clock evening meal. It was always about Seven O'clock, after they had all stopped faffing about to "let their dinner settle", as Steve put it, that we had the kitchen to ourselves until I had to leave by 9.50pm to be home by 10pm. The only slight interruption would be at 9pm when Steve's mum would come out to

make their suppertime cup of tea.
What was it about having a 9pm suppertime?
We would both have our own Subbuteo logbooks, and our own Leagues. Steve would have some strange fixtures such as, Blackpool vs Brazil, whilst mine included Alloa Athletic vs Mexico and Inter Milan vs Bishop Auckland. I would operate the goalies for his games, and he'd do the same for mine. Nobody else was ever invited to join us for these evenings. It was definitely a two-person hobby, and that was that.

*

November had Slade at number One with "Cuz I Luv You". They would have most certainly have been in the bottom group at school for spulling!
Soon, it was Yuletide once again, and as the saying went...
"Christmas is coming, Charlie Choops is getting fat", or it may have been something about a Goose!
Another festering Yuletide offering was at number One, this time it was about a milkman called "Ernie", and it was sung so beautifully by Benny Hill whilst wearing a lopsided milkman's cap. His little ditty just about outshone other classics like "No matter how I try" by Gilbert O'Sullivan, "Something tells me" by Cilla Black, and the first record that I ever bought. The classy (in my mind) "Softly whispering I love you" by The Congregation.
Don't knock it till you've heard it! And then, don't judge me!
The reason for purchasing my first ever record was that I had just been bought my first ever machine to play it on. Father Christmas (I'd put a bet on it being dad by now, but I didn't gamble) had left me a small Fidelity Record Player in a White imitation leatherette finish with a plastic smoked glass effect lid, along with the usual things that seemed to turn up every year now, such as annuals, Subbuteo,

football boots and kit, lovely shirt and tie combo's that still managed to find their way into Santa's sack when he was delivering to St. Georges Place, and the ubiquitous Games Compendium.

For the first time, I had to get up, go downstairs to the bathroom, get washed, go next door to number 5, let myself in, and go into the front room where my presents were all strewn beneath a scabby old Christmas tree, festooned with only a third of the needles that it arrived with, the rest already buried deep into the carpet, having avoided the authentic looking "grass" crepe paper surround at the base of the bucket that the forlorn stick stood in.

My new Record Player was removed from its box, and the tinny little White speakers were plugged in, so that I could listen to my very first ever record. I was so excited, I could have crushed a grape!

Hang on, it certainly didn't sound right to me. It wasn't the Congregation as knew them.

"This sounds like Pinky and Perky, mum!"

Lurch was cracked up, chuckling away while he moved his new Action Man figure into rude positions.

"Oh, hang on. It's on 78rpm, not 45".

I think thank my future DJ career may have got off to a less than auspicious start.

There were a few other old singles that Bett had given me from their large collection, so until I could get down to "Spin-a Disc" in Hythe high street, these would have to do.

I moved my nice, brand new White Fidelity Record Player with an imitation leatherette finish and a plastic smoked glass effect lid to my bedroom at grandad's so that my little brother couldn't get his little chubby, sticky fingers all over it, and then I carried on with Christmas day.

After our dinner, when grandad had taken his afternoon "siesta" as he called it, I spent the rest of the day with him watching TV and listening to his yarns about the olden days. Mum didn't want him to be on his own, especially as nan wasn't here anymore, but he was fine. It was almost like a normal day, except for the Christmas shows. Grandad and me had got into a sort of routine by now, where I would occupy the rug in front of the fire, playing out important Soldiers United games, once their opponents had arrived in their team handbag...I mean coach, and grandad would sit in his favourite chair at the table, either reading his Western book, of which he had hundreds, or just dozing or watching TV, until we were interrupted by inconsiderate relatives.

It was also, for obvious reasons, a very subdued gathering at Aunt Daisy and Uncle Bill's house on Boxing day, as there was a very important family member missing.

*

Barry and I were both serenaded into our birthdays by the New Seekers, who wanted to teach the World to sing. They could have made a start with mum!

They held off "Opportunity Knocks" winner, Neil Read singing "Mother of Mine", America's "Horse with no name", "Stay with me" by The Faces and Mr Presley, who just couldn't help believing.

Now that I had reached the princely age of Fourteen, I was eligible to go to any of the many major clubs in the region.

What a choice it was that was presented before me!

So, on a fairly nondescript dull Tuesday evening, along with Steve, Robert and Mick (Kim wasn't allowed to go yet), I pottered up to the glitzy establishment that was Palmarsh hall, and stood outside with five or six other "Groovers", for it was "Palmarsh Youth Club" and it opened it's door (just the one) at 6.50pm, or whenever Mr Gordon

Uden turned up from West Hythe, in his little two-tone Green Standard 10 car to unlock the aforesaid mentioned door.
I think that it was a 10p a week membership, or something like that. For that immense cost, we had the use of two, not one, but two table tennis tables and a half size Snooker table. We had to forage these tables out from under the stage and set them all up before we were able to fully immerse ourselves in the sheer joy of pointlessly whacking a ping pong ball backwards and forwards over a little net.
There was also a Record Player which was always set up on the stage so that we could play all the same records that we'd brought along, over and over, again. It was also an opportunity to dress up in the most garish fashion that was in your wardrobe but should have remained in your wardrobe.
It was a time of flared trousers and large collared, patterned shirts (minus any matching tie). To top off this trend statement, there was the Tank top jumper, in all sorts of patterns, colours and hoops. Gawd help you if you had a mum who was quite inept with the needles, knit you one!
I had one!
At the bottom of our attire, would be our shoes or boots. Doctor Marten boots were just starting to be fashionable in certain areas, and whenever new fashions or trends hit the main cities or towns of the land, Hythe could be seen to follow closely, only six months later. Another type of boot that was in favour at the time, was a lightish Brown one, with a type of cork heel and sole. It wasn't really cork though, but "Cork effect". A bit like plastic with a cork pattern on. The heels on these would wear down very quick, requiring "Blakeys" to protect further erosion.
We all had many trips to Ballad's shoe repairers, next to the Police Station in Prospect road, to get replacement Blakeys.

At the other end, on top of our attire was our hair.

Now, I loved my grandad in every way, but the one and only time to avoid him was when he had his hair cutting scissors and clippers out. If you ever saw a board being put across the arms of his big old Carver kitchen chair, then it was time to run and hide.

As a young kid, after my…er…slight accident at Chapel Street barbers, I would, along with any of the others caught in the round up, be made to endure one of grandad's haircuts. His styles, or style (there was only one) was about as up to date as leeches were for still treating ailments, although they were still being allegedly used on the Marsh!

My last visit to grandad's "Chair of Doom" resulted in the following…

"Er, grandad can you give me a "Rod Stewart?"

"Yup, young Kev. Just ee sit still".

Snip, snip, snip, clip, clip, snip, clip, snip, snip.

An awful lot of my hair seemed to be falling onto the floor, and he appeared to be cutting a long way up the back of my neck!

Snip, snip, snip, clip, clip, snip, clip, snip, clip, snip, snip.

"There ee go, young Kev. All done".

With a feeling of total dread, I jumped down from the board and clomped (I still had my calliper) to the bathroom mirror.

"Arrgghh!"

"That's not a Rod Stewart!"

"What's that, young Kev?" He replied, whilst relighting his pipe.

"That's not right, grandad, it's much too short at the back as well!"

"Shall I put some back on, matey?" he said, smiling.

"That's what your mum said to do it like!"

"It's not right".

"Innit?"

"No grandad. Rod Stewart don't have his hair all short like this!"

"He would if I cut it!"

My time for free home haircuts had come to an end.
I had a "Look" to establish!
The "Feather cut" hairstyle had come into fashion for some boys, although most still had very sensible short hair. That wasn't going to be for me though. As the years would progress, I would try to maintain a cross between My "Rod Stewart" and a "David Bowie" hairstyle. Sadly, I still have my own "Rod Stewart" hairstyle today. Hair fashion definitely peaked for me in the 1970s!

*

Anyway, back to Palmarsh Youth Club. It's at this point in my story that I must mention the man who ran this Club, for the youth of the area, for no reward, other than to see the kids enjoying themselves. In a World, at a time now, when numerous various club leaders have been exposed as vile creatures, who preyed on young vulnerable people, it has to be pointed out that there were also selfless, community spirited, helpful, delightful, brilliant folk, such as Gordon, or Mr Uden, as we would jokingly call him (He always called me Mr Pilcher, in return).
In his time running the Youth Club, he organized many trips to concerts or whatever for the older members of the club, and he gave up so much of his time for us kids. A great man in in every department, except size. I don't think that he's ever been able to look over too many walls, as he's only just about Five and a half feet tall, and I think I'm being generous to him there.
He still lives in the same house that he was born in West Hythe, and we always have a bit of a yarn about the Youth Club days if I go past on my bike and he's out in his garden, in his usual Blue denim dungarees. Blimey, he must be at least 150 years old now, but he still looks the same as he did back in the early 1970s. What a great chap!

In the kitchen of the hall, Gordon would sell Coca Cola, Mars bars, crisps, nuts and the like and there would always be a few of us, gathered around him, all "chewing the cud". I expect that he gave us all loads of good advice, in a way that none of us noticed.

As the weeks flowed by, I started to buy more and more singles like "Son of my Father" by Chicory Tip, "Telegram Sam" by T.Rex, and "Without You" by Nilsson. They were all number One hits. There was also "American Pie" by Don McLean, and Gilbert O'Sullivan's "Alone again (Naturally)". These were all played at the Youth Club, along with other kid's records. It was here, at Palmarsh Youth Club, that some of the Burmarsh mob, Steve Watts and Jamie and George MacPherson got to know us better, and we all became great pals. Kim's mum finally relented and let Kim attend on one Tuesday evening, although she escorted him the two hundred or so yards up the road at 7pm, then was waiting outside at 9pm to escort him back home again. Youth Club didn't end till 9.45pm. She even made him dress up in his smartest shorts. He was almost Fifteen, for the love of "Spotty Dog!".

He never turned up there again. Poor old Kim!

*

Chapter Nineteen – Who's nicked our Meadow?

Back at school, lively debates would be engaged in, at wet break times in the classroom about the latest chart music. Copies of "Melody Maker" and "New Musical Express" would be flaunted about, along with the "Disco 45" songbooks, with the words to all the hit records. It was a time when you played and knew off by heart the B sides of your records. They were important.

The ban on the "Out of school" trips was finally lifted on all the "Pegwell Bay Martyr's", and I could challenge Higgy Highland as school team goalie, which is just what I did.

Our inter house games at school almost became school team trials. I was in goal for Wakefield house, whilst Higgy was in goal for Becket. They had the best players in the year group, and they won more than they lost. That meant that, as a goalie, I had more to do than Higgy, more saves to make and, alas, more goals to let in. As I had been side-lined for so long, due to my incapacitation, Higgy had been given the jersey without any decent challenger. Now I was in his rear-view mirror, about to overtake him.

It should be admitted, at this juncture, that we weren't one of the best when it came to matches against other schools. In fact, if Harvey Grammar school were the top team, the "Derby County" First Division league champions, then we were at the other end of the league system, the "Newport County" Division Four, perennial strugglers.

Again, as a goalie, you were kept warm and busy. During my games in goal, in Third year, I can't recall any victories. It was the same when Higgy was between the sticks (except that I was smaller, yet far more agile, obviously).

Of the outdoor activities on a cold February or March morning, Cross Country running wasn't a favourite. These tortuous runs took place during P.E. mostly as early as 9.45am. At Brockhill, it involved running down into a valley, through thick gooey mud and cow pooh, crossing the Brockhill stream and then climbing around and up the hill the other side, through thick gooey mud and cow pooh, then a long trudge along the top of the far side of the valley, followed by a slip and slide, often on your bum, back down the hill through thick gooey mud and cow pooh, re-crossing the stream without the aid of either a bridge or ferry, then a long hard struggle back to the Five bar gate finish, by the school kitchen, through thick gooey mud and cow pooh!

A few of us cunning types decided not to bother!

We had worked out that once we had all departed from the start, instead of standing out in the freezing cold and (sometimes) rain in his very short shorts, Mr Kennedy would retreat, back into the warmth of his office by the main hall. We had also discovered that there was a cowshed, out of sight from the Five bar gate, that had to be passed on the outward and inward leg of the trail.

Do I need to draw a picture here?

Although the area surrounding the cowshed was submerged in thick gooey mud and cow pooh (obviously), it was a good place to withdraw from the torture for a while, and then re-join for the inward few hundred yards up to the finish. The secret to not getting caught out was to not upset any of the boys doing the full circuit, or they would "snitch" on you!

Also, it was imperative to always come back in the "middle" of the field, not too good, not too bad, and to always be puffing and blowing like the others. Some boys that hid in the cowshed really were puffing and blowing at the end, because they had used the time to have a cigarette break!

I would, at this point, hate to admit that I cheated...so I won't! I'd rather admit to using my noggin, saving my little spindly legs for proper sport.

*

Back on the music front, in the charts in April, there was a new foot tapping (not) number One with a reasonably short title. "Amazing Grace" performed by a very unreasonably long group name "The Pipes & Drums and The Military Band of The Royal Scots Dragoon Guards Band". There was, all sorts of music about in the charts. Even football clubs like Chelsea and Leeds United got in on the act (mind you, they weren't much cop!), TV theme tunes by Orchestra's, Eurovision songs, such as "Come What May" by Vicky Leandros, plus Glam Rock was now forcing its shiny stuff upon us. My main concern was, would my paper round money be able to keep up with all the records on offer? I'd even started buying LPs, mainly David Bowie ones like "The Man Who Sold the World" and "Hunky Dory". I had "Ziggy Stardust" to get soon, as well. Oh, life with the charts was bliss for us young 'uns.

*

As the clocks had changed to Summer time, Steve and I were told by his mum and dad that we could put a goal up in his back garden, to play out in the evenings. He had quite a long garden, with just a clothes line and pole in the way. We named the pole "Jackie Charlton". After we constructed a goal that was almost as wide as the garden itself (it was about 10 feet wide and five feet high), we decided that we needed a proper goal net, so we proceeded along to the Nursery, just off Old London road, where we bought a long length of hessian netting for about 30p a yard. It was a yard wide, so we joined it, quite professionally, as it was our first ever proper net (and our only paid for one). It looked absolutely brilliant. We'd even got the right amount of "bulge" for when the ball hit it. That was more important to two sad little boys like Steve and I than life, itself! It didn't take too much to please us in our World.

*

One evening, after getting home from school, we all noticed a change on the meadow. Someone had unloaded about three million large building blocks. Well, that's how we saw it. This mass of Grey was stacked right behind our goal, and a swathe had been cut, directly through the gorse from the end of the road, by the garages.
"What in Heaven's name could be occurring here?" Mick might have said.
"I'm dashed if I know!" I may have replied.
"Some Blaggard has deposited a certain amount of building material, directly behind our goal, the fiends" Steve definitely, did not say.
What we actually said was...
"We've got terracing behind the goal!"
We decided to climb up to the top.
"I can almost see up to Burmarsh playing field from here" pointed Mick.
"Look Brian, you can see your mum in her back garden!"
We all waved, and she waved back.
"What's it doing here?" Steve had finally questioned the logistics of the matter.
"Dunno, looks like they're going to build something" I replied, never stating the obvious.

"I feel sick up here" said Kim, whilst appearing a tad Green around the gills. It was time to return to ground level for a game. "Two and in" meant that once you had got through, you could sit up on the terracing and watch the others, although Kim didn't relish sitting too high up.

What was confirmed to us by our dad's, as more and more building stuff encroached on our domain, was that the erection of a new school, Palmarsh Primary school, was imminent.

In time, I believe that other major club grounds, such as those at Brighton & Hove Albion, Coventry City, Stoke City, Sunderland, Middlesboro, Arsenal, Tottenham Hotspur, Manchester City and others were given over to development. It just happens that ours was the first!

Although Palmarsh Angels, as a functioning club, were now defunct, the team lived on in all of us in all but name, and now it looked as if we would become homeless.

We could still play on the meadow for a while, but soon the entire wilderness of our youth would be torn from us by chain link fencing. Where would all the lizards go?

Those of us with bikes (Steve, Mick, Rob, Kim, me) became Nomads of the local footballing World. We would sometimes turn up on Burmarsh Rec. and play along with Steve and Paul Watts and Jamie and George MacPherson on their pitch. That was good fun, and sometimes, if we had a death wish, we'd have a kick around in one of the big goals on Halterne's pitch at Reachfields. Mind you, if the Paton's happened to come along and weren't in a jovial, sharing mood, then they'd have a kick around, using us as the ball!

There was a pitch, in the top corner of Hythe Green, nestled up against a hedge near the Infant's school and the large Portex Plastics factory, which backed onto Hythe Ranges. With proper schoolboy goalposts more to our size and liking, this became our pitch of choice. There was only one thing missing on the goal that we shot our old heavy leather football into, and that (you've guessed it) was a net.

We needed a cunning plan!

Alas, instead of a cunning plan, we just decided to have a good old mooch around the old fisherman's huts, where the Hythe fishing boats landed their catch on the conveniently named "Fisherman's Beach", as it happened.

Well, there were more nets there than you could shake a tortoise at! (we didn't shake sticks).

A wizened old fisherman pointed us in the general direction of a large pile of what we assumed were, old and torn discarded nets that would never see the depths of the English Channel again.

To be honest, most of these old nets were so torn and tattered that, even we would have been hard pushed to have made a decent goal net from them.

So, we didn't bother!

Instead, between a couple of the huts, we found a reasonable section of netting that, it was quite possible, would have seen the depths of the English Channel again, if it wasn't for the fact that we snaffled it!

We weren't entirely sure if we could take it or not, as it was near to where the wizened old man had pointed, and we didn't really want to bother him again as we could see that he was busy, lighting his pipe!

Not wanting to look at all suspicious, carrying this possible piece of "swag" away from the huts, we all persuaded Rob that, as he had the biggest baggiest jumper on, it would be a lot better if we shoved the fishy smelling mesh up the front of it!

"But I don't want it. It stinks!" He tried to say in protest.

"Just get it in there" instructed Mick, whilst pushing it up Rob's jumper.
"It shows" said Rob, again in protest.
And it smelled like a Grimsby trawler, on a bad day!

"Come on, we'll all walk together so it won't notice" said I, whilst really noticing that it stuck out like an extremely sore thumb!
"Quick Rob, get moving" Kim gave him an, ever so slight, nudge in the back to propel him forwards.
"It'll look great when we get it up" drooled Steve, as he kept back from Rob's bulging jumper, holding his nose.
"Look, we'll all surround you so nobody will even notice" said Mick, just as we were about to clear the line of fisherman's huts, where the wizened old man was puffing on his pipe and now chatting to another wizened old man on the roadway.
So, Rob, looking like a very pregnant lady, quickly walked past them, holding the bottom of his smelly, and now wet, bulging jumper in, whilst the rest of us watched, hiding behind the huts, just in case he was stopped.
He wasn't!
He kept on walking, going the direct route down Cinque Ports Avenue, to the Green, whilst we all took an alternative route down St. Leonards road.
Our group motto could have been...
"All for one, and one for all".
If we weren't such cowardy custards!
Anyway, most gangs of kids had a really, gullible member within the group. We were just lucky, we had two!
Good old Rob and Kim!
The net fitted perfectly, with a little bit of tinkering and fettling. It was almost like a goal at West Ham's Upton Park. After we played on

the Green, we'd sometimes leave the net in a black sack behind the hedge instead of taking it on our bikes, back to Steve's dad's shed, and it never got stolen (again).
I mean, who would want a smelly old fishing net, apart from us kids using it on a goal? Okay, perhaps some disgruntled fishermen might have wanted it back, but let's not go into that!

*

My Third year at Brockhill came to an end. In exams, apart from French where I got an "A", I appeared to have a monopoly on any grade between C- and C+. It seemed that I excelled at being absolutely, average in all subjects. I believe that the range of subjects marked upon, should have been extended.
I reckon that, in the "Noticeably visible trouser leg turn-up" category, I could have taken a cup or two, or in the "One leg much thinner than the other" section, I would have cleaned up with the highest mark available. Obviously, I would have also been a contender as "Cheeky Chappy of the year" as well.
Apart from the alphabetical gradings that we were forced to take home in our reports each year, the only other "incentive" throughout the term that we could obtain was a "Housepoint". Now, what's that all about?
If your work or attitude was sub-standard, you could be expecting a cuff around the ear, a slipper, cane, or even concussion from a thrown Black board rubber!
At worse, you could be looking at half an hour detention after school, where you'd be forced to inanely copy sections from a book, or to repeat a sentence over and over on the page, in the form of "Lines".
But, what could you expect at the other end of the Educational scale, if you excelled, over achieved, or you were just a "Yes Sir, No Sir, can I clean your Blackboard, Sir?" sort of boy?

I'll tell you.
You would be awarded a "Housepoint".
Not money or a nice sweetie, or even both!

No, the teacher would give you a meaningless, pointless "Housepoint", to be added to the total amount of "Housepoints" that your "House" collected throughout the school year.
At the end of this aforesaid mentioned year, Mr Setterfield would read out the total results to inform the entire school which "House" had the brainest, swottiest, well behaved, bum-licking boys in it! The "House Captain", (some nerdy prefect) would then be awarded a cup and every boy in that "House" would cheer. The other three "Houses" weren't permitted to boo!
The same "House", (Becket), won it every year, whilst my "House" (Wakefield), always came a well beaten second or third. Average again!
You even got "Housepoints" in sports like football, whilst proper footballers were getting paid money (and sweeties, I expect).
I think that it can be assumed from my derisory opinion of "Housepoints", that I was not, in fact, a great accumulator of them. I never lost any sleep over the fact though, after all, I still proudly held my "Bean Bag Winner" certificate from Primary school. Not many other boys could boast about that!

*

Our beautiful British Summer had turned up in all it's glory once again. Small fluffy White clouds set against a deep bright Blue sky, with wall to wall sunshine. It's funny how we never remember the dull, dreary wet days, isn't it?
Once more I can delve into some of the music of the time. There had been T.Rex's "Metal Guru" at number One in May, just pipping Elton

John's "Rocket Man" and David Cassidy's double A-side "Could it be forever" & "Cherish". In June, "Vincent" by Don McLean had hit the top, closely followed by those bad spillers, Slade, with" Take me bak 'ome". In July, a young Donny Osmond had some "Puppy Love" at the top, whilst Dr. Hook and the Medicine Show sang about "Sylvia's Mother", and The Sweet tootled on about their "Little Willy" (not "World Cup Willie!").

Now, we come to the elephant in the room.

No, not a real elephant. That's just a silly saying.

It seems that these days, one certain performer is never mentioned, his songs are never played, and nobody wants to be in his "Gang" anymore, despite his pleas to us 1970s kids.

Yes, his name is "Gary Glitter".

I make no apology for mentioning him here because, like it or not, (and it's "not" for most, if not all, folk), he was a major part of the Glam Rock era. His first chart hit "Rock and Roll Parts 1&2" made it to number two in July, and it was followed by many more chart successes. I know this because, along with thousands of other kids, I bought most of them. We were all taken in by the music and the times. We never imagined that he wore a "syrup" because he was as bald as a coot! We all thought it was his own "Barnet" (I appear to have turned into a cockney, now).

We'd all be at Palmarsh Youth Club, belting out the words to "Do you wanna touch me? (oh yeah)", and "I'm the Leader of the Gang", in the ensuing months without the knowledge that he was a predatory Paedophile. In 1972, we'd have thought a "Paedophile" was an Ancient Greek word for a "Collector of Peas", only it was spelt different!

Today, there are quite a few Idols of our youth that we now know to be repulsive, and not even 1% worthy of our adoration, but we didn't know then.

Who did?

I've already mentioned Jimmy Savile and Rolf Harris, but I expect you could add a page full, to those names if you really thought about it. I'd rather not think about it.

To us, at that time, it was our pop music and that was all it was! And he couldn't mime to save his life, the useless waste of space! Phew, I'm glad that I've cleared that up and got it out of my system. I'm wound up now!

*

Back to my life as a multi-talented sportsman and trend setter. Okay, perhaps I'm exaggerating on the "trend setter" bit there…alright, and on the first claim as well, but the two big things in any young lad's life in the early 1970s was sport, music and fashion…hang on, that's three things!

The look that turned a few heads, and quite a few stomachs, as well!

There were a few shops in Folkestone and Ashford where you could buy some of the more, snazzy attire, but for a poor little boy like myself, struggling to get by on a paper boy's wages, the bus fare wasn't worth the journey, plus that was valuable footballing and cycling time that could be wasted.

Instead, there were the advertisements at the back of "Melody Maker" and "New Musical Express" papers.

For only …Hmmm…some pounds, a person of a certain age and scrawny build could purchase a Satin bomber jacket and matching pair of wide flared trousers from these Music papers.

I bought a pair…er…I mean, somebody I know bought a set in Navy Blue!

The...er...person told me that they looked really cool, standing in the bedroom, facing the mirror and screeching out the words to "All the young dudes", but when I...er...I mean, when he bent over to put his shoes on, the trousers tore right across his bum cheek!
Phew! I'm glad I wasn't daft enough to buy a pair!
I think I may have got away with that.
The same person, obviously not me, also bought a pair of four-inch heeled Black shoes with a Pink star on the top, a pair of three inch Beige wedges (I know, ridiculous, it would have been like having my calliper shoe back on), I mean, it would have been like that, if it was me!
But the "piece de resistance" (that's French, that is) was a pair of Black five-inch heeled boots with two- and a half- inch platform Soles. The boy was an Idiot!
All these footwear items would be worn in the coming months, years, with some of the unbelievable outfits of the time.
I may mention, at various times in my story that I wore such ridiculous things as these, but you know that I'm only pretending, I mean, I wouldn't have been so stupid, would I?

*

It was towards the end of the football season that dad decided to take Steve and me up to London, to watch our first ever League game. It was Chelsea vs Crystal Palace at Stamford Bridge. I recall that the game ended in a draw 1-1, but the thing that stands out was seeing the players in real life, and not on the TV. We both sat in my front room, on the Sunday afternoon after the match the previous day, to watch it on "The Big Match". We tried to spot ourselves in the crowd, but we couldn't. The commentator, Brian Moore, didn't mention us being there, either. Ne'er mind, we knew we were there.

*

My Fourth year at Brockhill began, this time I would be in 4G, Mr Gant's form in N3, in the New building. This was going to be a momentous year for our school football team, of which, I was now the established goalie (poor Higgy never stood a chance against my, totally left sided, cat-like ability). We would be in the Chadwick Cup, a tournament for all the local schools. There would be five of us in total, with the top team taking the trophy. I think it's fair to say that we were fifth favourites to win.
As well as being our form teacher, Mr Gant was also in charge of our Chadwick Cup team.
There was also a new Music teacher. Mr. Richard Baulch had joined the school in this capacity. From the off, he was a fun person to be around. That was a major plus. He was also the step father of Steve Watt's girlfriend. Another major plus. He was also a young "Rolf Harris" look-a-like. Ah, not so good!
Apart from the usual French and Games, school was quite a chore. I still excelled in mediocrity, if only that could have been an actual subject. I had made up my mind that I wanted to leave school as soon as possible, because football gear, records and new togs didn't come cheap, and with only my paper round money to see me through, this wasn't a great situation. Mum and dad tended to agree that it wasn't worth me pursuing a University place, anyway, Cambridge didn't do any degree courses on Subbuteo!

*

We had a new addition to our little group of nomadic footballers. Ian Daffin's family had moved onto the Pennypot Estate, directly behind Steve's house. They originated from Sunderland, but we tried not to hold that against him. He was an ardent Sunderland supporter, and against all odds, he would have something big to cheer and brag about in the coming months.

In the light evenings after school, when Steve's dinner had "settled", Ian would climb over the wall from his garden, to join us as we recreated matches from the Watney or Texaco cup, that were played pre-season. There was also the Anglo-Italian cup, but most of those games seemed to end in violence or spark off fights among the rival supporters. It was now a common trend at football matches.

*

Despite the violence on the terraces and around the grounds, we did arrange to go up to a game by ourselves for the first time. It was Steve, Mick, Ian, Kim and me. Yep, Kim was reluctantly allowed to go with us. He did go, armed with strict instructions though. Come to think of it, I think that we all did. Four young country bumpkins and a Northern descendant of a ship builder. What could possibly go wrong?

The game itself, couldn't have been between two more friendly clubs or bunches of fans. It was West Ham United vs Leeds United. It was a frenzied war, with more kicks on legs than on the actual ball!

It ended in a bloody 1-1 draw (another one). When I say "Bloody", that was the state of some of the players, not an angry description of the result!

What stood out for us, and really shook us outside the ground, was the sight of about four young kids, younger than us (they all looked about ten years old), set about two elderly Leeds supporters who were doing nowt more threatening than just standing, eating their pre-match hot dog. They really did kick seven bells out of them, and they were then laughing about it. This was a completely alien World to us. We then spent the rest of the day in perpetual fear. We had

never witnessed this inner-city violence that seemed to explode at football matches before, so it was such a relief to get ourselves back to Charing Cross, and the safety of the returning train.
At last we could all feel easier, at least, we thought, nowt could go wrong now!
So, there we were, all chatting, laughing and joking as the train reached Ashford. We were all pleased to be getting back to Folkestone Central, where dad would be waiting to cram us all into his little car, and head for home and supper.
Kim knew that his mum wouldn't be happy until her young lad was in his pyjamas, safely tucked up in his bed with his teddy. Everything had gone smoothly on the trip and he'd be home soon. He wouldn't mention the trouble or the violence, or the sheer terror that he'd witnessed. No, that would be kept quiet by all of us, because we wanted to go to games again.
We waited, chatting and laughing, as the train shunted, then separated at the platform, then off we went...
We appeared to be branching off to the left, this wasn't the way, surely?...
"Hang on, where are we going?" asked a confused Mick.

"This way's Canterbury. That's our way" pointed Steve, as it began to dawn on us.
"I don't wanna go to Canterbury!" Shouted Kim, now starting to ever so slightly panic.
"Pull the cord! Pull the cord!" He made to grab for the communication chain to stop the train.
Mick shot up and half Rugby tackled him.
"What are you doing? You Idiot!"
"They've gotta go back. Tell him to reverse!"
"Kim, calm down. They can't reverse" Ian tried to reason with him,

but he failed.

"My mum'll go mad. I don't wanna go to Canterbury!"

Ian and Steve thought it was incredibly funny, so did I. We left Mick with the job of trying to calm Kim down.

"I've gotta jump off. We're going to Canterbury!"

"There's nowt we can do, so calm down!"

"I don't wanna go to Canterbury. My mum'll kill me!"

He then came up with a cunning plan!

"Let's see the driver and get him to take us back to Ashford!"

"Come on, it's worth a try. My mum'll kill me!"

He was starting to dribble, and frothy bits were coming out of the edges of his mouth. We could see that he was either losing it, big time, or we had a rabid Maycock on our hands!

That made us laugh even more!

The next thing we knew, he was bounding off to the front of the train, with Mick trailing after him.

The three of us left sitting there could see the funny side. We knew that dad would be waiting at Folkestone Central, but there was nowt we could do.

Then the conductor appeared...

"What are you lads doing here? You should be on the other half of the train!"

"Yeah, we know that now" said a contrite, yet smiling Steve.

"We got on the wrong half!"

"I can see that" said the conductor. (nowt got past him).

"Where are the other two? There were five of you!"

"Oh, they've gone to ask the driver to turn around" said Ian, as matter of factly as he could be.

"WHAT?"

"Oh Gawd, I'd better get up there sharpish. Now you sit tight".

With that, he was legging it through the carriage. His ticket machine

was bashing the seats (No, that's not a euphemism!).
He found Mick, and a frantic Kim at the door to the driver's cab.
"We need the train to go back to Ashford!" said Kim with a hangdog face and little pleading eyes.
"He can't go back, lads. You've got to go to Ramsgate!"
"Ramsgate? My mum'll kill me. We can't go to Ramsgate, please make him turn it round, please mister!"
He escorted them back to our compartment. Apart from Mr Panicky Pants, we all thought it was an adventure.
"Look". The nice conductor said...
"This train terminates at Ramsgate. I'll see that you get on the last train back through to London"
"No, I don't wanna go back up to London. My mum'll kill me" Kim was starting to get a teensy bit leaky around the eye department. The conductor let out a sigh...
"It stops at Dover Priory and Folkestone Central".
"Thanks mister" said Mick. We all concurred (apart from Kim who was rocking back and forth on the floor with his head between his knees).
"You can use a phone box at Ramsgate to call your parents, if they're on the phone"

"Yeah, thanks. My dad has a phone!"
Luckily, we had just had a telephone installed because dad was "On call" with his council job.
"Well, if he was meeting you, I expect that he's gone home again in case you call".
"Yeah, thanks for that. Sorry about the mistake" said Steve.
"No problem lads, you're not the first to do it, and you won't be the last!"
"What does "Terminal" mean?" asked an anxious Kim.

"Is he for real?" said the conductor, shaking his head.
"Oh well, nowt we can do about it now" said Ian.
All the while, slouched on his haunches in the corner, with his head in his hands, a little whining voice said…
"My mum'll kill me".
"Shut up!" we all shouted, as one!
We all alighted the train at Ramsgate, thanked the conductor, who put us on the correct train, and after a short delay, off we went.
I had phoned dad, who was understanding about it. He said that he would let the other mums and dads know what had happened, and he would meet us (again) at the station.
When we'd got back to Folkestone, and into dad's car, he told us that all the other parents thought it was funny, and typical of us.
Well, all except Kim's mum. Apparently, she was frantic with worry, climbing walls and spitting bricks!
Although it was almost midnight when we'd got back to St. Georges, after dropping Steve, Mick and Ian off, Kim's mum was pacing at the top of the road. She didn't even acknowledge dad's "Goodnight", instead, grabbing Kim by the ear, she frogmarched him home to his bed and teddy. He was kept indoors, staring out of the upstairs window at us playing football in the Square, for three days, and he was never allowed to go to a football match with us again! Such a shame.

*

My record collection was growing, "School's out", "Silver Machine", "Starman", "Run to me", and "10538 Overture" by the Electric Light Orchestra, along with "All the young dudes", "Wig Wam Bam", and those perennial bad spollers at number One with "Mama Weer All Crazee Now", were just some of the many 45s I bought in August, September and October.

In November "Clair" by Gilbert O'Sullivan reached the top spot, followed by Chuck Berry, singing about his "Ding-a-ling". I also bought "Donna" by 10cc, and "Goodbye to love" by the Glitter Band. It seemed that everything that was released, I loved. Well, everything that is, apart from the dancey, disco'ey songs from Motown or anywhere. Any type of music that involved moving about in a dancey fashion just wasn't for me.
The Jive, the Twist, the Locomotion, the Bump, the Hustle, Shaft, ABC, Love Train, any Motown, you name it!
As you may or may not be aware (you should be aware if you've been taking it all in, up to now!), I possess a left leg that could belong to Fred Astaire, but unfortunately, my right leg has about as much rhythm as a limp liver sausage sandwich, on a cold plate of indifference!
From that stance, I've never understood the "fun" or purpose of dancing, and I don't suppose that I ever will!

*

My paper round continued to run as smoothly as a heavily buttered bannister. Again, it was the routine that grandad and I had got into. He would always get up just after 6am (he laid in till 6.30am as he got older, the lazy so and so!). After what he called "his ablutions", he'd come to the bottom of the stairs and call...
"Kev, time to get up, matey".
"Alright grandad" I'd reply, and away we'd go on another day.
His alarm never failed, although sometimes I'd lay in bed, waiting to hear his voice, or hear any movement, worrying in case he'd had a fall. I could only relax when I heard him up and about.
As well as his call, there was the distinctive aroma of eggs, bacon and fried liver, that he had for breakfast on most mornings. It's a smell that stays in my memory, and when I smell anything similar it brings

back the thoughts of happy days with him. By the time I was ready to go up to Mr Nicholson's shop, he'd always have a cup of tea there for me. His early morning calls stayed with me for so many years of my life.

*

This Christmas, Aunt Kate was going to stay with another sister, my Aunt Jess, so nan Pilcher was able to come down to us for the festering period. It was handy that she was able to use my old room. It was great having nan down and she thoroughly enjoyed herself, especially when regaling one and all about her "Special" baby sitting ways, when she used to chase Lurch upstairs, leading her charge with an outstretched arm containing her teeth. Even Barry, who had recovered by now, found himself chuckling, despite him being the butt of the tale.
There was one very good deed that I did, this Yuletide. At school, we all gave food and Christmas goodies so that special Christmas hampers could be made up from the donations. We were asked to put forward any names of elderly folk that we deemed worthy of such a gift.

I put forward the name of a lovely lady called Miss Stephens, who lived round the Square. She was always doing so much for other folk, especially those less able than herself, despite her age. Everybody that knew her spoke so highly of her. She was certainly a very special lady in my eyes.
As luck would have it for a change, my choice was picked out to be a recipient of one of these hampers, and the pride that I had when I handed over the box and saw the look of amazement and gratitude in her eyes would have been difficult to surpass. What a lovely lady she was.

*

The Christmas charts had a very badly spulled "Gudbuy to Jane" by that Wolverhampton group, "Solid Gold Easy Action" by T.Rex, and "Happy Xmas (War is over)" by John and Yoko, but they were all held off the Christmas number One slot by little Jimmy Osmond, ranting on about a "Long Haired Lover from Liverpool".

My Subbuteo collection was enhanced further by the addition of some new goals, Partick Thistle, No. 29, Liverpool, No. 41, and Leeds United, No. 21. My annuals collection gained the usual culprits, plus "Goal" and "Shoot" annuals. My clothes (bought by mum), I feel it's better not to say too much about, other than the dodgy shirt salesman had appeared to have found a regular customer.

There was one present that Father Christmas couldn't get down any chimney, so it was left in the back porch at number 5, so that when I went into the house on Christmas morn, it was the first thing that I saw (that was a clever old Santa!).

A dark Golden 5 speed Raleigh racing bike was staring out at me! My very first brand new bike (I believe it cost £38).

That would certainly put the Games Compendium in its place. I couldn't wait to do my Boxing Day paper round with my new trusty steed. Yep, we delivered on Boxing Day, back then.

For some reason, I recall Barry got a Crystal Palace shirt despite him liking Manchester City at the time. Still, he didn't seem to mind, he had several Selection boxes to get through whilst he watched the Christmas TV.

My little brother and me. He's got his Crystal Palace shirt on and I appear to have a "John Denver" hairstyle!

We had "A Stocking full of Stars" featuring such luminaries as Basil Brush, The Goodies, Laurel & Hardy and Yogi Bear. Following on were "The Black and White Minstrel Show" and "Top of the Pops" in the afternoon. The evening's entertainment consisted of programmes like "Christmas Night with the Stars" (there seemed to be a lot of "Stars" about), "The Morecambe & Wise Christmas Show", "Opportunity Knocks", "The Comedians" and the "Val Doonican Christmas Show".

That was without all the new toys to play with and Christmas annuals to read.

Old Barney Rubble didn't do too badly on the present front either. As well as getting the usual sweeties, annuals, and Barbie doll (I may have made that one up), he got "Kerplunk", "Etch-a-sketch", "Spirograph" and some "Weebles". They were almost the same as him. "They wobble but they don't fall down".

His favourite pressie was a "Space Hopper", he loved bouncing around the room on it, smacking into the furniture, and when he sat down beside it, you could hardly tell them apart!

It was good to load myself up with snacky food and take it back to my room at grandad's so that I wouldn't starve in the night if we were attacked by Aliens.

Grandad and me, had plenty to feast upon during the evening as mum made sure our supper would be a treat. There were her sausage rolls, that looked like a lump of dog pooh had been shoved into the middle of some old crusty pastry, and mum's own version of a "Cheesey Puff", which had absolutely no "Puff" at all, but they all tasted brilliant. Mum was never one to go for presentation (as her sewing and knitting had proved), but the taste was second to none. It was faultless.

That was a rare treat for me and grandad, sitting at the table, tucking into our very own Christmas Day supper, accompanied by a large pot of grandad's tea. I had to leave my new "Racer" in the back porch, all ready for the morning, so I contented myself by just reading my new "Goal" and "Shoot" annuals, sitting by the fireside with my best mate!

Our Boxing Day jaunt to Aunt Daisy and Uncle Bill's house went without incident, apart from Charlie Choops going into the bathroom, only to find a certain Auntie, who shall remain nameless (to protect Auntie Phyllis's memory), legs akimbo, lying in the bath after she had toppled in when it jumped out in front of her. It gave most of the family gathering a good old chuckle, although it must have left a deep scar on the tortured mind of my little urchin brother. Ne'er mind, eh!

*

My fifteenth birthday passed with the indifference of one of Mr Duthoit's Friesians, slowly chewing grass.

I was slowly, very slowly, growing towards being an adult. I was still a boy, in every sense though. I mean, adults very rarely play Subbuteo

or kick a football around with their mates every waking hour, although, as I've found out in much later life, they do still like to go on bike rides!
One thing that a grown-up adult certainly wouldn't do was, to take Soldiers United on an Epic quest for domestic and European glory, from an old granny's handbag!
I did! Which proved that I was still a young teenage boy with a lot of growing up still to do.

*

The Sweet had "Blockbuster" at number One, and there was "Daniel" by Mr John, "Gene Jeannie" by Mr Bowie, "Do you wanna touch me (oh yeah)" by Mr Paedo Pervy Pants, and Status Quo had a "Paper Plane", whilst Wings had a double A-sided "Hi Hi Hi" & "C Moon". In February, we were all singing "Cum on feel the noize". What school did they attend? Certainly not Brockhill, as their speiling was atroshush!
Focus played the guitar based "Sylvia", and Thin Lizzy had some "Whiskey in the jar" (good job grandad and Uncle John didn't find it). There were also some classic comedy programmes that started in 1973 that would still be watched and chuckled at, almost fifty years on. "Last of the Summer wine", "Some Mother's do 'ave 'em", "Are you being served" and "Porridge", to name just a few.
Some well-known programmes ended as well. "Watch with Mother", "On the Buses", "The Fenn Street gang" (it was the follow up to "Please Sir") and "Follyfoot" all finished their runs.

*

Back to being me again. Our school Chadwick Cup started against Hillside Secondary school, from Folkestone. From between the sticks, I could see that our boys looked resplendent in the Brockhill colours of Green and White quartered shirts (Green again), and White shorts, as we got steamrollered by 5-2. Oh dear, that was meant to be our easiest game.

Pent Valley Secondary school were up next. This time we hammered in four goals to really shock and surprise them. They responded by putting seven past me, so another narrow defeat then, this time by 7-4.

Mr Gant though, was full of praise for our efforts. He said that he felt that we "held our own" in the match. It was when we were all "holding our own" that they scored seven goals!

Southlands Secondary school, from New Romney, on the Romney Marsh, wasn't a problem (for them). This time, nine of the beauties flew past me. We didn't bother scoring any ourselves because they were much better than we were, so we lost 9-0.

That only left Harvey Grammar school to play at home, on our "Rugby Pitch" football pitch, just to fool them!

Mr Gant missed the start of the match as he was out of school at a meeting, but I'll always remember our conversation, when he turned up behind my goal, all bouncy and confident about our prospects for the game…

"Hello Pilcher".

"Hello Sir".

"How are we doing?"

"3-0 to them, Sir"

"Oh dear".

"How long have you been playing?"

"Ten minutes, Sir".

We lost the match 10-0.

So, our Chadwick Cup came to an end with four defeats, six goals scored, and thirty-one goals conceded. I just couldn't understand it.

How could that have happened?
It was very difficult to put into words...
"How did we score six goals?"

*

Being in the New Building at school, up on the top floor, I could gaze out of the window and look down on the "Rugby Pitch" football pitch, and the "Rugby Pitch" cricket pitch, and even the "Rugby Pitch" rugby pitch, which helped to pass the time during the most boring lessons. Next door to our form room was the Art room, Mr "Baby" Martin's domain. I don't know how he got the name "Baby", because he had a moustache and babies tended not to have moustaches (I bet that Geoff did, though).

There was an extensive view, across to the Girl's school and their playing fields, and beyond to the sea. This was great for looking out at girls in the distance, over five hundred yards away, the size of leporyptic ants. I may have just made that word up. No, not "ants", the other one!

At the far end of the corridor, in the opposite direction, in N1, was Mr Smith, or "Poof" as he was known around the school. I couldn't be sure how he got his nickname either, other than perhaps, for the "camp" way that he moved and spoke. I did say that they could be vicious and spiteful with their insults and remarks at secondary school. The kids were just as bad!

Downstairs, next to the staff room and...er..."Poof's" library, was the office and Sixth year form room of the Deputy Head teacher, Mr Lloyd Stainer.

Now, Mr Stainer, when standing rigid and upright, which he always did, stood at about nine foot six inches (in our eyes). He always wore a crisp Black pin-striped suit, immaculately turned out, just like a

Regimental Sergeant Major, with a bellow to match his appearance (he didn't wear a cap, though).
He put the fear of a bedpan into every boy in the school, most of the teachers as well. To be singled out for any reason for one of his tirades was to be avoided at all costs. He would tower above you, and glare down with the eyes of a wind-chilled fox!
I do believe that he gave out more detentions than all the other teachers put together. They were all held in his Year Six form room, and that was where he also taught us Geography, by fear, of course.

*

My out of school activities were ambling along. Palmarsh Youth Club, playing football, riding my bike, you'd think that there wasn't any room for owt else, especially owt else with a physical element. I had remembered Mr Baird's words, but did I heed them?
Did I "Andrex puppies!"
I joined Seabrook Athletic, along with Steve Birch, to play in the Seabrook and District League again, on Sunday afternoons. I was, at the time, experimenting playing out on the pitch instead of in goal. Most Goalies have dreams of playing Centre Forward, I was a little Left Winger, or Left Back!
Seabrook Athletic, incidentally, played in White shirts with thin Green stripes (Green again).
Also, alongside Steve, Mick and Ian, I had started Weekday night training with Hythe Town. We'd form our own little group on the usual training run along Hythe seafront to the Hotel Imperial, and back to the pitch at Reachfields, where the training was held. None of the "Halterne" mob would dare attack us while we were surrounded by Hythe Town first team players. There was a large old wooden building where we all got changed, and for us lads, it felt very odd being in the company of grown men who we normally

cheered on Saturday afternoons at Hythe Recreation ground.
Ian was, by far, the best player in our little group, and he gradually made his way up to become Right Back for the first team.
What with this promotion to the first team, and Sunderland beating Leeds United in the F.A. Cup Final 1-0, his head could have grown, but it didn't (it didn't stop him going on and on and on and on about his little Second Division Club though, mind you, we were all cheering for them). No one liked Leeds, except Geoff.
The rest of us would be glad to get a game for the Reserves.
To be honest, Steve and Mick, being a year older than me, and having both legs the same size, were favoured more by the team management, so although I got picked for some games, I mainly played the part of the 12th man, the "Ball Boy", the "Gofor", the substitute.
I was Hythe Town Reserve's reserve!
One thing had changed though, Hythe Town played in White shirts, so the Green theme had been broken.
But then it came back...
A couple of Steve's schoolmates ran a 5-A-Side team called "Creteway". They played at the Marine Pavilion, down by Folkestone harbour on Thursday evenings, in the Friday League, Division Two (I know, it doesn't make sense!). Steve and I joined them, so it meant me walking down to Steve's house, wait for his dinner to "settle", then we'd catch the bus to Folkestone, walk down the road of Remembrance (if we could remember) to the venue. I was the goalie of the team, I could just about reach the 5-a-side goal crossbars without having to jump up!
There were two massive pillars holding up the roof, they were slap, bang in the middle, directly in front of the goals, about ten yards out, and they were a goalie's nightmare, deflecting many shots past

unsuspecting goalkeepers. Not me though, obviously.
Oh yeah, one other thing. Creteway wore Green shirts!

*

My time as a Year Four schoolboy was now complete. I would be looking to leave school at the end of next year, after the dreaded C.S.E. exams. How could I get out of them? A cunning plan was needed.

My highlight on the music front was that Ian had loaned me T.Rex's album "The Slider". He was a big Marc Bolan fan, and now, so was I. Playing my favourite "Ballrooms of Mars" over, and over, again in my bedroom till I knew all the words without checking the record sleeve. I still play it, today.

During the past weeks in the charts, there was "All because of you" by Geordie (Ian loved that one), "Crazy" by Mud, "Drive-in Saturday", Wizard's "See my baby jive" at number One, followed by "Can the Can" by Suzi Quatro, "Broken Down Angel", "Good Grief Christina" by Chicory Tip, "Rubber Bullets", "Albatross", and in July, getting even worse (or "worserer") with their smelling, it was Slade with "Squeeze me Pleeze me" at the top, holding off songs like "Life on Mars", and the pervy paedo's "I'm the Leader of the Gang".

It was the love of these tunes and many others like them, that encouraged Jamie MacPherson and me to clomp (once again, high up) down to the Light Railway Disco's on Wednesday nights, wearing our big platformed shoes or wedges, high waisted, three buttoned Oxford or Birmingham Baggies in Beige or Light Blue (so that they showed every wee wee drip!), wide wing collared, flowery or otherwise patterned shirt and snazzy Tank top jumper.

We obviously, didn't stand out too much on the two-mile clomp along the main road from Palmarsh.

Upon arrival at the hall, behind the Light Railway Café, we would blend in with all the other teenage boys and girls, all wearing the same, or similar outfits. During the Winter months, Jamie and I would clomp down there wearing large checked Trench coats, to top the ensemble off.

These days, so called "Know-it-all's" or "Experts" say that the 70s was the decade that fashion forgot!

I say, "Now hold your donkey's", in the 1970s we had a fashion "Overload", and that was all before the mid to late 70s Disco gear, and Punk attire as well. Don't forget the Bay City Rollers Tartan infestation, either. I mean, how could you sing along with the Sweet, playing "Blockbuster", without platform shoes, shiny bits and a gallon of Glitter?

Long live Glam Rock!

Me and Jamie thought that we looked "The Gnat's nadgers" as we bowled along (despite many twisted ankles).

*

Our Nomadic football life carried on, mainly on our pitch on the Green. Those fisherman's nets were the business!

The days were full of football, cycling, Subbuteo and Soldiers United. The furthest that I can recall us cycling was, up to Dover and back that Summer, only this time we all had Racing bikes except Rob, who had a dodgy old one.

One day in this holiday, we'd cycled up to Court at Street again (on my insistence), and on our return, going down Lympne hill, hands firmly on the brake levers because it was an average 11% grade, going to almost 16% in places, Rob zoomed past us all, screaming… "My brakes don't work!"

We all laughed as he overtook, thinking that he was just "tugging our leads".

"Where's he gone?" Shouted Kim, as we rounded a bend, about half way down.

"I hope nowt's coming up the hill" I yelled.

"He'll go straight into the garage or he'll hit the canal bridge at that speed" Steve chucked in for good measure.

He was now so far in front that he'd disappeared from our view completely. As we all slowed, towards the steepest bottom section, we couldn't see him crashed into, either the garage or the bridge.

We all pulled up by the bridge, assuming he had made it around the bend, and gone on, still brakeless, and then…

From a gap between some bracken and a rotten piece of fencing by the bridge, came the creature from the deep lagoon!

Sopping wet, Rob shouted up to us…

"Give us a hand with my bike!"

"Where is it?" Said Kim, asking the obvious (we did worry about him, sometimes).

"Where do you think, you Idiot?" Said a disgruntled, dripping Rob.

"I'm not the one that's wet! You are" Said Kim.

"You will be in a minute!" Rob didn't seem to see it the same way that we all did.

With much chuckling and merriment at Rob's expense, we got his half- submerged bike out of the canal, and with much squelching around Botolph's Bridge corner, leaving a trail of stinking brown water in his wake, he managed to get HMS Hyson home again. I think that it was the first time it had ever had a wash (not Rob, he'd had several during the past year).

Chapter Twenty – It's all Greek to me!

After the glorious holiday sunshine, with "Yesterday once more" by the Carpenters hauntingly resounding in my ears, not to mention "The Ying Tong Song" by the Goons (I said, not to mention that), it was back up Barrack hill, to school. Only this time, I had an additional burden to bear. Yes, yet again, my little nose picker of a brother would be joining me at school. I lectured him about not leaving with any newspaper wrapped parcels, telling him that I was a fifth year, a responsible, mature, almost, sixteen-year old, and that he wasn't to show me up as a first year. He just stuck his tongue out at me and ran off. Mind you, he didn't stick it out as far as his sticky out ear! I didn't reciprocate by sticking my tongue out because I was a mature fifth year…I just chased him!
Another thing that I'd noticed was that all his new school attire and equipment was of a much higher quality than I'd ever managed to obtain. Mum told me that it was because I'd had enough spent on me with the calliper and shoes, and all my Hospital visits.
For the love of Demitris. It wasn't my fault!
Any further discussion on the subject was dissuaded by mum going off to the Ritz Bingo hall on more pressing business. I certainly knew my place in the pecking order!
I think that I was just above Peter the cat (who we'd still got), but I wasn't too sure.
I talked to grandad about it. He understood, but he wouldn't let me wallow. He said…
"You'll be leaving school soon Kev, you'll be able to buy your own clobber an' that".
"I know, grandad, but it does pee me off sometimes. It's like I don't

matter at times".

"Don't ee worry, young Kev. I know that you'd rather be you, than 'im"

I think that he was trying to point out something to me, that despite me still getting some hip pains, or "hippy shoes" as I call them, my World wasn't too bad.

To prove my own theory though, a couple of things would soon happen to enhance my view, before I left Brockhill behind.

*

I did do some things with my little brother. I took him down to "Spin-a-Disc" Record shop, in Hythe, on the bus (obviously, as he didn't ride a bike). Our musical tastes differed slightly as I bought "The Ballroom Blitz", "Angie", "Angel Fingers", and "The Laughing Gnome", and he purchased "Eye Level" by the Simon Park Orchestra. By now, the Pilcher household had acquired a second-hand Radiogram from Bett and Pete, with the capacity to stack, and play eight records at a time, that's if you wanted them all to fall onto the playing deck in one heap, because that's what always happened when I had a go. It wouldn't worry the little chimp though, with his one Orchestral offering!

Mum and dad lived next door, the other side of the alley, to the "Warren's", and Barney Rubble's best friend at the time was David Warren. He was a nice chubby lad, the same age as Barney, but he had to have several insulin injections each day, as he suffered from Diabetes. His poor old mum had to administer these, among her many other jobs in the house. She was a lovely older lady, with many troubles, mainly looking after David's health and, also her father, who lived with them. When she smiled, she showed the lines of sacrifice, but she would watch over her brood like a caring mother hen, and she'd always give out a cheery greeting.

Poor old David also had another affliction which, of course, the other kids would mock. He had a stutter.

He would knock on mum's door...

"I I I I I I Is B B B B B Barry c c c c c c coming out?"

"No"

I do hope that he's still around and coping with life today. Yet another young lad having to live with a disability, a handicap, that other folk either didn't understand or care about, back then. So long as it wasn't them, they could ridicule.

*

My form room for this year was R5 in the Old Building, which was down a few stairs from the ground floor (half ground floor, half cellar?), my form teacher was Mr "Taffy" Lewis. No guesses where he came from. No, it wasn't Ireland! His one little foible was that he liked to pronounce his S's. He would say something like...

"My name isss Missster Lewissss, and I will be your Hisssssstory teacher. He almost whistled as he spoke.

*

Little Lurch (or "Baa" as mum still called him) made it through his first term without one pooh parcel being brought home, although I suspect that he may have dumped several in the bushes, along the canal, and mum was constantly being told how well he was doing, by the teaching staff, as they collected their dinner from her at the serving hatch. Me, on the other hand, well, Mr Setterfield, the Headmaster called me over to him as I was wandering past with my friends, on our way to our next lesson, one day...

"Pilcher".

"Yes Sir".

"What have you been up to?"
"Pardon Sir?"
"What have you been doing, lad?"
"Me Sir? Nowt Sir!"
"You must have been up to something, Pilcher".
"Why Sir?"
"Because you're always smiling!" He gave me a slight grin.
"Now get off to your next lesson".
"Yes Sir".
Now, mum told me later at home, that he'd gone into the school kitchen and told her what had happened. He said that I'd always got a cheeky grin, as if I'd been up to something.
So, The Curly Wurly Kid was being praised for his work, and I was being rebuked for smiling. Unbelievable!

*

Let's now have a Christmas number One that nobody will ever remember. It was by that group called Slade, and it was the correctly spelt "Merry Christmas Everybody". Can you recall how it went? No, 'nit me (as grandad would say). Who would have thought that over forty-six years on, it would still be the most played Christmas record? There are some sad old folk now, jumping around, singing it, just as we were back then. "Holy Smoking Socks" they've earned some money out of that song!
Another Christmas hit, just behind Slade, didn't do too badly either. "I wish it could be Christmas every day" by Wizard. Blimey, hadn't Roy Wood come a long way since singing "Blackberry Way" to me, and to me alone, in Ashford Hospital, that February long ago, in 1969!
Our festivities took on much of the same as the previous year (except I didn't get a bike this time). I got Subbuteo, annuals, naff clothing,

Top of the Pops LPs and the "timeless" Games Compendium. Nobody fell into Aunt Daisy's bath this year, as the sherry bottles were carefully hidden away by Uncle Bill.

We had a lovely visit to see Aunt Kate and nan Pilcher in East Langdon. We always went over at least once a month, unless nan came down to stay with us.

Grandad and I continued to plough our happy furrow by the fireside. He'd enchant with yarns about when he went to Lympne Primary school, around 1898, and of when he was a "Cellar Boy" at the County Members Public House in Lympne. He said that he even started smoking at the ripe old age of Five!

I think that he also partook in the odd pinch of snuff, as well. Yuk! There was one story he told me regarding a headless horseman, riding over the fields from "The Carpenter's Arms" pub, I believe he said, in West Hythe one night, many moons ago. I asked if it wasn't him that had been in the pub, and had one too many, but he said that it was a true yarn. If he said that there was a headless horseman, then there was a headless horseman.

Grandad didn't tell lies!

*

The new year, 1974, began what would be my final full term at school. I didn't know it at the time, but the wheels were in motion for me to start a Painting & Decorating apprenticeship alongside Steve, who had started the previous October for S.J. Sharp & Sons, in Hythe. I don't know why I opted for this type of work, as it wasn't something that I was at all interested in. I think that I possibly chose the trade because, both Steve and Mick were already doing it. Mick worked for Charliers, another building company, almost next door to Sharp's.

When the Careers Officer visited the school, I saw it as a way of getting out, into the big wide World and, also a way to earn some money. I didn't realize though, at the time, that as an apprentice, you earned very little buggly, and the only things that you would be trusted to do, was to sweep up, or to rub down rough wood and rusty old metal window frames, and to paint some horrible smelling primer on (not undercoat, but primer!).
Still, we live and learn and, anyway that was in my future life and not a part of this story, so forget all that I've said about it. I didn't like it anyway, in fact, I hated it, so there!

*

I reached the grand age of Sixteen, as The New Seekers informed the World that "You won't find another fool like me", Leo Sayer told us the "The show must go on", and The Sweet were in the middle of a "Teenage Rampage".
Mum and dad though, were in the middle of a quandary!
Little Charlie Choops had brought home from school, a large brochure and consent form regarding a late Summer term Cruise around the Greek Islands. It was, basically a couple of weeks school trip on a Cruise ship, to be funded by parents.
Well, I must have been out playing football when Barry whined, pleaded, begged, grizzled, and finally cajoled mum and dad to pay up and allow him to partake in this Mediterranean extravaganza, because as I went to park my racing bike in the back porch, out came Lurch, beaming from ear to sticky out ear…
"I'm going on a Cruise" He boasted, unable to contain his joy in telling me.
"Yeah, right" I replied. I knew that mum and dad couldn't afford for him to go on a Ferry to France, never mind a Cruise.

"Mum. Tell him what I'm doing" His beam had changed into a malevolent smirk, by now.
"Ah, Todd. Barry's going on a Mediterranean Greek Island Cruise. Now, where have you been? You're late for your tea!"
"Whoa! Hold on a cotton-picking minute!"
It was just starting to register.
"What do you mean, he's going on a Cruise? No, he's not!"
Dad then came out to the kitchen, The Sun newspaper under his arm, determined to put the matter to bed.
"Yes, he is, Todd. It's a chance of a lifetime for him, so we'll have no more arguments".
"He's only been at Brockhill for five minutes!"
Mum then chucked her fivepence worth in
"As dad says, it's a chance of a lifetime"
"How can he go? You can't afford it" Said I, starting to get ever so slightly angered.
"We'll have to make cut backs on things. You included".
"What?" I couldn't believe what I was hearing.
"If you want sweets, you'll have to use your paper round money from now on, Todd" Said dad, going back to his armchair in the front room.
"Why do I have to pay for him to go swanning around the Greek Islands?" My anger was rising even more.
"He hasn't got much, Todd. He doesn't go out like you do, with your friends all over the show".
"That's not my fault, is it? I don't go to the Greek Islands with my friends!"
Dad shouted from the front room…
"Todd. Shut up! He's going, and that's that!"

"So, he goes on a Cruise liner around the Mediterranean Greek Islands, and I went on a Viking Longboat in Pegwell Bay!"
"They didn't have this trip then, and you know it, Todd".
"If they had, you wouldn't have let me go".
"He never stole any George Best stickers, you did!"
Ooh! That was below the belt, and totally irrelevant as well.
With that, I stomped off to grandads.
"I could 'ear, you've 'eard then?" Said my wise guru as I sat at his table.
"Oh, I've heard, grandad. What I can't understand is why he's allowed to go".
"Nit me, matey. It's their way I s'ppose".
"What do you mean? He gets everything".
"That's exactly what I mean. Yer see Kev, ee's their baby, ee's the little 'un".
"Little? Have you seen the size of him lately?"
"Ee is a bit of a porker, in ee?"
"That don't change the fact, grandad. He's going on a Cruise ship, I'm not going anywhere!"
"Ne'er mind matey. Yer won't change it so no use fretting. You 'ad yer tea?"
"Oh bugger, I forgot that. It'll be in the bin now, anyway".
"Or shovelled down Barry's gullet!" Grandad laughed.
I did too, at that image.
"You wanna cuppa, grandad?"
"Good Idea matey. Bring them biscuits in as well".
So, there it was. A done deal.
I'd been to the Isle of Thanet, he was going to the Island of Crete (among others).
It wasn't fair, or "den itan dikaio" as they say in Greece.

Yes, I can speak Greek, but not very well.
"Neh, boro' na miliso ellinika', alla' ochi poly' kala'".
The Curly Wurly Kid didn't know diddly squat!
It was then a taboo subject at number Five. Luckily, I lived at number Six, so me and grandad could "chew the cud" over it, with me always hoping that Lurchio would come back the colour of a bloated lobster! My own malevolence was fighting back.

*

As mum and dad saved, Barney Rubble gorged, and I faced a sweetie shortage, my burgeoning career with Seabrook Athletic knew no bounds. From my new outfield position of Left Back, I had helped us to reach the Semi-Final of the District cup against Martello (the team who were the opponents in my very last Palmarsh Angels game). Dad had always driven me to matches and stayed to watch, but on this special Sunday afternoon, the "lobster to be" had something on, so dad took him instead, leaving me to cycle up to the Shorncliffe stadium pitches on my own. On my arrival, Bill Ward, our manager told us that our usual Centre Forward was ill, and as he wanted somebody tall, big and bulky, to fulfil the role, he came up to me...
"Well, Kevin. What about it?"
"What about what, Bill?"
"How do you fancy playing Centre Forward today?"
I looked up at him, attempting to find any sign of mental illness in his face.
"Me?" I said, incredulously!
"Yes. You. Why not? They won't be expecting that" He said, in his best "Bill Shankly" impression, although he actually looked more like "Selwyn Froggitt".
"But they're massive" I gulped.

Yes, but they're all big and cumbersome, and you're small and nippy"
He lied.
Nobody else wanted to play Centre Forward. In fact, most of them had disappeared behind their parents, trying to avoid Bill's gaze. I didn't have that luxury, and he knew it.
"Okay, I'll give it a go" I said, as I realized that he must have had some faith in me to even suggest it.
For the first half, we were "under the cosh" and we went back for our half time oranges 1-0 down, but then...but then... Seabrook Athletics new, pint-sized Centre Forward scored...not one...not two...not three...but four goals to carry us through to the Final 4-1. As we all ran from the pitch in celebration, I looked around, but of course, I had nobody there to celebrate with, so I just wandered over to Bill, who had his "I told you so" grin on. He was correct in every way. What a manager!
Of course, when I arrived back home, cycling on the wings of a cloud, and told of my four goal heroics, nobody believed me. It wasn't until the game on the following Sunday, when I had reverted, back to Left Back, that dad truly believed what had happened, and that was only because Bill and several of the players told him.
Why couldn't he believe me the week before, when it really mattered to me?
Hey Ho!

*

"Tiger Feet" by Mud, had been at number One, with such classics as "The air that I breathe" and "The Wombling Song" (joking) pressing hard for top spot. Then, later in March, Paper Lace were telling Billy not to be a hero, at number One, with "Jet" by Wings, "Rebel Rebel" & "Candle in the wind" by Mr Bowie and Mr John, also high in the charts.

*

I didn't know if anyone important had been watching my, to be honest, totally stupendous performance in the Semi-Final, or any other game, for that matter, but a letter on the Club's official headed paper, came through the letter box for me.
Now, I had never received a letter before. Birthday cards, yes, but not a letter.
I gazed at the headed paper and, with shaking hands, I read the contents.
I was officially being offered a trial at "United"!
I couldn't believe it. Me, offered a trial to become a professional footballer, and with such a prestigious club, as well.
This couldn't get any better, surely?
"Mum, dad. Guess what?"
"What is it, Todd? What was the letter about? Are you in trouble?" Asked mum, more out of nosiness that genuine interest.
"I've been offered a trial!"
"A trial, why, what have you done? Have you got to go to court?"
"Not that sort of trial" I said, looking at her relieved face.
"I've been asked for a football trial!"
"Where?" Asked dad.
"For United!"
"What?" Replied dad, half choking on a bacon buttie.
"Give me that letter, let me look!"
"It's for Southend United, you wind up merchant!"
He said, whilst spitting out sections of burnt pig.
"Yeah, I know" I replied with a grin.
I pointed out a few facts about the letter.
"It's addressed from their manager, Arthur Rowley, and it's at Roots Hall, that's their ground. They're a 4th Division Club.

"It's where?" asked mum, getting a smidgeon confused now.
"Roots Hall, mum. That's Southend's ground".
"Is that in London?" Mum's geography wasn't too good.
"No mum. It's in Essex. It doesn't say what position they want me for though. Goalie or Left Winger" I studied the letter again.
"Well, you can forget that" Said dad, abruptly dismissing the notion completely.
"What? Why?" I responded, thinking that he was having me on.
"I'm not driving all the way to bloody Essex, so you can forget it!"
"What? Why?" I was despairing now, unable to fathom any logic in his statement.
"It would cost a bloody fortune in petrol to get there and back. You're not bloody going!" Dad was shouting at me now. His bacon buttie left on the table.
"It's only about sixty miles dad, this is my big chance to be a footballer, to do what I've always dreamed of" I was shouting at him now.
"It's too far, you're too small, we're not going, and that's that!" With that final declaration he slammed the door, went out to the car and drove off, down to the "Oddfellows" club for a lunchtime pint or two. I was left devastated. I was sixteen, yet tears were streaming down my cheeks, only these tears were tears of anger and frustration. My letter had been dismissed without any thought or discussion.
"Mum, how come you can afford for Barry to go on a Mediterranean Cruise, but you can't afford for me to go to Southend?" I pleaded with her.
"Your father has told you, Todd. It's too far".
"It's Southend! He's going around the Greek Islands" Somehow, I knew that I wouldn't win.
"Just do as you're told, or you'll get a clout when he comes back!"

At least Lurch had the sense to stay upstairs in his room whilst all this was going on.

"This is my chance to be a footballer, mum. It's all I've ever wanted to do" I tried, one last time.

"Do you want a smack?" (Why do they ask that?)

"Now just get out with your friends" Conversation over.

I showed grandad the letter as I passed his shed door. He put down his pipe on the bench and read it through...

"A pretty "Rum Do" Kev" He said, handing it back and shaking his head.

"Yer don't 'ave much luck, do yer?"

"Not really, no. What should I do, grandad?"

"Not much ee can do matey, you're not "top dog", see".

I think I understood what he meant.

My bonfire had been wee'd on again, only this time before I'd even managed to light it.

"Ain't you got that football match coming up?"

He'd remembered Seabrook Athletics Final against the top team, Folkestone Youth Club at Hythe Recreation ground, on Sunday.

"Yeah grandad, but everyone reckons that they'll win by at least 10-0. They're much bigger and better than we are. They've already thrashed us twice and they've won the League".

"You just give it yer best shot, matey. You can only do what you can do!" That was some statement (I think).

"Now, can yer 'ear kettle boiling?"

I strained to hear owt.

"No, grandad".

"Well, yer best get it on then" He smiled.

"Alright grandad".

My little "sticky out eared" urchin brother (with his sticky out ear on display) laughing his large baggy pants off in the knowledge that he'd be cruising around the Mediterranean whilst I would be cycling around Court at Street!

*

Back at school, I had been called for an appointment with the Career's Officer. I was told to go down to an office in Hythe, near the Police Station, whereupon I was offered the salubrious position of "Apprentice Painter & Decorator", not just "Painter", but "Decorator" as well! I was informed that the position would commence after the Easter holiday.
It wasn't something that I really wanted to do, as I've already stated, but it meant that I only had a few weeks to go until I could finally join the adult working World. My "Season in the Sun", as Terry Jacks sang, was coming to an end. I was also informed that I would earn

the princely sum of £11.39p per week. What I didn't realize at the time was that £5 of that would be snatched by mum and dad for my "keep".

I lived with grandad, for Johan Cruyff's sake!

Still, I suppose it would help fund my little urchin brother's jolly jaunt. I wondered if he would get sea-sick?

Fingers crossed!

When I told Andy Maytum, Steve Watts and Geoff that I would be leaving, and not doing any C.S.E. exams, they were disbelieving, and they called me some choice names for getting out of all the studying that they still had to do.

*

I watched my last major football occasion as a schoolboy, as Brian Moore commentated on Wolverhampton Wanderers beating Manchester City 2-1 in the League Cup Final at the beginning of March.

By the time that my team, Liverpool, beat Newcastle United in the F.A. Cup Final 3-0 in May, I would be a working man (well, a little working apprentice, anyway). I would watch the 1974 World Cup in West Germany, this Summer, as a working man (Nope, wrong again. Still a little apprentice).

*

My own Cup Final was now upon me. As I, along with all my friends, turned up at Hythe recreation ground for the big showdown with Folkestone Youth Club. I noticed quite a gathering of support for both teams. I thought that it must be deemed an important game because the Council had given us pitch number One to use, right next to the pavilion and changing rooms. It was the pitch that Hythe Town first team used, hallowed turf indeed (except for the bits with dog's doodah on them!).

There was one big surprise for our team in the changing room. Bill Ward, in his wisdom, had hired us a new kit for the match. Shiny Red and White striped shirts and Black shorts (Southampton Subbuteo team No. 9), instead of our old loved and trusted White and Green. I didn't like this at all. The new shirts felt uncomfortable to wear. Their new crispness seemed at odds with our scrawny bodies. A lot of the team wished we were playing in our usual gear. We also thought that it made us appear "Flash".

A new kit for a Final that nobody gave us a hope in. In my mind, we were tempting fate. The mood in the changing room was ominous! "If it ain't broke...er...make your grandmother suck an egg!"

Oh, I don't know. I was nervous, okay?

Dad was stood on the pavilion veranda with the other anxious, hopeful parents. My mates, Steve, Mick, Ian, Rob and Kim all stood on the touchline, near to my Left Back position, then they all moved behind our goal when the game kicked off. After all, that's where all the action was meant to be. In our goal.

Somehow, either by hook or by crook, we reached half time without Folkestone Youth Club breaching our defences. We, on the other hand, had scored from a penalty, and were 1-0 up.

Our half time talk, amidst the sound of sucking and slurping of oranges, was positive...

"Keep going boys. You can win this" Said Bill, hardly daring to believe his own words.

The predicted second half onslaught on our goal commenced, as we all knew it would. I now had Jock Paton on the side line, yelling at me to...

"Stop the blighter at all costs, Kev. Don't let the scoundrel past!"

Or perhaps nearer to what he really shouted, in a mixture of Glaswegian abuse, threats and swearwords was...

"Kick tha' flogging bustard up 'is flogging hearse, Ye kin, Kev"
followed up by...
"Dinnae let tha' flogging bustard beat ye! Ye bustard!"
There was no way that I was going to be beaten by any Right Winger, not with Jock there by the touch line.

No way, Hamish!

What we had noticed during the second half was that every time any of us got near to one of the Youth Club players, the Referee was giving them a free kick, so Bill Ward sent out instructions that, on no account, must we touch anyone in or near our penalty area, as it looked clear to most folk watching, which side his bread was buttered!

Every time they threatened our goal, either our goalie or one of us got a body part in the way. They threw everything they had at us, but we held out for the entire ninety minutes...

Unfortunately, the Referee decided to add on a teensy weensy bit too much injury time for our liking, as they burst our dam in the ninety fifth minute...then blow me down with a parsnip flute, as a shot flew towards our goal, it hit Steve Birch full in the "parchment pocket", leaving him doubled up on the ground thinking that any future chance of fatherhood may have gone by the wayside, in the line of duty for his team.

What followed next was a shrill blow on the Referee's whistle. We thought that it was the final whistle, but our hopes were dashed by the sight of him pointing towards the penalty spot for "Hand ball" by Steve!

By witnessing the writhing around on the floor that Steve was currently engaged in, it was obvious that he hadn't managed to get a hand anywhere near the region he was struck.

Never the less, the man who should have been wearing a Folkestone Youth Club shirt had awarded a penalty, and that was that!

It was no surprise to anybody present that, seconds later, after the ball had again nestled in our net, he decided to blow the final whistle!

We had lost 2-1!

Amid boos from a great proportion of the crowd, the Referee disappeared into his changing room as Folkestone Youth Club boys celebrated their (undeserved) victory. Bill Ward had a face so Red with rage, that you could feel the heat and anger rising from him. He felt, along with many others, that we had been cheated.

There was nowt that could be done now though, other than to complain to the relevant footballing Authority, so that was it!

As the teams went to collect their medals from the Hythe Mayor on the pavilion veranda, I chose to stay, sitting on the pitch in the far goalmouth, with my friends. This was the goalmouth where we had been robbed of victory. I felt desolate at that moment. My mates all gathered around me, as good mates do, to offer an arm around my shoulder, some consoling words, a lot of angry words, and then...a few chuckles.

I didn't want a loser's medal, not this way. Bill collected it and handed it to dad. I didn't mind losing, I was used to it. I'd lost out a lot in my short life so far. But it was the way that we lost that I couldn't handle. We all felt robbed, cheated. I finally separated myself from my friends, but only for a short time, just long enough to get that "Lucky" shiny new strip off, then it was straight back out to join them for a kickabout in the goal, while the net was still up.

Any thoughts about spearing the Referee with a harpoon gun soon vanished as we laughed, joked and generally took the micky out of each other (mainly Kim), as we kicked the ball about. Anyway, Rob had pointed out to me that we didn't have a harpoon gun at our disposal, so that was out, and the apology for a Referee was safe.

There were questions asked, regarding some of his decisions and the vast amount of time he added on until they were in front, but nowt came of it so...Hey Ho!
I still have the loser's medal that Bill collected for me, somewhere in a drawer. It was a proper little plastic job, in a case. The winners all got a little Subbuteo type plastic cup for their efforts.
Ne'er mind eh!

*

My last week at school was just a time when I was told to clear my stuff away, ready to be taken home each day, and to keep out of the way of the other boys who were all studying deeply for their C.S.E. exams (I knew of several who weren't!).
My apprenticeship papers had all been signed and I had been given a start date, a few weeks on. I had given Mr Nicholson enough notice to finish my paper round so he could find my replacement. I would really, genuinely miss that early morning round, I had been doing it for so long now. Some of my customers came out to see me, and they all gave me a few Bob to say, "Thank you". I was very touched and very grateful. I would always remember those days, especially, as I've stated earlier, I now live in that Avenue.
My last day at school. Some teachers took the trouble to wish me well and bid me goodbye, others couldn't be bothered. Mr Riley, my French teacher, came up to me and shook my hand. I had already told him that French was the only subject that I enjoyed (apart from sports), and the only one that I would have carried on with. He confirmed that I would have done quite well, but you can't stay in school for just one subject so, early in the afternoon, I was permitted to slip away after I had my final interview with Mr Setterfield.?

It was strange, having the knowledge that this would be my last engagement as a schoolboy and also, a bit daunting as I knocked the big oak door, and entered on his summons...
"Ah Kevin, are you all set to go?" He called me "Kevin!"
"Yes Sir, I've got the last of all my things".
"Have you handed everything in that you should?"
"Yes Sir".
"Well Kevin, you've been through quite a lot here, haven't you? Especially with the calliper and all that entailed" This was nice, and friendly.
"Yes Sir".
"I do know what you had to put up with during that time, and I think that you handled it incredibly well".
"Thank you, Sir. It was really bad at times".
"I know it was, but hopefully it'll stand you in good stead for the outside World. How is the hip now?"
"It still hurts quite a bit at times, Sir, but I don't want to go through all that again. I've just got to get on with it and hope that the pains go away" (If only I knew!).
"Yes, I see. Well, good luck in the future Kevin, and please come back to see us".
Not on your nelly, I thought.
"Yes Sir, I will".
He got up from his large desk and shook my hand.
"I can always keep updated on your progress if I ask your mum" He smiled, as I turned to leave.
"Cheerio then".
"Cheerio Sir".
I was now a free person. It felt scary!
Mr Addison, a new teacher, was on duty at the end of the school drive. He shook my hand and wished me luck, then I was on my way

home, down the hill for the last time.

I had been at school since 1962, not all the time obviously, but as far as the learning tank was concerned, mine was now full to brimming with so much pointless knowledge, it was spilling out of my ears!

*

Who needed school? I had my Grandad!

As it was a sunny mid- April afternoon, and ages until the others would be about, I thought that I'd get my bike out and go for a ride. There was only one place that I wanted to go though, Court at Street, where my story began. I thought that it would be fitting for me to pedal off up there, alone with my own thoughts and memories. Just as I was about to push off, grandad came out the back to see me...

"That it then, young Kev?"

"That's it, grandad" I replied.

"So, you're all done wi' school now?"

"Yep, no more homework" I smiled.

"Where yer off to now then?" He asked.

"Court at Street, grandad. I feel that I want to go there".
"I understand, matey. Watch them cars though".
"I will. Grandad, can I ask you something?"
"Ask away matey" He replied.
"All the things that happen to me, the good stuff and the bad stuff. You know what I mean? Growing up at Court at Street, my friends, football, my bike, living with you, and then there's my knacked hip, the calliper and the bullying, and being picked on and singled out because of my bad leg. All that stuff. Does everyone get stuff like that, growing up?"
He pondered my long question, rubbed his bristled chin, knocked out his pipe on the fence post and answered...
"Nope, Kev. That's just "Todd's Luck""!

****

The End

Epilogue

Well, as things happened, little Charlie Choops enjoyed his Cruise around the Greek Islands. He didn't fall overboard and drown, he didn't get sunburnt like a lobster, and he didn't bring me back a present!

My apprenticeship didn't last the full three years (two and a half, to be precise). The lead in the paint made me feel ill and gave me bad headaches.

Oh, Woe is me!

My hip continued to deteriorate as the years went on. The pains got worse, almost unbearable at times, culminating in me having to get an emergency hip replacement in 2009, when there was hardly any hip left to replace.

Mr Baird's Traction & Calliper remedy that I had to endure was proven not to work, and future treatment for Perthes disease changed completely, so that was lucky for me, wasn't it?

Mind you, my luck regarding this particular joint has carried on, as my new hip has caused me all sorts of problems, and it still continues to do so, but mustn't grumble, there are lots of folk worse off than me.

A while back, I returned to the place of my birth. The two cottages have been converted into one large house "Well Cottage". I showed the owners my photographs of me sitting on the well by myself, and with my grandad Pilcher. They graciously insisted on taking a photograph of me at the time, over fifty-five years later. There's still no Blue plaque to say that's where it all started, though!

Most of me grew up into an almost mature person, although I have found no fame whatsoever, in my life as a former Bean Bag Race winner, all-round "Good Egg", or part-time Adult! Still...Hey Ho!

****

Back to where it all started. The well may now have a newer look but it's the same one, I'm the same one as well.

****

Also, by this Author...

"JUST FOLLOW THE MAP"

How hard can it be?

A cycling misadventure across Britain (Eventually)

Printed in Great Britain
by Amazon